A.K.A. Jesus:

*22 Sketches For Recognizing The
Present-Tense Christ*

Hope Douglas J. Harle-Mould

CSS Publishing Company, Inc.
Lima, Ohio

A.K.A. JESUS

FIRST EDITION
Copyright © 2021
by CSS Publishing Co., Inc.

Library of Congress Control Number: 2022930178

For more information about CSS Publishing Company resources, visit our website at www.csspub.com, email us at csr@csspub.com, or call (800) 241-4056.

e-book:
ISBN-13: 978-0-7880-3017-8
ISBN-10: 0-7880-3017-5

ISBN-13: 978-0-7880-3016-1
ISBN-10: 0-7880-3016-7   DIGITALLY PRINTED

Dedication

To "Bunches,"
my companion, wife, and true love:

The Reverend Linda M. Harle-Mould,
the Windy of my dreams,
the Spirit-Dove of my convictions,
the Mom of our countless adopted children,
the Francis-hands for injured critters,
the Storyteller of Wakantaka,
the Singer of folksongs still needing to be sung,
the Living Sacrifice poured out for many,
holy and acceptable.

He comes to us as One unknown,
without a name,
as of old,
by the lakeside,
He came to those men who knew him not.
He speaks to us the same word:
'Follow thou me!'
and sets us to the tasks
which he has to fulfill for our time.
He commands.
And those who obey Him,
whether they be wise or simple,
He will reveal Himself
in the toils, the conflicts, the sufferings
which they shall pass through in His fellowship,
and as an ineffable mystery,
they shall learn
in their own experience
Who He is."

—**Albert Schweitzer,**
The Quest of the Historical Jesus

Contents

Prologue: A Composite Sketch

Do We Fail To Recognize The Present-Tense Christ?

The Anonymous Gift-Giver.
Years ago when my wife was seriously ill, she received a small, hand-addressed, purple-wrapped package in the mail with a postmark from a distant city. The strange thing was that we didn't know anyone in that city, not anyone in the entire state. Who could it possibly be from? She opened it up. Inside was a recording of music and a note:

> *You do not know me and I do not know you. Your name was given to me by a friend of yours who knows you are in a time of suffering. My gift to you is the enclosed recording. It is full of music; music with which you might meditate, be uplifted, or simply enjoy. Each song was composed with you in mind and was recorded while holding you in prayer. It is my fervent hope that as you listen, the Spirit will touch you with strength and healing.*

After reading this, my wife wept. It was like holding a miracle in her hand. Then I wept. The gift had come precisely when she needed it most. To this day, we have no idea who the sender was, but if you pressed me, I would have to say it was *The Anonymous Gift-Giver*, A.K.A. Jesus.

What if we failed to recognize Christ at all?
Other times in our lives, Jesus comes to us in quite a different guise, in the form of someone who challenges us to go into new geographies of faith, to places of risk, to strangers we fear: *The One Who Invites Us Into Danger*, A.K.A. Jesus.

Too often we live our lives protected from Jesus. We keep him in the past, carefully embalmed. We may allow him into the present — conditionally — but only if he stays within the boundaries of our current assumptions, the borders of our current worldview. But what if Jesus unexpectedly walked up to us in our daily life today and we failed to recognize him at all? That would be the greatest of tragedies.

Perhaps we can be better prepared to see and sense Christ's surprising presence if we learn to ask one question: "Who is Jesus Christ for us today?" Such a question opens a crack through which Jesus can approach us in ways we cannot predict or control.

Dietrich Bonhoeffer And The One Who Invites Us Into Danger.

Dietrich Bonhoeffer once asked this question: *Who is Jesus Christ for us today?* And he taught his students to keep asking this question: *Who is Jesus Christ for us today?* And where did it lead him? To a costly discipleship. To a sacrificial life exemplifying the way of Christ.

Dietrich was just a twenty-seven-year-old Lutheran pastor when Adolf Hitler was elected Chancellor of Germany on January 30, 1933. Two days later, Reverend Bonhoeffer gave a radio address warning that if a leader (Führer) allowed his followers to make him their idol, he would be a "misleader" who mocked God and committed idolatry. His radio broadcast was only halfway complete when it was abruptly cut off by the authorities.

When Hitler required clergy to sign a loyalty oath to him and 70% of Lutheran ministers pledged their allegiance, Bonhoeffer resisted, helping to form a new Lutheran denomination, the Confessing Church, which asked him to create and lead an illegal seminary to train its new ministers. The Gestapo shut it down in 1937.

In 1939, at a time when Bonhoeffer was about to be conscripted — and knowing that his refusal to fight for the Third Reich would mean prison — Bonhoeffer received an invitation from theologian Reinhold Niebuhr to come to New York City and study for several years at Union Theological Seminary (the author's seminary), which he accepted.

But just ten days after arriving in New York he wrote Niebuhr an astonishing, personal letter, as he sat in the garden of the country house of the seminary president:

I have had the time to think and to pray about my situation and that of my nation and to have God's will for me clarified. I have come to the conclusion that I have made a mistake in coming to America. I must live through this difficult period of our national history with the Christian people of Germany. I shall have no right to participate in the reconstruction of Christian life in Germany after the war if I do not share the trials of this time with my people...

Christians in Germany will face the terrible alternative of either willing the defeat of their nation in order that Christian civilization may survive or willing the victory of their nation and thereby destroying our civilization. I know which of these alternatives I must choose; but I cannot make that choice in security. (1)

Bonhoeffer returned to Germany, joined the underground resistance, and served as a double agent in the German intelligence service, the Abwehr. In 1942, he traveled to Stockholm, Sweden, to secretly meet England's Bishop Bell and tell him of a plan by generals and government leaders to stage a coup de tat against Hitler if the Allies would accept a conditional surrender. England would not agree.

In 1943, Bonhoeffer was arrested for helping Jews escape to Switzerland. While in prison, his role in a plot to assassinate Hitler was uncovered, and he was sent to Buchenwald concentration camp in February, 1945. Later he was transferred to Flossenberg camp where he was hung on April 9, just weeks before the camp was liberated.

In *The Cost Of Discipleship*, Bonhoeffer described his experience of the grace of Christ:

Costly grace is the treasure hidden in the field; for the sake of it a man will gladly go and sell all that he has. It is the pearl of great price to buy which [sic] the merchant will sell all his goods. It is the kingly rule of Christ, for whose sake a man will pluck out the eye which causes him to stumble, [sic] it is the call of Jesus Christ at which the disciple leaves his nets and follows him...

Such grace is costly because it calls us to follow, and it is grace because it calls us to follow Jesus Christ. It is costly because it costs a man his life and it is grace because it gives a man the only true life." (2)

Dietrich Bonhoeffer faithfully and courageously followed *The One Who Invites Us Into Danger*, A.K.A. Jesus.

Sketches from eyewitnesses: Recognizing things only the Risen Christ could do.

Perhaps we can be better prepared to recognize Christ if, together, we create a collage of sketches of Jesus — like those made by police artists from eyewitnesses.

Each one of us are eyewitnesses of Christ. Each one of us have caught glimpses of Christ's visage and movement in our age. Each one of us have found evidence of the healing and hope he has brought into our circumstances. Each one of us have experienced some way in which his presence has transformed us and transfigured our world:

> *Since that day so long past,*
> *I've been on the move.*
> *Everywhere, I notice,*
> *Things only **he** could do.*
>
> *He's in the prisoner, the child abused,*
> *The outcast and refugee.*
> *I reach out my hand to them… to help,*
> *But it's **their** hand…heals me. (3)*

Perhaps if we combine our descriptions with those of the biblical witnesses, we might be able to create a composite sketch to help us see, hear, and meet Christ in the present tense when he enters our lives once again.

The face of Christ in the faces of us all.

There is a poignant painting by William Zdinak (*In His Image*, 1969) in which, as you examine it close up, you see faces of people of all ages and races. Some are famous faces: Mahatma Gandhi and Martin Luther King, Jr, Pope Paul VI and Bobby Kennedy, Alexander Graham Bell and Jonas Salk. But most are faces of everyday, beautiful people: mothers and girls, uncles and infants, strangers, and those of the artist's family.

Yet if you slowly back away from the painting, another pattern emerges. Stepping back eight or ten feet, the faces of the many blend together to form a singular face, a visage we instantly recognize, a man with a crown of thorns on his head. From a distance, you cannot pick out any of the individual faces that comprise *his* face. All you can see is Christ.

This is our religious task: to learn how to walk through our life and world with senses spiritually attuned with Christlike focus and Christlike perspective, until something hidden emerges, something more, something holy — the radiance of God's face shining on you, giving you grace and peace.

A composite sketch.

This book offers 22 sketches of Jesus. May it move you to add one of your own, so that together we might say with Thomas, *My Lord and my God!*

ENDNOTES

Prologue: A Composite Sketch
Do We Fail To Recognize The Present-Tense Christ?

1. *Christian History* 32, vol. X, no. 4, (January 2018), 15-16, 32.

2. Dietrich Bonhoeffer, *The Cost of Discipleship* (New York: The Macmillan Company, 1969), 47.

3. From the song, "He Has Gone On Ahead of You," composed by the author.

Sketch #1 ...Jesus, Our Player-Of-A -Different-Game

A Higher Game On A Wider Field

Luke 5:27-32 — At a banquet of tax collectors and sinners

Luke 6:32-36 — Love enemies, do good, and lend

Luke 7:31-35 — Like children playing at the marketplace

> *"They are like children sitting in the marketplace and calling to one another, 'We played the flute for you, and you did not dance; we wailed, and you did not weep.' For John the Baptist has come eating no bread and drinking no wine, and you say, 'He has a demon'; the Son of Man has come eating and drinking and you say, 'Look, a glutton and a drunkard, a friend of tax collectors and sinners!'"*
> Luke 7:32-34 (NRSV)

One Game to Play, by Hope Harle-Mould

> *Once you clear away all the world's distractions —*
> *all the falsehoods,*
> *all the clutter of things,*
> *all the noise of competition,*
> *all the confusion of purpose,*
> *all the emptiness of spirit —*
> *there is only one game to play,*
> *and that is peace,*
> *there is only one teacher to teach us,*
> *and that is Christ,*
> *and there is only one strategy to perfect,*
> *and that is love.*

A higher game on a wider field.

In a world where we are taught to play the game of *Diminish Others* and *Accumulate Stuff*, Jesus is calling us — is enticing us

— to play a higher game on a wider field, with deeper goals and surprising rules, using a multitude of hidden players and a timescale long enough to win every time.

What kind of game is Jesus playing? The game of *Up* and the game of *Holy Hugs*, the game of *Astonish Others* and *Give Away Stuff*, the game of *Lost and Now-Found* and *Adopt Your Whole Family*, the game of *Bridges to Everywhere* and *Everybody Around One Table*.

Children playing wedding, playing funeral.

One day Jesus is watching children play in the marketplace. He notices the first group of kids start to play the game Wedding, pretending to play flute music and have a bride and groom come together, but the other group of children say, *Boring, we don't want to play that.* Then he observes the first kids start to play the game Funeral, pretending to weep and wail and tear their garments, but the other children say, *Boring, we don't want to play that either!*

Jesus sees in this an answer to his critics' constant criticisms of his ministry. The respectable clique was always pillorying him for the kind of people he welcomed and served. So Jesus responds this way:

> *"To what then will I compare this generation, and what are they like? They are like children sitting in the marketplace and calling to one another, 'We played the flute for you, and you did not dance; we wailed, and you did not weep.' For John the Baptist has come eating no bread and drinking no wine, and you say, 'He has a demon'; the Son of Man has come eating and drinking and you say, 'Look, a glutton and a drunkard, a friend of tax collectors and sinners!' Nevertheless, wisdom is vindicated by all her children'"*
> Luke 7:31-35 (NRSV)

A banquet for a bunch of tax collectors?

On an earlier day, Jesus was walking along the shore of Lake Galilee and saw a tax collector named Levi, whom we know as Matthew, sitting at the tax booth; and he said to him, "Follow me." And he got up, left everything, and followed him.

"Then Levi gave a great banquet for him in his house; and there was a large crowd of tax collectors and others sitting at the table with them. The Pharisees and their scribes were complaining to his disciples saying, 'Why do you eat with tax collectors and sinners?' Jesus answered, 'Those who are well have no need of a physician, but those who are sick; I have come to call not the righteous but sinners to repentance'"
Luke 5:29-32 (NRSV)

These Pharisees were playing the game of *Keep Out the Lowly Unworthy*. These scribes were playing the game of *Condemn the Perverts*. But Jesus was playing the game of *Potluck Dinner Affirmations*, and *You'll Find Me Only among the Forsaken*.

Jesus' strategy.

Jesus' strategy was to use feasts and banquets as places to invite the unwanted and the unworthy, as well as to associate with the bigots, the self-righteous, and the rich. And by accepting them all at one table — affirming each one's inner beauty and hidden gifts — he brought them into a change of heart, a transformation of lifestyle. Jesus challenged them to accept one other and to find salvation in one another's eyes. We see this so poignantly in the story of Zacchaeus, who gave to the poor half of his wealth and vowed to repay fourfold anyone he had defrauded! "Today salvation has come to this house, because he too is a son of Abraham. For the Son of Man came to seek out and to save the lost" (Luke 19:9-10 NRSV).

The pick-up artist.

When Linda and I were studying for the ministry, we got to hear and meet the Reverend Paul Moore, Episcopal bishop and rector at St. John the Divine on the upper west side of Manhattan, a man of immense commitment to bringing Christ's love into the streets. Only later did I learn about one of Bishop Moore's most unusual spiritual practices.

Every so often, Moore would go for an intentional walk through one of the tougher surrounding neighborhoods just to see who or what he might encounter in his city. One day as he did so, a young woman with gaudy makeup and a very short skirt approached him: "Do you want to go out?" "Yes," he answered,

"What's your price?" She told him. He gave her the money and said, "Go home right now. But I want to meet you for lunch someday soon. Here's my card with my number." Bewildered, the young woman replied, "I've never met anybody like you." He replied, "Yes, you've never met me!" He smiled and they agreed on a date to meet at a restaurant.

As they talked, Reverend Moore discovered she was from Minnesota and had suffered a difficult life. He asked, "What would you dream of being? She replied, "I had been thinking about becoming a teacher." "Why don't you become a teacher?" She laughed, "Well, look at me, I can't." Why?" "I have no resources, I have a pimp, I have no place to stay, I have no money to go to school, I have no job." But at each problem she mentioned, he said, "I can handle that, I can handle that, I can handle that." And he did. She became a server in a restaurant, studied at a college for teachers, got married, and raised a family of beautiful children.

You might say Paul Moore was playing the game of *Pick-Up Artist for Christ.*

A non-zero-sum Savior.

Jesus is calling each of us to a new life and a new world that is a **non-zero-sum game**.

Most games, from checkers and chess to tennis and football, are zero-sum games: there is one winner and one loser, a plus one (+1) and a minus one (-1), all adding up to zero (0). But with Jesus, there are multiple winners on multiple sides, and nothing adds up to zero! It's a non-zero-sum game.

Christ accepted the cross, the ultimate sacrifice, choosing to go down in ignominious defeat — which spectators might score as a minus one (-1) — in order to redeem us all. Christ took on the utter loss and forsakenness of the cross to emancipate us, freeing us from sin's prison, making us new victors, giving each of us a score of plus one (+1), plus one (+1), plus one (+1), plus one (+1), plus one (+1), plus one (+1), plus one (+1), plus one (+1), plus one (+1), plus one (+1), and so on. So Jesus' costly defeat at Golgotha became a reverse-engineered triumph for us all.

You might say that Jesus is our Non-Zero-Sum Savior of the world.

Spontaneously playing a new game of lasting worth.

Here in Buffalo, New York, on New Year's Eve, 2017, the Buffalo Bills had earlier in the day won their NFL football game and were on the verge of making the playoffs for the first time in seventeen years. All they needed now was for the Cincinnati Bengals (who mathematically could not make the playoffs) to defeat the Baltimore Ravens in the evening game. The Bengals were behind in the score, with only 45 seconds left on the clock. But then, when the ball was hiked, Bengal's quarterback Andy Dalton dropped back and completed a 49-yard pass play for a touchdown that won the game. At that very moment, all of Western New York erupted in shouts of amazement and joy. And everyone broke out in singing the fan-favorite song, "Shout!"

But then something astonishing happened. Just as swiftly and unpredictably, our City of Good Neighbors began to play a Jesus game, the game of *Prodigal Generosity*, and *Contagious Giving*. Spontaneously and with joyful abandon, Buffalonians suddenly began to call in personal donations to Andy Dalton's foundation for children with special needs. It started with one donation, but within 24 hours there were more than 2,500 donations totaling over $57,000. As Andy began to notice the flood of donations, he was quite puzzled by one thing: many of these donations came in the odd amount of $17. But as Andy thought about it, he realized that people were simply grateful for finally making the playoffs after that many years. Many donations were in far larger amounts, for in only 48 hours the total reached $100,000. In the end, over $300,000 was given.

In gratitude, for several months following, the homepage of Andy's foundation website featured a picture of the Bengal's stadium with words written across it: "Thank you, Bills fans! — Andy and J.J. Dalton."

Think about this. One game involving moving an elongated pigskin ball across a designated line on a field had been transformed into a spontaneous outpouring of generosity for a different game, one of lasting worth: providing support, resources, and opportunities for physically challenged children and their families. You might even name this game, *Special Children Up!*

Transmute the Enemy.

In Luke's Sermon on the Plain, Jesus taught:

If you do good to those who do good to you, what credit is that to you? For even sinners do the same... But love your enemies, do good, and lend, expecting nothing in return. Your reward will be great, and you will be children of the most high; for he is kind to the ungrateful and the wicked
      Luke 6:33, 35 (NRSV)

In saying this, maybe Jesus was teaching us to play the game of *Transmute Enemy into Friend.* We all know we should practice this, but it can be very hard. Yet what if we could inveigle our imagination to change dark feelings and negative thoughts into empathetic perspective and forgiving spirit?

Imagining an alternate ending.

Surgeon and teacher Bernie Siegel, in his book *Prescriptions for Living,* shares a time when he experimented with this kind of spiritual transmutation. He was at a hotel once when his room was broken into and robbed. And he was pretty sure who did it, as when he and his wife were heading out of the room to go down to the hotel restaurant, there was a suspicious looking man loitering in the hallway near their room. As they waited for the elevator, Bernie got a good look at him.

When they returned, their belongings were gone: Bernie's clothes, a fur coat he had bought once for his wife, and her jewelry that had been handed down by family loved ones were all gone. They reported the crime and gave a detailed description of the burglar.

When Bernie tried to do his meditation exercises the next morning, he was still upset and obsessed by the clear picture of the thief's face and by thoughts of the kind of revenge he wished for him. The next morning, he had the same fixation, and the next and the next. Even when they returned home, his mind kept being disrupted by this violation.

After several weeks, Bernie came to new realization. He was tired of having the robber in charge of his peace of mind, so...

That morning I decided to reclaim my life and thoughts. I spontaneously visualized the man bringing his children Christmas presents that he had purchased with the money he made when he sold our possessions. As I pictured the scene I thought, if I had known what he was going to do, I would have left a few dollars on the bedside table for him so he could bring his children some really lovely gifts. I finished the visualization smiling and never again did the man in the hallway trouble my thoughts.

Now and then I smile thinking of him and his children. You can point out that the robber probably spent the money on drugs rather than his children. Maybe he did. It makes no difference to me what he did with our belongings. I am free because of the change in me. (1)

Sometime later, when Bernie's son, Jeff, had his home robbed, Bernie helped him to leap directly to a reframing visualization of the theft, only this time the thief purchased his mother a birthday present! Jeff made fun of his dad's crazy way of thinking, but he had to admit that it worked like a charm.

A higher game on a wider field.

In a world where we are taught to play the game of *Diminish Others* and *Accumulate Stuff,* Jesus is calling us — is enticing us — to play a higher game on a wider field, with deeper goals and surprising rules, using a multitude of hidden players and a timescale long enough to win every time.

What kind of game is Jesus playing? The game of *Up* and the game of *Holy Hugs,* the game of *Astonish Others* and *Give Away Stuff,* the game of *Lost and Now-Found* and *Adopt Your Whole Family,* the game of *Bridges to Everywhere* and *Everybody Around One Table.*

Christ's circle.

Finally, imagine you are in a circle around Christ's communion table, a great circle extending from your church's chancel out into the sanctuary, as far as needed to include everyone.

Now imagine everyone is invited to echo back the following words of commitment, words that pledge us to play the Jesus game, words that express our vow to become the kind of faith community Christ calls us to be.

Imagine, and respond now, line by line, with the echo-response of your commitment:

21

*May our circle
become Christ's circle,
Where all are welcome
and none forgotten,
Where our uniqueness is affirmed
and our hidden gifts freed,
Where we begin again
to care for the suffering
and rebuild the world,
Where we deepen in faith
and discover our part
in the drama of God's redeeming love.
May our circle
become Christ's circle. (2)*

ENDNOTES

Sketch #1 ...Jesus, Our Player-of-a-Different-Game:
A Higher Game On A Wider Field

1. Bernie Siegel, from the audio recording of his book, *Prescriptions for Living* (New York: Harper Audio, 1998).

2. "Our Circle" is a poem-prayer by Hope Harle-Mould, first published May 1993 in *Church Educator*.

Sketch #2 ...Jesus, Our Wounded-Hands Healer:

Saying "Jesus" With Your Hands

Mark 6:53-56 — Healing wherever he went

Luke 22:39-42, 45-53 — A last healing in Gethsemane

"Thenoneofthemstrucktheslaveofthehighpriestandcutoffhisrightear. ButJesussaid, 'Nomoreofthis!' Andhetouchedhisearandhealedhim."
Luke 22:50-51 (NRSV)

"There is a sign each of us wears... invisibly hanging around our necks, a message candidly declaring our need for personal connection, for palpable caring, for skin to skin contact, for human touch. We keep this sign hidden, far from prying eyes, to protect our vulnerable inner child, to camouflage our fragile sense of self, to deny our isolation and exile, to disguise our aching need and open wounds. And yet hoping against hope, we pray that somehow, someone may see our sign and give us what we most long for but cannot ask: 'Please touch!'"
— Hope Harle-Mould

Jesus made house calls.

Jesus was not just a teacher or preacher; he was a healer. His ministry was holistic. Jesus not only taught new truths for our minds and preached new trust for our souls, but he also cared for our broken bodies. His was a ministry of healing, wholeness, and hope.

In the world Jesus grew up in, the sick were often written off as expendable. People with disabilities were reduced to beggars. People with chronic illness were cast out and condemned as getting their due punishment from God. People with contagious disease had no hospitals to go to, nowhere to turn. So Jesus came to them:

When they had crossed over, they came to land at Gennesaret and moored the boat. When they got out of the boat, people at once recognized him, and rushed about that whole region and began to bring the sick on mats to wherever they heard he was. And wherever he went, to villages or cities or farms, they laid the sick in the marketplaces, and begged him that they might touch even the fringe of his cloak; and all who touched it were healed.
Mark 6:53-56 (NRSV)

When Jesus announced that the kingdom of God was at hand, he didn't just use words; through his hands he demonstrated it with signs of power: *The reign of God has dawned in your midst!* Jesus didn't just preach about heavenly things, he *practiced* bringing heavenly things to earth. Jesus didn't just teach scholarly points of scriptural interpretation; he waded into crowds of sick people who needed the word of God to be made into the Word become flesh.

Jesus made house calls. He healed Peter's mother-in-law of a high fever. He healed the epileptic young man who was thrashing about. He healed the little girl who was beyond coma and declared dead. When he was in a crushing crowd and the woman with the flow of blood touched the hem of his garment for healing, he stopped and called for her and spoke to her with compassion. Jesus healed the blind and mute man with spittle and mud, with a groan toward heaven, and with the Aramaic word, *"Ephphatha!"* — be opened! He healed the widow of Nain's son, who relied on her son for survival. Even as Jesus was leaving Jericho to journey toward death in Jerusalem, he stopped and noticed and healed the blind man, Bartimaeus.

The last person Jesus ever healed.

But who was the last person Jesus ever healed? The healing happened at his weakest moment, on the night before his death, in Gethsemane, just after he had prayed that he might not have to die — but *not my will but thine be done*. It happened just after he found his disciples asleep again, despite his imploring them to stay awake and keep vigil with him. It happened just after Judas arrived and betrayed Jesus with a kiss, and the armed temple guards of High Priest Caiaphas rushed forward to seize him. It happened just after one disciple drew a short sword to defend Jesus and ending up slashing off the ear of the servant of Caiaphas. It happened just after Jesus rebuked his disciples, shouting, "Enough!" meaning, *Put down your swords!* **That** *is not the kind of Messiah I am.* **This** *is the kind of Messiah I am...* and he reached out his hand, touched the servant's ear, and healed him, a man named Malthus.

Liberated from illness.

One of the primary ways Jesus went about curing people from disease was by liberating them from illness. A disease is the organic problem within the body which a doctor diagnoses. An illness is the patient's experience of the disease, both as an individual and as one is treated by society.

John Dominic Crossan, in his book, *Jesus: A Revolutionary Biography*, said:

> *Think, for example, of the difference between curing the disease or healing the illness known as AIDS. A cure for the disease is absolutely desirable, but in its absence, we can still heal the illness by refusing to ostracize those who have it, by empathizing with their anguish, and by enveloping their sufferings with both respect and love.... Seen from those perspectives, the leper who met Jesus had both a disease (say, psoriasis) and an illness, the personal and social stigma of uncleanness, isolation, and rejection.... I presume that Jesus... healed the poor man's illness by refusing to accept the disease's ritual uncleanness and social ostracization. Jesus thereby forced others either to reject him from their community or to accept the leper within it as well. (1)*

In first century Palestine, religious law often ostracized people with open skin diseases, people with bleeding disorders, and people with mental illness. Social barbed wire and cultural brick walls were put up to keep sick people out and religious people in, to keep ill people prisoners and the pious people pure. That is what is depicted in the parable of the Good Samaritan: the Levite and the priest walk by on the other side because they believe the beaten victim's blood would have made them unclean.

By treating broken people as pariahs and wounded people as untouchables, religious authorities had created the experience of illness. That is what Jesus attacks in his ministry. He breaks through the barriers of socially created illness to touch the sick, to embrace the broken, to hug the hopeless. Does this cure their disease? Not always, but by healing these people from ostracism, by inviting these people to join him at table, Jesus liberates them from the experience of illness, forcing the disease into a corner where it could wither and die on its own.

A ministry of presence.

How can we participate in Jesus' healing ministry? One way is through the ministry of presence, by simply being-there for others in their time of need. Henri Nouwen described it this way:

> *The friend who can be silent with us in a moment of despair or confusion, who can stay with us in an hour of grief and bereavement, who can tolerate not-knowing, not-curing, not-healing and face with us the reality of our powerlessness, that is the friend who cares.* (2)

My father was 24 and fresh from seminary when he began serving his first church. Shortly after he arrived, a young person in the congregation committed suicide. People in the church were devastated. Dad barely knew the family, but he headed over to the house as soon as he heard the news. As this young minster walked up toward that home — where inside was such a magnitude of anguish — he could only do one thing: admit he was stepping into a situation beyond his competence, beyond his experience, beyond his wisdom. Their need for God's word of comfort was so dire and his words so unsure. As the grieving mother opened that door, he prayed that God would use him somehow, in some way — a healing balm of Gilead. Inside the house, my father said very little. He didn't have to. Just by his presence, the family received a sign: that God was there, that God cared, that God's grace would carry them on. They thanked him profusely. They had received what they needed. And my father had, too.

Old Anna.

How can we participate in Jesus' healing ministry? Through the power of touch.

In the early 1900s, infant mortality at some of America's orphanages soared, some approaching 100%. It was at that time that Dr. Fritz Talbot of Boston visited the Children's Clinic in Dusseldorf, Germany. There he noticed an old woman always roaming the hallways, sick children always on her hip. They explained:

> *That's Old Anna. When we have done everything we can medically for a baby and it still is not doing well, we turn it over to Old Anna, and she cures it. (3)*

Talbot introduced "tender loving care" to Bellevue Hospital in New York over the skepticism of its modern-thinking medical staff. But the statistics converted them all. Infant mortality dropped from 35% to less than 10% when every child was carried and cuddled several times daily. All thanks to Old Anna.

A child's crayoned name.

How can we participate in Jesus' healing ministry? Perhaps by making homemade greeting cards and giving them to the sick, the grieving, and the lonely.

This is something I always ask the children in my churches to do. They draw flowers, animals, and rainbows, and glue on glitter and cut out hearts with scissors. They write a few endearing words of greeting and sign their names in big letters. Then they give them to me to take to people on my home or hospital visits.

When I hand them to someone, their eyes light up with appreciation. Often these are the first cards patients receive in a hospital and are usually the first bit of artistic color to be tacked up in their sterile room. People treasure these cards and never fail to smile at them. Inside the card, below the child's crayoned name, I always add: "From the children of our church, as their hands join Jesus' hands in healing."

You, too, can make homemade cards of blessing. You, too, are a child of God. You, too, can join Jesus' hands in healing.

In our woundedness...pools of healing for others.

How can we participate in Jesus' healing ministry? By finding in our very woundedness a source of healing for others.

This should come as no surprise to us, for we follow a man who wore a crown of thorns and was nailed to a cross. The crown of thorns was one way the Roman soldiers mocked Jesus: *You, the king of the Jews? Well, where's your royal crown? Here, let's make one for you!* And they took the branches of a thorn bush and shaped them into a cap like Caesar wore, and they pushed the crown of thorns down into his scalp, wounding him with this sign of humiliation, rivulets of blood dripping down his face. Yet even then, as he hung in pain upon an instrument of capital punishment, Jesus spoke words of healing that have reverberated down the centuries, words meant not only for those soldiers but spoken directly to you and me as well: *Abba, forgive them, for they know not what they do.*

One way our suffering finds meaning is as the Holy Spirit links us in caring to another person. There are many people who can offer support to us in times of tragedy, but the person who may help us most is the one who has been there before, who has personally experienced what we are going through. That is why groups like Make Today Count, a support group for persons with cancer, are so effective. Such a person can come to us through our tears and anguish and say, *I know the depth of your loss; I know the anguish of your pain; I've been through it; let me weep with you; and we will walk through this together.* Such a person can show us, as no one else can, that there is hope, that we can endure, that we can go on and build a new life.

Making the world safe for marigolds.

How can we participate in Jesus' healing ministry? By inspiring others with the way we live and way we die.

In his book *Peace, Love, and Healing,* surgeon Bernie Siegel tells of a 78-year-old landscape gardener named John Florio. Complaining of abdominal pain, an upper GI series revealed an ulcer. A month later, a biopsy revealed the enlarged ulcer to be malignant stomach cancer. Bernie recommended immediate surgery, for he would soon be out of town on vacation. But

John, wanting to hold off on surgery, told the doctor that he had forgotten something. Bernie was puzzled and asked what he had forgotten. John said, "It's springtime. I'm a landscape gardener, and I want to make the world beautiful. That way if I survive (until you return and can do surgery), it's a gift. If I don't, I will have left a beautiful world."

Two weeks later, Bernie returned from vacation and John told him that the world was now beautiful and that he was ready. After the operation, the pathology report was grim. The cancer had penetrated the gastric wall and seven of sixteen lymph nodes tested positive for the tumor. Siegel recommended chemo and X-ray therapy. John told him that he had forgotten something. Bernie asked what he had forgotten this time. John replied, "It's still spring. I don't have time for all that." And with this kind of serenity, John recovered quickly from surgery and went back home.

Four years later, Bernie saw John Florio's chart on his rack. Thinking that John must have died by this point, he told the nurse that she had gotten out the wrong chart. She said she had not. Bernie wondered if there was another person by the same name. No, the nurse replied, it was indeed the same old John Florio sitting right out there in the waiting room. When it was John's turn, Bernie asked him why he was there. He replied that he had a hernia from lifting boulders in his landscape business. Bernie treated him for the hernia. Two years later Bernie heard he was still alive in the beauty of nature doing what he said was his life's work: "Making the world safe for marigolds." (4)

John Florio reminds us that it is by living passionately with purpose, by staying grounded in the joy of nature, that we can connect with the sources of holy healing.

Not everyone with cancer or heart disease or HIV can be cured. Life is a terminal condition. If we try to live forever, we're going to fail. Death is part of life. But the greatest tragedy of all is to stop living in the midst of life while we are still alive, as Norman Cousins reminds us..

If you had only six months left to live, how would you live? If you answer that question by saying, *Just the way I am now*, then you are living your calling: to a vibrant, fully alive life.

"Wounded Hands."

Our Savior's name in English is pronounced "Jesus." In Hebrew it is Yeshua (or as we might say, Joshua). But what is it in American Sign Language (ASL)? What symbol did the deaf community improvise and evolve to say the name of Jesus? It had to be something immediately recognizable, something that would instantly remind someone of Jesus. The symbol they ended up choosing is one that profoundly expresses Jesus' entire mission and meaning. They called him, "Wounded Hands," depicting his name by depicting the pierced hands of his sacrificial love.

How to say "Jesus" with your hands.

How do you learn to sign "Jesus" in ASL? Hold your hands up in front of you, palms facing each other, about a foot apart. With the middle finger of the right hand, quickly strike the center of the palm of the left hand. Then with the middle finger of the left hand, quickly strike the palm of the right hand. That is how you say "Jesus" with your hands.

When anyone sees you signing this, they will immediately know who you are speaking about, for in all of history there is but one person whose hands are remembered so uniquely. His hands were marked by wounds, wounds there were received in unmerited suffering, to reconcile the world to God, to be the bridge for the estranged to come home: "But he was wounded for our transgressions…and by his bruises we are healed" (Isaiah 53:5 NRSV).

This is our Savior, the one we believe in, the teacher we follow, the healer who heals us, the man known down through the ages as Wounded Hands. In the hands of this one man, the wounds of our world are redeemed. And so are we.

A Jesus high-five.

How can we participate in Jesus' healing ministry? By taking on the burden of our neighbor's suffering, so that we may become be an instrument of God's peace.

One way we can symbolize this is through a ritual I call the Jesus High-Five. The idea is to form the name of Jesus in ASL, but with one crucial difference. It must be formed by using two people at once.

The Jesus High-Five begins by two people facing each other, with the first person holding up their right hand toward the one in front of them. Then the second person raises their right hand toward the first person's hand, keeping it about a foot away. Now the first person uses their middle finger to quickly strike the center of the palm of the second person's palm. Then the second person uses their middle finger to quickly strike the center of the palm of the first person. Together, the two have formed the word "Jesus," but in poignant way.

What is the meaning here? The first person opens their palm — representing their life — to accept and help bear the pain and suffering of the other person, and the second person opens their palm — representing their life — to take on and carry the hurt and anguish of the first person. In the act of offering each other our empathy, vulnerability, and love, we depict and say "Jesus."

What if our religion no longer allowed us to speak the name of Jesus by ourselves? What if the only time we were spiritually permitted to say "Jesus" was when two persons came together and offered to share the wounds of the other, when two persons *were* Jesus to each other? If that was so, if we said "Jesus" only at such moments, then Jesus' name would not only be fully honored but fully practiced. And Christians might become known in a new way, as... *those people whose wounded-hands heal.*

ENDNOTES

Sketch #2 ...Jesus, Our Wounded-Hands Healer:
Saying Jesus with Your Hands

1. John Dominic Crossan, *Jesus: A Revolutionary Biography* (San Francisco: Harper San Francisco, 1994), 81-82.

2. Henri J.M. Nouwen, *Out of Solitude: Three Meditations on the Christian Life* (Notre Dame: Ave Maria Press, 1974), 34.

3. Paul Brand and Philip Yancey, *Fearfully and Won-*

derfully Made (Grand Rapids: Zondervan Publishing House, 1980), 138.

4. Bernie S. Siegel, MD, *Peace, Love and Healing* (New York: Harper and Row, Publishers, 1989), 9.

Sketch #3 ...Jesus, Our Dead-Raiser:

Talitha, Koum! — Little Girl, Arise!

Mark 5:21-43 – Jesus raises to life the twelve-year-old girl

"Do not fear, only believe" Mark 5:36 (NRSV)

"He took her by hand and said to her, 'Talitha, koum,' which means, 'Little girl, I tell you to get up!" Mark 5:41 (TEV)

"Sometimes our light goes out but is blown again into flame by an encounter with another human being. Each of us owes the deepest thanks to those who have rekindled this inner light."
— Albert Schweitzer

My not-exactly-raising-the-dead experience.

I had been the Associate Pastor of a church in Ohio for less than a year when I got a phone call from one of our members. It was a thirty-year-old woman whose father had just been admitted to the Coronary Intensive Care Unit (CICU) and was in critical condition. She told me the family had just returned home from seeing him at the hospital and asked if I would be able to visit him. Though I had never met her father, I said I would be happy to go at once.

Entering the CICU, I approached the main desk and said to the nurse, "I'm Pastor Hope, and I'd like to see Gabe Berryman (1), please." She replied, "Oh, I'm sorry, pastor, but Mr. Berryman just died a few minutes ago." I was stunned. I stood there not knowing what to say or do. I had never been in this situation before. Then I realized that I was the first to know, and that I would need to go to his daughter's home and break the news to them.

Taking a step to leave, I turned around and said, "I'd like to pray over the body." She told me his room number. I entered through the already-opened door and stood near the foot of his bed. As I solemnly folded my hands and bowed in silent prayer, I noticed that something didn't seem quite right. It appeared Gabe's foot was moving. Then it appeared his chest was moving. Then it appeared the room was moving!

I must have turned pale as a ghost — or looked like I had just seen one — because a different nurse swept into the room and asked me, "Are you okay?" "Never felt better," I lied. She continued: "I'm sorry, pastor, but we gave you the wrong room number. The man who just died is in the next room, the room to your right."

Moving toward the door, I said, "Thank you, yes, I'd like to pray over his body. You see, I'm the pastor of Gabe Berryman's daughter." The nurse replied, "Well, you may if you like, but the dead man in the next room is not Gabe Berryman; he's John Doe. This man here is Mr. Berryman."

Now I was really ready to pass out! Any moment would have been fine. I thanked the nurse for how uniquely helpful they all had been and returned to Mr. Berryman's bedside to pray. I held onto the bars the whole time.

Less than three hours later, I got a call at my home saying that Gabe was dead. This time he really was.

Throughout the evening, I imagined with horror what would have happened if I had gone to the daughter's house and declared her father dead while he was still alive and kicking. Of course, if I had, I would have been off by only three hours! Maybe they would have thought I had psychic powers. On the other hand, they might have assumed I was working as an agent in a euthanasia conspiracy.

The next day I met with the family to prepare for the funeral, my first at that church. To this day, they still don't know that I almost pronounced dear old Gabe dead slightly ahead of his time, like Mark Twain being erroneously listed as deceased in the obituary columns of a newspaper and his quipping, "I assure you that reports of my untimely demise are highly exaggerated."

Every so often since then, when my wife and I find ourselves driving along the highway past the cemetery where Mr. Berryman is buried, my wife invariably turns to me and asks, "Are you *sure* Gabe is really in there?"

Why does Jesus raise the dead?

At Bethany, Jesus weeps at the tomb of his friend Lazarus, the brother of Mary and Martha, and despite four days of bodily putrefaction, Jesus commands the stone be rolled away and calls out: "Lazarus, come out!" (John 11:43 NRSV.) And Lazarus does, still wrapped with grave-clothes around his hands, feet, and head (John 11:1-44).

At the Galilean town of Nain, as Jesus approaches the town gates, a dead man is being carried out — the only son of a widow, her only means of support — and out of compassion Jesus brings her son back to life (Luke 7:11-17). Two of the witnesses who were in the crowd that day are disciples of the imprisoned John the Baptist, who sends them back with a question: *Are you the anointed one, the Messiah, or should we wait for another?* Jesus answers, "Go and tell John what you have seen and heard: the blind receive their sight, the lame walk, the lepers are cleansed, the deaf hear, the dead are raised, the poor have good news brought to them" (Luke 7:18-23 NRSV).

Why does Jesus raise the dead? Not to deny or delay death at all costs — for Jesus clearly invited people into dangerous discipleship, to take up their cross, as in the end he does as well. And not to perform spectacular public miracles to seduce observers into believers — for he told people not to publicize these wonders. Rather, Jesus raised the dead for the same reason he healed and preached and shaped a community of faith: to be a sign, a sign pointing to something more, and that more was the kingdom of God.

The central message of Jesus was this: the reign and realm of God was now at hand, breaking into human history, dawning in their midst in his ministry. Raising the dead was one of the signs that here and now the liberated zone of God was being established, a spiritual area where God's will was being done on earth as it is in heaven.

But there was another reason. Death is the ultimate destroyer. It ravages our world. It annihilates our loved ones. It diminishes our faith. It destroys our hope. But when Jesus raises the dead, he puts the powers of death on notice. Evil may do its worst, but in the end God's promises cannot be killed. Even in defeat, God's truth triumphs still. And so Jesus raises the dead, and the forces of darkness are once again dethroned and defeated.

Entering the scriptural story.

There's a modern proverb that warns, if something seems too good to be true, it probably is. But when it comes to the promises of God, there are some things that are too good *not* to be true. And this is one.

How does Jesus' raising the dead connect with our lives? To find out, we must enter the scriptural story from Mark 5.

One day after returning from across the Sea of Galilee, Jesus is surrounded by a crowd along the shore at Capernaum. Jairus, the dignified administrative leader of a nearby synagogue, comes — as a last resort — to this controversial Jewish teacher, throws himself at his feet, and pleads again and again: *My dear daughter is tottering at the brink of death! Come and lay hands on her that she might recover and be whole and live again.* Moved by this dad's devotion, Jesus turns from the lakeside and without a word goes with Jairus up the path and into the town.

On their way, they are interrupted. A woman hidden in the crushing crowd around Jesus reaches out, touches the hem of Jesus' cloak, and is immediately healed of her twelve-year-long hemorrhage. Sensing power has gone out of him, Jesus calls the woman forward and pronounces, "Daughter, your faith has made you well; go in peace and be healed of your disease" (Mark 5:34 NRSV).

But by the time Jesus is ready to go on, messengers from Jairus' home rush up and tell him every parent's worst nightmare: *I'm sorry. It's too late. Your daughter is dead.* Jairus begins to weep. The messengers say, *Why bother the Teacher any longer? There's no reason. It's hopeless.*

Jesus overhears this exchange. How does he respond? He ignores their despondency. He gives no power to their despair. Instead, the Teacher teaches them the teaching they most need at that moment to learn: "Do not fear; only believe!" (Mark 5:36 NRSV).

36

Allowing none of the crowd to follow him but Peter, James, and John, Jesus approaches Jairus' house where a cacophony of mourners are wailing loudly and weeping pathetically outside the door. As he come nears, Jesus asks, *Why all this chaos and carrying on? Why all these tears? The child needs not a funeral but an awakening.* Some of the people there think to themselves, *What a terribly cruel thing to say to a grieving family.* Indeed, the text says that many people angrily made fun of Jesus, mocking him to his face.

Then Jesus commands: *Get out of this house, everyone, now!* And they obey. Then with the father and mother and three disciples, Jesus goes into the room where their daughter's limp body lay. There he takes her by the hand and proclaims in Aramaic these exact words: *"Talitha, koum!"* — meaning, *"Little girl, arise! Little girl, get up!"* And she does. She stands. Then do you know what she does next? She begins walking round and round the room.

The parents are so overcome with amazement, they don't know what to say or do. So Jesus gives them a hint — and a wink: *Well, give her something to eat!*

Jesus says to the dead places in you and me: "Child of mine, arise in hope!"

Sometimes life makes us die inside while we are still living. At those times, we hit the wall of despair; we sulk despondently. But it is then that we see the unanticipated hope Jesus brings across the threshold of our days. It is then that we experience this truth: in every situation no matter how dismal or desperate, in every circumstance no matter how seemingly closed, there's always hope. And when, in hope, we step out onto the thin air above the abyss, we will find underneath our feet a bridge of angels we cannot see but only sense, and in hope we will walk across to the other side.

Famed cardiologist Dr. Bernard Lown (professor of cardiology at Harvard University School of Public Health) once had a patient named Mr. B who suffered a massive heart attack. His cardiac muscle was irreparably damaged, his lungs congested, his heart rate wildly rapid, heart rhythm out of sync. The doctors had nothing left to try. One morning, Dr. Lown was explaining Mr. B's condition to a group of medical students while Mr. B, breathing through an oxygen mask, seemed unaware of what was going on. Dr. Lown matter-of-factly stated that Mr. B had a "wholesome, very loud, third-sound gallop." In medical jargon this meant a critical condition, indicating that the heart muscle was failing. The doctors exited.

But remarkably Mr. B began to recover. His chart no longer read irreparable, incurable or terminal. Soon he was released and smiling. Dr. Lown was stupefied. Only months later did Mr. B tell him that he knew the exact moment he started to recover:

> *I was sure the end was near and that you and your staff had given up hope. Then I heard you tell your colleagues that I have a "wholesome gallop," so I figured that I still had a lot of kick to my heart and I could not be dying. For the first time my spirits lifted, and I knew that I would recover. (2)*

There is no such thing as hopeless hope. Hope is so powerful that when we live by hope — even if by mistake — extraordinary things are possible.

Fear not — Just believe!

Sometimes fear paralyzes us. Fear imprisons us, walling us within our homes, far from the love-starved world. Fear inhibits us from going out and serving those whom Christ calls us to go out and serve. Fear conditions us to hide our gifts and bury our goodness from those we are in relationship with, week to week. But Jesus says to the fearful places in you and me: *Fear? Not! Just believe!*

During the war in Bosnia, Francika Redzepagic (whose family was sponsored and resettled as refugees by my former church in Springboro, Ohio) was only 23-years-old the day soldiers came into her house and pointed their guns at the heads of her daughters, four-year-old Anja and six-week-old Ena, demanded all of their deutsche-marks (money) and demanded that Sasha, her husband, come with them to be incarcerated in a prison camp.

Francika was terrified. All she wanted to do was cry out for her mama to come and make everything better. But she knew that Sasha was in grave danger and might be executed. It was up to her. She had to be brave and without fear. She decided to save her husband.

The next day she walked through the streets — despite the occasional gunshots of snipers — to the police station and said, "I must use a phone." They said, "What are you doing here? Are you crazy? Don't you know it's dangerous to go through the streets? Stay at home." She said, "I must use a phone. My brother is with the Croatian forces. He might help persuade the military commanders to let my husband go." They let her use the phone, but her brother said there was nothing he could do; the commanders wouldn't listen.

Again, the same day Francika went back to the police station and asked to use the phone to speak to her brother. Later that day she went back a third time and tried to phone once more. At the end of the day she returned a fourth time and phoned again.

The next day she did the same, and the next, and the next. For nine consecutive days, four or five times every day, Francika risked her life on the streets to save the life of her husband. Why was Sasha finally released? It's not clear, but I have a theory. Perhaps the police and her brother and the military commanders and even God were so worn down by Francika's relentless protests that in the end they had no choice... but to surrender to Francika and release her husband. And they did.

After Sasha told me this story, he said of Francika: "My wife is a strong and brave woman. But sometimes when I act up, she says, 'Maybe I shouldn't have saved you after all!'" (For more about Sasha and Francika, see Sketch #13, Jesus, Our Foreigner-Lover.)

All in a day's work.

Let me end with my poem, "All In A Day's Work."

> At the village of Nain,
> Jesus sees the funeral procession
> of the widow's son
> and he simply raises the dead.
> At Bethany, Jesus sees the tomb of his friend
> Lazarus

and he simply raises the dead.
At the home of Jairus,
Jesus sees the room in which the little girl
lies
and simply raises the dead.
In our community and in our homes,
Jesus sees our places of fear and hopelessness
and simply raises the dead.
It's really no big deal —
all in a day's work.
Jesus simply walks into the dark places in
our lives
and raises the dead,
then says to you and me:
"Now... how about something to eat?"

ENDNOTES

Sketch #3 ...Jesus, Our Dead-Raiser:
"Talitha, Koum! — Little Girl, Arise!"

1. A pseudonym.

2. Maurice Lamm, The Power of Hope: The One Essential of Life and Love (New York: Rawson Associates, 1995), 108.

Sketch #4 ...Jesus, Our Stranger:

Meet-Me-at-the-Neighbor

Matthew 25:31-46 — Parable of the Last Judgment

"How can I help but think of these things every time I sit down ... and look around at the tables filled with the unutterably poor who are going through their long-continuing crucifixion. It is more surely an exercise of faith for us to see Christ in each other. But it is through such exercise that we grow and the joy of our vocation assures us we are on the right path. The mystery of the poor is this: That they are Jesus, and what you do for them you do for Him. It is the only way we have of knowing and believing in our love. The mystery of poverty is that by sharing in it, making ourselves poor in giving to others, we increase our knowledge of and belief in love."
— Dorothy Day

"For I was hungry and you gave me no food, I was thirsty and you gave me nothing to drink, I was a stranger and you did not welcome me, naked and you did not give me clothing, sick and in prison and you did not visit me." Matthew 25:42-43 (NRSV)

A DRAMATIC DIALOGUE

NOTE: Imagine that you were called into a court of law by a hostile prosecuting attorney to give testimony as to whether or not you have truly trusted and followed Christ's teaching in Matthew 25:31-46, the Parable of the Last Judgment. How would you answer? Would you be convicted or exonerated? This is what I imagined happened to me.

"Meet-Me-at-the-Neighbor"

Attorney: I have just a few questions for you this morning. Are you familiar with the Parable of the Last

Judgment, also known as the Parable of the Sheep and Goats, found in Matthew 25:31-46?

Hope: Yes, of course, it's one of Jesus' greatest teachings.

Attorney: And why would you say that?

Hope: Well, he's teaching us what it means to love our neighbor as ourselves, and how loving God with all our heart is intertwined with loving our neighbor. And he does with such memorable metaphor and surprising twists.

Attorney: I see. Now in the parable, the righteous are surprised to hear the king say that they are deemed righteous. Why is that?

Hope: Well, the righteous did deeds of mercy for their neighbors simply out of empathy and compassion for those who were suffering, not out of any obligation or the seeking of reward. They didn't do it because the hungry person was someone famous or a close relative but because they truly cared. What they didn't realize was that in doing so, they were actually caring for Christ in disguise, God coming to us in the form of the poor.

Attorney: And in the parable, the unrighteous on the king's left are surprised to find out they are deemed unrighteous. Why is that?

Hope: Well, the unrighteous were highly pious but thought that was enough. They knew that Christ was king, said they believed in him, promised they would do anything for him if he asked, but when he came to them in the form of the downtrodden, they failed to recognize his face. They were blind. They did not see him.

Attorney: And which are you?

Hope: What's that?

Attorney: Which are you, the righteous or unrighteous?

Hope: Well, it's not for me to say; it's not even for others to say; it's God judgment in the end.

Attorney: But whom do you most identify with in the parable?

Hope: I believe we're supposed to learn from them both of them.

Attorney: Let me remind you: you're still under oath.

Hope: Okay, well, if I'm honest, I probably identify most with the righteous.

Attorney: And why is that?

Hope: Well, I do think it's very important to care for the hungry and the suffering.

Attorney: Do you think the king in the parable *cares* what you think or believe in your mind? Or does he only care about actions that show that your faith is not dead?

Hope: Well, deeds do reveal what's inside us. I do try to be intentional about this.

Attorney: And do you think the king in the parable *cares* about your good intentions — that you'll get around to taking compassionate action someday, that you'll get around to giving generously someday — or only about whether you have in fact done so?

Hope: Well, I think Christ cares about inner motivation as well, which only he can see.

Attorney: Please limit your responses to answering the question. We're talking about this parable.

Hope: Could you repeat the question?

Attorney: Let me rephrase. Do you think Jesus told this parable to make complacent people feel good about themselves — to help self-righteous people feel they deserved commendation, when in reality they had done so little for so few, and at the last minute?

Hope: No.

Attorney: Would you say Jesus told this parable to challenge people to consider how often they've been oblivious to inconvenient neighbors, how often they've turned their backs on the dregs of society, while at the same time pleading with God to help *their* family and *their* relatives get even more?

Hope: Probably so.

Attorney: And didn't Jesus often use surprise endings in his parables to wake people up, to make people indict themselves, to show them a different path in being religious?

Hope: Yes, that was a hallmark of his.

Attorney: So, do you think Jesus is using this parable today to wake *you* up, to make *you* realize the benign neglect you've shown toward the sick and the stranger?

Hope: I believe you're right about that.

Attorney: Now, when you care for the hungry, do you see them as Christ?

Hope: Sometimes.

Attorney: And when you *fail* to care for the hungry — when you intend to act but do not, when you are asked to get involved but you pretend not to notice someone in need, when you — without a second thought — spend frivolously on yourself the very money that others are praying for …when you fail to care for the hungry, do you see them as Christ?

Hope: No, I guess not.

Attorney: Could I see your wallet, please?

Hope: What?

Attorney: Your wallet.

Hope: Okay, sure, I guess.

(Hope hands his wallet to the Attorney, who peeks inside, quickly pulls out a card, and holds it up.)

Attorney: This is a rewards card from Subway. Does it belong to you?

Hope: Sure does. I love Subway.

Attorney: I see you have received eight out of ten points, after which you can earn a free foot long sub. Is that correct?

Hope: Yes.

Attorney: And who were you planning to give that free sub to?

Hope: Well, ah...me or my family.

Attorney: I see. And every autumn, when your denomination takes its special Neighbors In Need Offering, do you always give the equivalent of ten subs?

Hope: No, I can't say I do.

Attorney: Exactly. You can't say that you do. Now... when Jesus says, *I was sick you didn't visit me,* could this refer to those who are depressed or who might be suffering chronic illnesses? Could it refer to those who hide at home, or to those who have such negative or troubled personalities that others find it easier to forget about them than to visit them?

Hope: Yes, it certainly could.

(The Attorney walks back to his table, picks up a flash drive in a clear plastic bag, and holds it up.)

Attorney: I have here a surveillance log based on video camera footage outside the home of one person whom you know who is suffering depression and chronic ill-

45

ness. On the casing of this flash drive is recorded the number of times you have visited this person in recent weeks. Would you care to read aloud the total number of your visits?

Hope: No, I'd rather not. It's not enough, not nearly enough.

Attorney: Now, when Jesus says, *I was a prisoner and you abandoned me,* could that refer to a prisoner-of-conscience, held illegally by some nation for years without charge, without trial, and forced to endure enhanced interrogations?

Hope: Yes, it could.

Attorney: And have you done anything in the last year to publicly and personally speak up for such people?

Hope: I gave a donation to Amnesty International.

Attorney: Just answer the question! Did you publicly and personally do anything in the last year to speak up for such prisoners? Anything at all?

Hope: No.

Attorney: So, in as much as you did nothing for these, your brothers and sisters — incarcerated, tortured, or alone in unspeakable conditions — you did nothing for Christ. Correct?

Hope: You might say that. I could have done more.

Attorney: So, in light of your answers, do you still claim to identify most with the righteous?

Hope: No.

Attorney: And can you honestly say that you have you ever met or personally known *anyone* who is an example of the righteous, anyone who, as in the parable, might be surprised that their deeds were actually done to Christ?

Hope: Well, yes, in fact I have.

Attorney: Oh, really. And who could that be?

Hope: Meet-Me-at-the-Neighbor.

Attorney: No, I was asking you the name of someone you've known who is a righteous example.

Hope: Meet-Me-at-the-Neighbor.

Attorney: I don't understand.

Hope: That's her name.

Attorney: That's what I'm asking.

Hope: That's what I'm telling you.

Attorney: What are you telling me?

Hope: Meet-Me-at-the-Neighbor.

Attorney: Why do you keep saying that?

Hope: Because that's her name!

Attorney: Who's name?

Hope: The righteous woman.

Attorney: Meet-Me-at-the-Neighbor?

Hope: Now you've got it.

Attorney: What do I got?

Hope: The woman's name.

Attorney: Meet-Me-at-the-Neighbor.

Hope: Bingo!

Attorney: What kind of name is that?

Hope: It's her spiritual name.

Attorney: But not her given name.

Hope: It *is* being given her.

Attorney: When?

Hope: Today.

Attorney: By whom?

Hope: By me.

Attorney: So what does this name, Meet-Me-at-the-Neighbor, actually mean?

Hope: I believe this is something Christ says to you and me: "Meet me at the neighbor." It means that the place where we might encounter Christ most vividly is in and with the neighbors.

There are times when we're struggling to return to God or to sense God's presence and suddenly a neighbor appears in our life and becomes for us a teacher of sacred insight or new perspective. There are times when we're crying out in anguish for a miracle in our lives and suddenly a stranger appears and becomes for us a godsend of compassion or just a silent solace. The neighbor is where we meet Christ incognito.

Attorney: And so this woman you are naming — she has no idea how much she has done for Christ?

Hope: No, no idea at all.

Attorney: Is she here today?

Hope: Yes, as a matter of fact she is.

Attorney: What's her given name?

Hope: Meet-Me-at-the-Neighbor.

Attorney: No, I mean, what's her birth name?

Hope: That would be... Roberta Farkas-Huezo. Or, as all her friends call her, Robbie.

Attorney: And why did you give this woman this name?

Hope: Three reasons.

First, Robbie's faith in Christ is so deep and compassionate that she has, since childhood, felt a clear call to the priesthood, though her Catholic upbringing made that path impossible.

Second, from the time she was a young woman, she has worked to resettle refugees from throughout

Latin America, using her courage and her fluent language skills. She even married one of those refugees, an extraordinary Salvadoran soul named Oscar, and together they had two amazing children.

Third, despite being an extremely busy social worker, working in both child protective services and family services, she still finds time to be a prominent leader and member of our local Protestant church's work in sheltering asylum-seekers and supporting refugees from around the world. And on alternate Sundays she continues to be involved in a Spanish mass service at her favorite Catholic church.

Attorney: That is quite commendable.

Hope: It is. In fact, Robbie exemplifies Jesus' parable in the present tense. On a wall of her home is a sculpture of Christ she once rescued from the trash when it was being thrown out because Jesus' hands were broken off. And she always says, "We are the only hands Christ has in this world, to reach out to our neighbors in love."

So, Mr. Attorney, I would like to call forward Robbie Farkas-Huezo to stand before us all. And I want to recognize and affirm her unrelenting Christlike life.

[Robbie comes forward and stands next to Hope.]

Hope: Robbie, I have here in my pocket a small, symbolic gift for you. But it is not for you to keep. It is for you to give away. In the days ahead, you will undoubtedly meet someone in desperate need of Christ's healing and hope, someone who needs an extra dose of encouragement. This gift is for that person. It is a small, spiritual resource to support and recognize your ongoing ministry.

And please remember this. In the moment when you give this gift away, you and the stranger shall become God's holy place. And together, you shall form Christ's holy face.

(Hope hands her the small box as the court erupts into sustained applause. Finally, Hope continues.)

Hope: Finally, Robbie, I have with me an excerpt from a sermon you once gave, which I would like this court to hear. And I would like them to hear it in your own voice. Would you be so kind?

(Hope hands her the folded sheet of paper. After several moments of humble embarrassment, Robbie replies.)

Robbie: I can't believe you still have a copy of this, Pastor Hope, and I don't deserve all this attention. But I do strongly believe what these words say. So here they are, for you and me:

Christ calls us — every one of us — to be his partners in liberation. He calls us, as unworthy as we are, to be his eyes and his hands and his mouth in this world.

He asks us to use our eyes to see suffering and injustice in our midst, to use our hands to alleviate some, to use our mouths to speak words of comfort to the afflicted, and words of challenge and reconciliation and peace to the inflictors.

That this Christ, this son of God, would use my unworthy eyes and hands and mouth to further God's plan of salvific liberation... that is perhaps the most amazing thing of all.

Hope: Thank you so much, Robbie. And as your final word to this court, would you please state, to one and all, your given name.

Robbie: Meet-Me-at-the-Neighbor!

Sketch #5 ...Jesus, Our Coach:

Bodybuilding For An Unexpected Test Of Greatness

Mark 9:33-37 — Arguing on the road; Jesus and a child

"...What were you arguing about on the way?" But they were silent, for on the way they had argued with one another who was the greatest...Then he took a little child and put it among them; and taking it in his arms, he said to them, "Whoever welcomes one such child in my name welcomes me...." Mark. 9:33-37 (NRSV)

"To me, teamwork is a lot like being part of a family. It comes with obligations, entanglements, headaches, and quarrels. But the rewards are worth the cost... Teamwork is what makes common people capable of uncommon results..." —Pat Summit

"What were you arguing about on the road?"

Jesus was glad to be back home, the only home he had during his ministry, the house of Simon Peter and his family in the city of Capernaum, a fishing town on the north shore of Galilee.

But Jesus was not glad about what was happening among his disciples. He sensed a spirit of divisiveness, a conflict of aims, a confusion of vision. He feared the relationships between the twelve were becoming competitive rather than communal. So, despite his exhaustion, and with a sigh every parent understands, Jesus asked, *What were you arguing about on the road?*

This is how the passage begins, but this is actually Scene II of the drama. Scene I has already taken place offstage prior to this, on the road. In Scene I the disciples are splintered into cliques debating which of them is greatest. Let's listen in:

Peter, James, and John: "Jesus invited only three disciples to go with him to the mountaintop to witness his transfiguration — us!"

Andrew and Philip: "We were the first to follow Jesus, and if not for us, most of you would still be out fishing."

51

Matthew: "My personal conversion experience was more dramatic than any of yours."

Simon the Zealot: "No, mine was, from violent revolutionary to a nonviolent one!"

Thomas: "But I have the kind of systematic, theological mind a new religion needs...in my opinion."

And **Nathaniel:** "Don't forget: Jesus himself once called me the humblest Israelite he had ever seen. How about that?"

This debate was exactly the opposite of what Jesus was trying to achieve on the road with his disciples!

On the road. That was where Jesus always was bringing his disciples. Why? The word "disciple" in Aramaic, the language Jesus spoke, literally means "apprentice." Like a master artisan showing an apprentice the intricacies of one's craft, Jesus was teaching by demonstrating. Jesus took his apprentices everywhere he went, not just to see his hands as they healed or hear his voice as he taught but to absorb the spirit of his work, to learn by osmosis.

But Jesus took his disciples on the road for something more: to mold them into a *koinonia*, a community of faith. Jesus was fashioning this motley crew of strangers and former adversaries into a *koinonia* that reflected in its relationships his healing and teaching ministry, a community of faith that lived out a new social order in the midst of the old, a community of faith about which outsiders would one day say with amazement, "See how they love one another!"

On the road, Jesus was doing a new thing: sculpting the body he would leave behind — not the carcass of a dead Nazarene but the living body of the risen Christ. Jesus was bodybuilding.

In his book *Fearfully and Wonderfully Made*, Dr. Paul Brand said:

> *Jesus departed, leaving no body on earth to exhibit the Spirit of God to an unbelieving world — except the faltering, bumbling community of followers who had largely forsaken Him at His death. We are what Jesus left on earth. He did not leave a book or a doctrinal statement or a system of thought; He left a visible community to embody Him and represent Him to the world. (1)*

Bodybuilding the body of Christ.

Building the body of Christ is not unlike coaching a college basketball team in the NCAA tournament. Yes, I confess I am a lover of basketball and every year I get March Madness. Now I don't claim to watch all 63 games every year, but I would appreciate it if you didn't bring up the subject with my basketball widow, Linda. Okay?

What I find most mesmerizing is watching an accomplished coach from a little-known school with marginally talented players going up against one of the dominant university powerhouses... and whipping them. To watch such a coach inspire his players to achieve beyond their personal best is like watching a symphony orchestra conductor meld previously-bickering musicians into an ode to joy.

Jesus was an incomparable coach. He took ordinary followers and turned them into extraordinary apostles. He took leftover and left-out peasants and fashioned them into heroic martyrs who changed the course of world history. That's coaching of the highest order.

In our scriptural story, one of the things I failed to notice is that Coach Jesus does not tell his disciples to stop striving to be great. On the contrary, he says he's counting on it. Listen again to Jesus' words as paraphrased by Reverend Dr. Martin Luther King, Jr:

> *Oh, I see, you want to be first. You want to be great. You want to be important. You want to be significant. Well, you ought to be.... Don't give up this instinct.... It's a good instinct if you don't distort it and pervert it.... Keep feeling the need for being first. But I want you to be first in love. I want you to be first in moral excellence. I want you to be first in generosity. (2)*

One of the ways we can be bodybuilders of Christ's *koinonia* is to challenge one another to use the gifts each of us have within. On the Pastoral Search Committee of one of my previous churches, there was one member who asked the most questions, the most theological questions, the most eccentric questions. His name was Mike. The rest of the committee tried to protect me from his

53

barrage of off-the-wall questions — even to the point of trying to stuff a napkin down his throat! But I took an immediate liking to this gentleman and relished his challenge, for his questions were intended not to trap me, but to see how my mind worked.

Later I told the congregation that if they chose me as their pastor, Mike's questions probably would not abate but only intensify, but I trusted that he would be one of those important folks to keep me on my theological toes — so whenever my monthly copy of *Biblical Archaeological Review* arrived on my desk and I noticed an article about an arcane but interesting topic, I would have to say to myself, "I better read this now; Mike probably read it last week!"

Mike was a bodybuilder. But the body of Christ needs you and me as well to offer our personal best. We dare not withhold it. Christ needs us to be great.

The test when dreams die.

There was once a young boy from the French mountain village of Val de Zair. His name was Michel Arpan. Almost before he could walk, he learned to ski. His boyhood dream was to become a member of the French national ski team and compete in the Olympic games. One day, his dream came true. He was one of eight named to represent France at the tenth winter Olympiad (February, 1968) to be held in Grenoble, France, in front of his President and tens of thousands of his countryfolk.

But two years before the games, a car crash ended Michel's skiing career. His dreams were dashed. At that moment, Michel made the most important decision of his life.

There was a boyhood friend Michel had when he was growing up in Val de Zair, a friend whom he always skied with and competed against. This friend had had the same dream as Michel and had also made the national team. Michel decided that from this moment on he would devote all his energy and expertise to help his friend accomplish what no one had dreamed possible: winning three gold medals in the three Alpine skiing competitions: slalom, giant slalom, and downhill. His friend's name was Jean-Claude Killy.

Michel became Jean-Claude's personal assistant, confidant,

54

and coach. He designed new kinds of skis, tested new boots and gear. He even went as far to go the factory and change the assembly line just to make Jean-Claude better skis. Jean-Claude described their partnership this way:

I really had the feeling that this was a tremendous advantage over anyone else. And of course when I won, I would refer to it as "we won," and Michel would say, "We won it, we did that, we lose there." But it was never his fault or mine if we lose, and it was always him and myself who had won.

History was made at that Olympics. Three gold medals were won by Jean-Claude... and Michel.

We may never become an Olympian like Jean-Claude Killy, or a world-renowned poet like Maya Angelou, or a Nobel Peace Prize winner like Malala Yousefsei, but we can be a someone: a church school teacher or a mentor, a benefactor or a friend, who helps a future heroic human being to accomplish his or her dreams.

The test of how far we can go together.

In the life of a church, the unexpected test of greatness is not to see how far a few of us can go alone but how far all of us can go together.

On day number seven of the 1989 Iditarod, the great dogsled race from Anchorage to Nome, Alaska, rookie Mike Madden had fallen sick in twenty-five degrees below zero weather. Suffering from shock and hypothermia, his life was in the balance when six mushers stopped to help. Two of them sprinted 25 miles to the nearest outpost to radio Anchorage for a MED-EVAC helicopter. Four others stayed with him all night to keep him warm and alive. Eventually, Madden made a full recovery.

Several of the six who stopped to help had been in position to win the coveted rookie-of-the year prize. The person who did win it had passed by without even pausing to see what was wrong. I've never heard the name of that so-called winner, but I have frequently heard the names of those who have become known in Iditarod lore as the Selfless Six: Jerry Austin, Mitch Brazen, Linwood Fiedler, Happy Halvorson (the only woman),

Jamie Nelson, and Bernie Willis. These were the winners of the unexpected test of greatness.

The unexpected test of greatness.

But what, you may ask, is the unexpected test of greatness? Let me illustrate with a children's sermon I once wrote and had the kids act out:

There once a boy named Yaw who participated in his school's all-day Field Day competition. Unfortunately, the boy came in last in almost every event. At the end of the day, he had to watch as other, more athletically gifted kids received medals to wear around their necks. When the boy came home, his father was quite surprised to see his son carrying a shiny new trophy.

"What event did you win, Son?"

"I didn't win any event, Dad."

"Then, did you come in second or third place in one?"

"No, I didn't."

"Then whose trophy is this?"

"Mine!"

"I don't understand," the father replied.

The boy explained. "You see, Dad, all day long the teachers and principals were watching how each kid treated the other kids in between the events. They were looking to see which kid helped the other kids to do their best, or if they didn't do too good, to cheer them up and encourage them to try again."

"Are you telling me that they thought you were the best?"

"They did! But they said something else, too. As I stood in front of the whole school, they said, 'Of all today's competitions, this was the most important of all. And you, Yaw, were the greatest encourager of all.'"

The father took the trophy from his son's hands, held it up before his eyes, and read aloud with pride the words engraved on it: "You make others great!" (3)

No altar, but a circle on the floor.

Jesus called the Twelve together, moving them from separateness and cliques to a circle of unity, and said, If any of you want to achieve excellence, you must be willing to come in last. If you want to succeed over others, you must serve beyond others.

Jesus could see they weren't getting the sermon, so he thought, how about a children's sermon? He noticed a child off in the shadows. (Jesus always noticed children.) He called the child into the center of the circle, whisked the young one up into his arms, and said, *Whoever adopts this child, adopts me. Whoever opens the door to the excluded, opens the door to me. Whoever embraces the ones who do not count, embraces me.*

There they were: Jesus and a child in the center of a circle, one person lifting up another, and the two of them lifting up the Twelve. It was almost as if the two of them had become — in that moment — an altar.

Herbert Brokering wrote:

Once there was a church that had no altar. Instead, there was a circle on the floor. Every week it was someone's turn to be in that circle and be an altar. Once two boys covered with mud who had been fighting stood in the circle. They hugged each other and smiled. No one told them to leave. Everyone agreed it was an altar. There always had to be at least two in the circle. That was the only rule there was. (4)

Imagine Christ calling you into the center of your church, putting his arms around you, and saying to all those gathered: *As I have let **my** life be disrupted for this child of mine, let **your** life be disrupted for this child of yours.*

One body.

When Dr. Paul Brand was a junior doctor in a London hospital on night duty, one of the patients was Mrs. Twigg, a spry 81-year-old with a great sense of humor, despite her cancer of the throat. Earlier in the day, Brand's professor had removed her larynx and the surrounding malignant tissue. She seemed to be making a superb recovery until 2:00 am when Brand received an emergency summons to her room.

There was Mrs. Twigg, sitting on her bed with blood spilling from her mouth. Brand instantly realized that an artery in her throat must have eroded and that if the blood flow was not soon stopped, she would bleed to death. He put his left hand into her slippery throat and carefully felt for the one pulsing spot. He found it and pressed gently against the artery, stemming the flow. Mrs. Twigg's eyes were wide with terror as she struggled to breathe through her nose and fight the gagging reflex. As she began to trust this young man with the hand down her throat, the fear gradually left her face and her breathing returned to normal.

After ten minutes, Brand tried to remove his finger and replace it with an instrument that would keep her from bleeding, but every attempt resulted in more bleeding and more panic in the eyes of Mrs. Twigg. Finally, Brand promised he would not move his hand again until a surgeon could be reached at home to come patch her up. Her eyes smiled a thanks as they heard his assurance.

Dr. Brand and Mrs. Twigg relaxed in their unusual pose. As his left arm remained in her mouth, Brand crooked his right arm behind Mrs. Twigg's neck to give her support. Neither could move an inch. For nearly two hours, they stayed intertwined. During the first hour, Brand's hand was twice seized with muscle spasms and he moved his finger slightly, but Mrs. Twigg's grip on his arm told him that the bleeding had not ceased. Brand had no idea how he lasted during that second hour when his finger went totally numb, but he never moved it, perhaps finding the strength in Mrs. Twigg's eyes, which never left his eyes during the entire ordeal.

Finally, Brand and Twigg were wheeled down to the operating room, still unmoving in their strange embrace of life and death. At the surgeon's signal, Brand removed his finger. And from Mrs. Twigg's beaming face, the news was clear: the bleeding had stopped.

> Dr. Brand later commented, "She knew how my muscles had suffered; I knew the depths of her fear. In those two hours in the slumberous hospital wing, we had become almost one person." (5)

Being an altar.

God calls us to take turns being an altar... two by two... a living altar to a living God: like Jesus and the child, like Simon

58

Peter and Simon the Zealot, like the two mud-covered boys, like Dr. Brand and Mrs. Twigg, like Mike and me, an altar where we can offer our best to God — our caring, our creativity, our conviction — as bodybuilders of the unexpected test of greatness.

ENDNOTES

Sketch #5 ...Jesus, Our Coach:
Bodybuilding For An Unexpected Test Of Greatness

1. Dr. Paul Brand, *Fearfully and Wonderfully Made* (Grand Rapids, MI: Zondervan Publishing House, 1980), 205.

2. James Washington, editor, *Testament of Hope* (San Francisco: Harper San Francisco, 1986), p. 265.

3. An original story by Hope Harle-Mould, copyright 2005.

4. Herbert Brokering, *"I" Opener: 80 Parables* (St. Louis: Concordia Publishing House, 1974), 9.

5. Brand, 203.

Sketch #6 ...Jesus, Our Nonviolent Rebuker

The Day Jesus Experienced Racism

Luke 9:51-56 — Should we call down fire from heaven?

Acts 1:6-8 — To Judea and Samaria and ends of earth

"When his disciples James and John saw it, they said, 'Lord, do you want us to command fire to come down from heaven and consume them?' But he turned and rebuked them. Then they went on to another village"

Luke 9:54-56 (NRSV)

"Peacemaking doesn't mean passivity. It is the act of interrupting injustice without mirroring injustice, the act of disarming evil without destroying the evildoer, the act of finding a third way that is neither fight nor flight but the careful, arduous pursuit of reconciliation and justice. It is about a revolution of love that is big enough to set both the oppressed and the oppressors free."

—Shane   Claiborne,
Common   Prayer:
A Liturgy for Ordinary Radicals

Why the detour?

When Jesus was twelve, his family took him on his first pilgrimage to the Passover Feast in Jerusalem. But the route they traveled was bizarre. Instead of going directly south on the roads from Galilee to Judea, they headed east, crossed to the other side of the Jordan River, traveled far to the South, then turned west, re-crossed the Jordan near Jericho, and headed up the road to Jerusalem. Why? What would make Jesus' family take such a long, circuitous route? Only one thing: racism. The Samaritans were of mixed race and mixed religion. The Jews hated the Samaritans and the Samaritans returned the favor. Like most pious Jews from Galilee, Mary and Joseph went out of their way to avoid contact with and contamination by *those unclean Samaritans.*

When Jesus was growing up in Nazareth, if one of the other kids called him a Samaritan, he knew it was the worst epithet he could be called.

Jesus never got his racial lessons correct.

But Jesus never got his racial lessons correct. During his ministry, he intentionally leads his followers through the heart of Samaritan territory again and again. He takes no discriminatory detours. On one occasion narrated in John's gospel (John 4:1-42), when Jesus encounters a Samaritan woman at the well, he not only treats her with compassion but offers her living water. And after she tells everyone about him, the whole Samaritan village opens their hearts and minds to him. In response, Jesus stays with them for two more days!

Another encounter with Samaritans occurs in Luke 9:51-56, the briefest of incidences, passed over by most preachers and readers of the gospels, but I consider it to be a defining moment in Christ's teaching and action. Why? Here is the one place where our Lord and Savior is the victim of racism. And here is the one place where we can see how our Lord and Savior decides to respond to this racist attack. On this most contentious of contemporary issues, scripture has gifted us with a case study. And if we truly believe that Jesus is humanity's role model for God-like living, we better pay attention — and seek the courage to follow wherever Christ leads.

Bigotry bars the way.

As Jesus passes through Samaria and approaches a village, he sends two disciples ahead of him to find food and lodging. How do the Samaritans greet these two Jews? They are refused entry: *Go back where you came from. Your kind is not wanted or permitted here. Only people of our ethnic group and our religion are welcome, and definitely not your pretend Messiah, Jesus. You need bread? Make your own out of stones.*

61

Racism blocks Jesus' path. Bigotry bars the way. Hate has constructed a roadblock. Jesus cannot continue forward. He will have to retreat.

The first to react are the disciples James and John, two of Jesus' inner circle. How do they respond? With fury! Their Teacher Jesus was willing to bring salvation to these unworthy Samaritans, and these sinners slammed the door in his face. Jesus was risking his reputation, doing what no other Jew would do, going out of his way to reach out to these "Gentile dogs" — these outcasts — and Jesus himself is cast out! What an insult to their Lord.

Incensed, James and John are ready for revenge: *The only good Samaritan is a dead Samaritan!* Then they recall something from scripture — 2 Kings, chapter 1: The king of Samaria dispatches a captain and fifty men with a question directed to a false prophet of a false god. When the prophet Elijah hears of this, he calls down fire from heaven and destroys the Samaritans. The king orders another fifty to go and again fire from heaven destroys all the Samaritans. So James and John, in their rage, prepare a similar retaliatory strike: "Lord, do want **us** to command fire to come down from heaven to consume them? (Luke 9:54 NRSV)

In fury, a righteous rebuke.

Now Jesus is furious, not at the Samaritan's racist rejection of him but at his dearest and most devoted followers turning to violence instead of turning the cheek. Have they understood nothing of what he has taught? *Do not take eye for eye, love your enemy, pray for your persecutor, pick up your cross, go the second mile, give your cloak, be merciful as your heavenly Abba is merciful.* What does he have to do for them to get it? Die on a cross?

In righteous indignation, Jesus rebukes his disciples. As Jesus once **rebuked** the winds of the storm at sea, **rebuked** the evil spirits representing mental and physical illness, and **rebuked** Peter for tempting him *not* to be a suffering Messiah, so Jesus *rebukes* James and John. With all his authority and purpose, Jesus rebukes them for siding with Satan and not understanding the redemptive power of unmerited suffering.

Then Jesus shows them — and us — how to respond. He neither attacks nor retreats. He moves forward, continuing through Samaria by another path, going onward to another Samaritan village. Jesus doesn't destroy, doesn't surrender, and doesn't go home. He pursues his course to the end, undeterred by those who oppose him. Jesus doesn't become like those who hate him. He simply goes on... to another Samaritan village... and another... and another.

And on the way, Jesus has a long time to go over a few things with the Twelve. They were so quick to recall scripture passages to support their self-righteous rage and so quick to forget what Jesus had instructed them when he sent them out two by two: "Wherever they do not welcome you, as you are leaving that town shake the dust off your feet as a testimony against them" (Luke 9:5 NRSV).

That's all. No fire from heaven to destroy Samaritan soldiers. Just go on, without hate or violence, loving your neighbor all the way. And who is my neighbor? That is the question someone asks in the very next chapter of Luke. How did Jesus answer? With a parable for James, John, and the rest of us — the Good Samaritan.

Colorblind Christ.

Each of us, when we were growing up, were taught who we were supposed to hate — if not by parents, certainly by society. But what if our eyes possessed the sight and the vision of Christ — *achromatopsia?* What if we became *achromats* like Christ? What if our eyes could not distinguish chromatic differentiation of skin pigmentation? What if we were **colorblind?**

Achromatopsia was the subject of an intriguing book by Oliver Sacks titled, *The Island of the Colorblind,* about the Pingelapese people of the eastern Caroline Islands in the Pacific. Their rare genetic condition forced them to learn to adapt to life seeing only in black, white, and shades of gray.

Our world is full of prejudice and bigotry based on color and shades of color, on shapes of faces and types of hair. But what if we actually could not distinguish these differences? What if we could not see society's prejudicial color schemes?

I once had an experience of this a young father. When our first child Jennifer was three years old, I was showing pictures of her to a close friend. Now, you must understand that we were very

63

proud that our oldest two children are adopted from Korea, we often attended Korea festivals, and we hoped to travel to Korea one day. But I had a candid question for our friend: "When I look at his picture, Jenny doesn't look Korean to me. Does she to you?" She replied, "Yes." Then I asked, "Here, look at this one; it really looks like Jen." My friend replied, "Yes, she does look Korean." I tried again: "How about this one?" Finally, my friend said, "Give it up, Hope." To me as Dad, I simply could not see the color of my daughter's skin or the shape of her face and eyes. I could only see the Jennifer I love.

What would the world be like if every time a baby was born, the parents had no idea what color skin their child would be given? Imagine. For some, it would be a shocking reality. But for our world, it would be the advent of hope, the birth of God with us in each and every community.

Adopting our multi-hued family.

When we were ready to adopt a third child, we decided to seek a domestic adoption in Ohio where we were living at the time. We met with the social workers at the adoption agency and went through the home study and approval process. We told them we were interested in an infant adoption. And they asked us if we open to a biracial child. We said we would be happy to receive and love a baby of any color. They said that in some cases the mother did not know who the biological father was, so the baby might be born with dark skin or Caucasian skin. We said that was perfectly fine with us and they put us in a special program to prepare us for this eventuality.

We were required to meet several times to hear staff presentations and to meet parents who had already adopted across color lines. One of the things that struck me most was when, in one of the sessions, a white mother made it clear that we, as white parents of a Black child, would be treated as if we were Black as well, and would need to be prepared to be on the receiving end of the prejudice and hard-heartedness that African Americans have to deal with on a daily basis in our land. Again, we were willing, but how tragic was it that the adoption agency had to have "the talk" with us to prepare us for the racism that would inevitably greet our family as we embraced this future child? In this moment I had to choose to relinquish some of the white privilege I was born into.

"How would I possibly know which family was yours?"

About a year later, we were at the national assembly of our denomination at a large convention center with our children and my wife Linda's dear friend, Richard, an elder of the Santee Dakota people (of Northern Nebraska), and pastor of Bazile Creek United Church of Christ, which his father had founded on the reservation years ago. Richard and Linda had first met on the national mission boards of our denomination and over the years had become like the brother and sister neither had. When Richard was ordained, we traveled to Nebraska for the laying on of hands. On that occasion, Richard and his relatives chose to adopt our family into the Santee Dakota people, a great honor.

At this assembly, Richard had flown out to meet us, and we prepared to go into the convention center together. At the last second, Linda had to go back and get something, so I said that I would go on in with Richard and the kids and watch for her to join us. When Linda came to the convention entrance we had used, she asked the usher if he had seen which way her family had gone. The man said, "Lady, there've been hundreds and hundreds of people going through this entrance this morning; how could I possibly know which family was yours?" Linda replied, "Well, did you happen to see a Native American man in a wheelchair, holding a Black infant, with two Korean kids at his side, plus a white guy with a beard?" The man started laughing and said, "Okay, yeah, I remember them; they went off over in that section."

What if...

What would the world be like if predominately white churches began to call as their pastors young Black or Latinx men and women, or if predominately African American churches began to call Asian pastors? What would the world be like if we did not live segregated by neighborhood and separated by economic class, but we simply lived side by side and got to know one another as next-door neighbors?

What would the world be like if our institutions were colorblind, if we were treated the same by police and the courts, by banks and employers, by schools and government? What would the world be like if we could choose to become a darker color and knew it would make absolutely no difference in how we were treated by others? I guess we'll never know — until God brings it about, until you and I repent and change and enter the kingdom of God.

Mosaic eyes.

As much as we may strive for Christ's colorblind eyes, we as flawed humans cannot attain this. We see differences, and we even see the differences differently. So perhaps we should strive for a different kind of vision, a way that perceives all the colors in all their diversity, a way that cherishes how each unique hue adds to the wonder of the whole. Perhaps we should strive for Mosaic Eyes.

Just as a mosaic creates a whole picture by assembling small pieces of various colors, maybe we need to value each fragment and its story as it adds its part to create the greater story of the whole canvas.

Jesus' parable of the Good Samaritan and his choosing to travel through Samaria are fragments of a mosaic. Jesus' rebuking the disciples' desire for vengeance against Samaritans and his embrace of the Samaritan woman at the well are fragments of a mosaic. It is a mosaic that portrays an amazing grace transfiguring lives, a mosaic that reveals a holy hope transforming our world.

Nonviolence as a gift of God for the people of God.

In Samaria, Jesus showed us a new way to respond to racism or our desire for violent revenge. Instead of calling down fire from heaven to consume those we hate or fear, Christ calls us to call down love, a love that overcomes evil with good, a love that is nonviolent and yet a powerful weapon of justice.

The Reverend Dr. Martin Luther King, Jr, once said:

Nonviolence is a powerful and just weapon. It is a weapon unique in history, which cuts without wounding and ennobles the one who wields it. It is a sword that heals. With a practical and moral answer

*to the oppressed people's cry for justice, nonviolent direct action
proved that it could win victories without losing wars. (1)*

It is my belief that nonviolence is a gift of God for the people
of God, meant for our time — and given just in time.

Calling down nonviolence from heaven.

Calling down nonviolence from heaven, the workers in
Poland stood alone against the Soviet Union's Warsaw Pact tanks
and refused to surrender, until all the people of Eastern Europe
rose up and broke down the Berlin Wall.

Calling down nonviolence from heaven, Archbishop Desmond
Tutu galvanized international boycotts and protests until South
Africa's racist regime was forced to set Nelson Mandela free,
until the people, united, dismantled the apartheid.

Calling down nonviolence from heaven, the people of Tunisia
sparked the entire Arab Spring in 2011 with their Jasmine
Revolution, which ignited many hopeful struggles across the
region. Most did not succeed or last, but the people's movement
of Tunisia was not only victorious in overthrowing tyranny but
also in building a pluralistic democracy. And in 2015 the Tunisian
National Dialogue Quartet (labor/industry/human rights/law)
was awarded the Nobel Peace Prize for its work in forging societal
justice and reconciliation.

Calling down nonviolence from heaven, women in 2017
America began marching in historic numbers and courageously
speaking out, demanding an end to sexual harassment and sexual
assaults, demanding a beginning to equal rights in the work place
and in the halls of power.

Jesus' very last teaching.

The last word about Samaria is Jesus' last word to his disciples,
one final message, perhaps the most remarkable of all. In Acts
1:8, when the risen Christ appears to the apostles one final time
— even then — Jesus makes it crystal clear that they are not to
by-pass their bigotry, are not to detour around the despised, are
not to forget the forgotten. The Risen One's final words are these:
"And you will be my witnesses in Jerusalem, in all Judea **and
Samaria**, and to the ends of the earth" (Acts 1:8b NRSV).

Extraordinary! The eleven might have assumed Jesus would say *Jerusalem, Judea **and Galilee**, and to the ends of the earth*, but Samaria? Even at the holy ascension itself, Christ reminds them that just as he led them through Samaria during his ministry, they are to go back through Samaria in their ministry.

And soon after this, one of the seven deacons, Philip, makes Samaria his special calling, eliciting an amazing response from the people there to his preaching and healing in Christ's name (Acts 8:5).

When Jesus says to us, "And you will be my witnesses in... Samaria" (Acts 1:8), he means all the places that we fear and avoid that he chose to enter and embrace. And he means all the people we stereotype and write off but for whom he chose to live and die.

Our Christian mission is to go to those who are vilified, laughed at, excluded, and condemned to hell — just the kind of person Jesus would make a hero in a parable and call good. And our Christian mission is to go out and find where the Risen One is already present — inviting us to join our hands with those different than ourselves and discover that together, you and I and they *are* us.

What will you call down from heaven?

Living near my youngest daughter's former high school, I often see teens walking home from school in the late afternoon. And almost every time I see them, I see something astonishing: African American and Caucasian kids, South Asian and Middle Eastern kids walking down the street side by side, laughing together as best friends... and thinking nothing of it. A whole new world is not only possible, it is already on the way, walking down the sidewalks of our streets.

Who will be Christ's witnesses in Samaria? May it be you. What will you call down from heaven? May it be nonviolence. What song will you sing? May it be love.

ENDNOTES

Sketch #6 ...Jesus, Our Nonviolent Rebuker:
The Day Jesus Experienced Racism

1. Martin Luther King, Jr's Nobel Peace Prize acceptance speech, Stockholm Sweden, 1964.

Sketch #7 ...Jesus, Our Namegiver:

What's Your Spiritual Name?

Isaiah 49:14-16 — Inscribed you on my hands

Matthew 16:13-20 — You are Peter, and on this rock...

> *"Simon Peter answered, 'You are the Messiah, the Son of the living God.' And Jesus answered him, 'Blessed are you, Simon son of Jonah! For flesh and blood has not revealed this to you, but my Father in heaven. And I tell you, you are Peter [Petros], and on this rock [petra] I will build my church'"* Matthew 16:17-18 (NRSV)

> *"To be nobody-but-yourself — in a world which is doing its best, night and day, to make you everybody else — means to fight the hardest battle which any human being can fight; and never stop fighting."* —E.E. Cummings

"How did you get your unusual first name, Hope?"

There is one question I've been asked most often: "How did you ever get a name like Hope? You must have had cruel parents to make you go through childhood with a name like that." Now, I must admit my name is quite unusual — I've only heard of one other male in the entire country named Hope (a sportscaster in the DC area), and I do get some interesting junk mail — addressed "Ms. Hope" — but I want to set the record straight: I do not have cruel parents. They named me, Douglas, a very popular name at the time, and I was actually quite happy being Doug growing up, and I've kept this as my middle name, but from an early age I yearned for a name that meant something deeper.

I actually became Hope quite unexpectedly. All thanks to church camp. I was 21, and it was the beginning of my second summer working fulltime as a camp counselor (my dream job) at three Presbyterian / United Church of Christ church camps in Wisconsin. Before the first week of camp, during our week of training, all of us counselors decided to pick a nickname which we would call each other throughout the summer and by which the campers would come to know us during the week they were there. Most of the counselors chose charming or fun names, but I wanted something more. Here was my chance to be named the very thing I was trying to communicate to the kids. But what could it be? Finally, it came to me. I knew exactly what my name had to be.

Back at college, during my first two years there, there was a phrase I was always saying: "There's always hope; there's always hope." I said it as I sat with classmates who struggled with personal pain and needed the hope of healing. I said it to my friends — as I became aware of the oppressed in our world who needed us to care and participate in their liberation. And I said it as part of a group of us who designed campus worship services to express our understanding of the Gospel's central message — the power of hope in the cross and resurrection. So, Hope it was! After all, I reasoned, why should women get all the best names?

Throughout the summer, the name grew on me. It felt so meaningful, and the kids responded to me as Hope in amazing ways. That fall, my brother Dave and close friends back at college continued to call me Hope, and I loved it.

Gradually it dawned on me that this was my spiritual name, this was my personal calling, this was my day-by-day challenge to live out. Christ had named me through the voices of church camp kids.

Two years later, the day after graduating from college, I appeared in court before a judge who asked in a monotone voice, "So, why is it that you want to legally change your name to Hope?" I talked about church camp, but also about how critical it is for the suffering to hold onto hope until healing comes, and for the oppressed to struggle on in hope until liberation comes. The judge could have cared less. The proceedings lasted just five or six minutes, but when he mumbled, "So ordered," I felt as if a sacred wreath had been placed on my head.

Being Hope has been a profound adventure to incarnate, and I've certainly failed spectacularly often enough, but it's also been a rare and precious blessing at the core of my being. At times of personal as well as professional crisis in my life, my name has been for me an ever flowing stream of strength, as if an intimate umbilical bond to the love that will not let me go.

God, the Name above all names

In the Hebrew scriptures, names were believed to contain great power.

At the burning bush, God calls to Moses saying, "I am the God of your father, the God of Abraham, the God of Isaac, and the God of Jacob" Exodus 3:6 (NRSV). But Moses wants to know God's personal name, so that if the people ask, he will be able to tell them something deeply revealing that will unveil who God truly is. So, God replies, "I AM WHO I AM," which with equal accuracy can be translated, "I WILL BE WHAT I WILL BE" Exodus 3:14 (NRSV) — as is specified in the footnote of that passage.

What does this signify? It points to God's always-on-the-move presence and providence — a pillar of cloud by day, a pillar of fire by night, always toward the Promised Land. And God concludes by telling Moses to call him by a personal name, Yahweh or YHWH, a Hebrew form of the word "to be," implying that God is manifested as Being-on-the-Move.

This name is so holy to Jewish believers that they will never utter it. Instead, whenever they come upon YHWH in scripture, they substitute the word, Adonai, meaning Lord. Most English translations of the Old Testament have traditionally honored and followed this pious practice in solidarity with our Jewish sisters and brothers, substituting LORD in capital letters to designate where the text reads Yahweh. To this day, faithful Jews consider the name YHWH such a holy of holies that when referring to God they will often call God Ha-Shem, meaning "The Name."

The One who gives names

Throughout the early narratives of scripture, God is often portrayed as the One Who Gives Names. Abram becomes Abraham and Sarai becomes Sarah.

When Hagar, Sarah's servant, is alone in the wilderness, having been expelled by a spiteful Sarah for carrying Abraham's child, the angel of the LORD confers on her son the blessing of a holy name: "Now you have conceived and shall bear a son; you shall call him Ishmael [meaning, God Hears], for the LORD has given heed to your affliction" (Genesis 16:11 NRSV).

When God tells Sarah she will bear a son, she laughs in response. When their son is born, he is named Isaac, *One Who Laughs.*

But perhaps the most significant name-giving of all was Jacob. Bolder than most of us, Jacob fervently desires something from God, not wealth, power, or fame but blessing, and he wants it badly enough to demand it. On one sleepless night, a man whom Jacob believes to be an angel wrestles with him for hours, unable to overcome Jacob. Even after the angel dislocates his hip, Jacob still holds on fiercely: "I will not let you go, unless you bless me" (Genesis 32:26 NRSV). So, the angel blesses him. But how? With a new name: "You shall no longer be called Jacob, but *Israel* [that is "the one who strives with God"], for you have striven with God and with humans and have prevailed" (Genesis 32:28 NRSV).

Think of it: Jacob's twelve sons and their descendants, who become the twelve tribes of Jacob, are known from that ancient day to the present as Israel, *The Ones Who Struggle with God for Blessing.*

And since Christian faith grew out of Jewish faith, we, too, are children of Israel. We are all Jewish Christians. Therefore, we should come to realize that our full name as Christians is *God-Wrestling Christ-followers.*

Isaiah, the name-giving prophet

The prophet Isaiah made name-giving a stunning part of his prophetic message, as he gave his two sons names of deep hope and dire warning. The first son he christened, *A Remnant Shall Return* (Isaiah 7:3 NRSV), and the second son, *The Spoil Speeds, the Prey Hastens* (Isaiah 8:3 NRSV). In addition, when Isaiah encourages King Ahaz to ask God for a sign but the king refuses, Isaiah says that God will give him a sign anyway: "Look, the young woman is with child and shall bear a son and shall name him *Immanuel*" (Isaiah 7:14 NRSV), meaning, as the footnote explains, "God is with us."

Jesus the Name-Giver

When the Israelite Jesus began his ministry in this world, he, like his Abba, became known as *The One Who Gives Names*. He chided the disciples James and John, the sons of Zebedee for their hot-headed temperaments by giving them the nickname, "Sons of Thunder." He invited Matthew's transformation from tax collector to follower by choosing to call Matthew by his Hebrew name, Levi. And on the road to Damascus, the Risen Christ turned the persecutor Saul into the missionary Paul.

Jesus names Peter

But perhaps the most significant name-giving by Jesus was to the disciple Simon, son of Jonah. Today we know this disciple only by the name that Jesus gave him, Peter, which in Greek means "rock."

"Simon Peter answered, 'You are the Messiah, the Son of the living God.' And Jesus answered him, 'Blessed are you, Simon son of Jonah! For flesh and blood has not revealed this to you, but my Father in heaven. And I tell you, you are Peter [Petros], and on this rock [petra] I will build my church'" (Matthew 16:17-18 NRSV).

Simon was, in reality, anything but a rock. He was volatile and unreliable, at one moment courageous, the next without belief. Simon was the one who walked out onto the water with Jesus until he saw the waves and sank. Simon was the first to recognize Jesus as the Messiah but immediately tried to talk Jesus out of suffering. Simon was the one who defended Jesus with a sword at his arrest in Gethsemane, but a short time later tried to evade his own arrest, saying *I never met the man!*

But Jesus saw something in Simon that Simon did not see in himself, something that did not emerge until after his greatest failure as a follower, after his denial of his Master. Yet from Jesus' resurrection on, Peter incarnated his name.

Peter was actually known in the early church as Cephas (pronounced KAY-fus), the Aramaic form of the name Rock, since Jesus and the disciples spoke Aramaic, the common language of the Jews in Palestine. We can see this in 1 Corinthians 15:5, where the apostle Paul lists all those who had witnessed the risen Christ, and the name associated with the first resurrection appearance is "Cephas."

So, if we seek to hear the actual voice of Jesus as he first christened Peter, we can hear the echoes of that encounter whenever we pronounce aloud this Christ-given name: *Cephas.*

Aldonza or Dulcinea?

The transformative power of a name is depicted unforgettably in the dramatic musical, *Man of La Mancha.* Don Quixote meets the kitchen maid and prostitute, Aldonza, but sees in her only the pure lady of his dreams, Dulcinea, which is what he calls her. At first Aldonza just laughs at this foolish man's blindness, but after a while, she gets angry, trying to force him to see reality: "I am a nothing," she says. "I am a whore." But Quixote will hear none of it. "Why is my lady speaking thus?"

In the end, on his deathbed, Don Quixote has lost all memory of his identity and glorious quest. Aldonza must tell him the words he once sang about dreaming the impossible dream. Then for a brief moment, Quixote is himself again, ready to return to the battle for good. He shouts, "Onward to glory I..." and collapses in sudden death. In the moments that follow, the squire Sancho weeps openly: "My master is dead." Aldonza replies, "Don Quixote is not dead. Believe, Sancho, believe!" Surprised, Sancho asks, "Aldonza?" She replies, "My name is Dulcinea."

Do you have a spiritual name?

I believe each of us as children of God have a spiritual name. By spiritual name I mean, first of all, a name by which God knows and cherishes you, a name that affirms and celebrates the inner qualities that make you unique. Second, by spiritual name I mean a name that describes and calls forth the gifts of the Spirit which God has created within you which the world so desperately needs. When God voices your spiritual name, I believe it unleashes from within you something that can transform everyone and everything you touch.

Yet there may be times in life when you feel your self-worth ripped to shreds, when you look into the abyss of personal crisis, or when you suffer disorienting change or tragic loss. It is at those moments that you will need to hear and believe in your name. And I believe that in those moments, your name *will* be there to hear and believe in.

Perhaps your spiritual name may come to you on a retreat, as it did for my wife, as you walk along a tree-lined road and suddenly hear a clear-as-a-bell voice from above saying, "You are *Spirit*."

It may come to you after a long hospital stay — as it did for a friend of mine — as you lay in bed at home during your long recovery from a serious illness and a certain friend comes to visit and names what he sees within you: "You are *Amazing Grace*."

It may come to you — as it did for another friend — as you struggle with past abuse and suddenly feel reborn to embrace the world, when a new image bursts into your mind and christens you: *Butterfly*.

Each of these naming experiences changed these persons' lives forever.

"I believe Christ is naming you this new name..."

Early in my ministry as an associate pastor, I helped to lead our year-long confirmation program which culminated with a weekend retreat. One year the idea came to me of giving each confirmand a spiritual name. It would be based both on my years of knowing them as well as my observing them closely throughout their confirmation year.

At the final campfire of the retreat, I called each of them forward one by one, describing what God-given qualities I had glimpsed within them, and what future purposes I sensed Christ was calling them to live out in the world. For some, I pointed to a moment during the retreat when we had witnessed their deepest character emerge for all to see. Then I put my hand on their shoulder and said, "I believe Christ is naming you...," and pronounced aloud their spiritual name for the first time. And everyone would applaud in celebration and affirmation.

I didn't know how much those names might have meant to them at the time, but I always prayed that in the future, when they needed it most, in the midst of some trial or turmoil, they might remember their spiritual name and feel held in holy hands.

Let me share with you some of the unique names I've given to my confirmation kids over the years:

Names pointing to some inner quality: Giver of All, None Forgotten, Carry-My-Kids-Through, Running with God's Breath, Friend of the Friendless, and Sees Unseen Light.

Names describing a deep devotion to serving Christ: Little Sister of Christ, Caring Hands Pray, Christ's Sixth Man, New Creation Eyes, 13th Disciple, Sent with a Scroll, Deep Living Water, and Goes the Distance.

Names illustrating commitment to making a difference in the world: Bright-Eyes for Others, Stands-For, Freed to Free, Why Not, Hands to Heal the World, Send Me, Performer of Sacred Words, Servicio con Risa, and Eddie Would Go.

Names praying for the overcoming of doubts and fears: Knows Storm's End, Only Connect, Seeker of Inner Good, Snakewise Dove of God, Rock-Shaping Water, and Must Know God.

Remembering one name when tragedy struck

When one of my confirmands had, after four years, gone off to college and I had gone off to a new church, I one day received heart-rending news. This bright young man of promise, in his first year of studies, had died in a horrific accident, a college prank gone out of control. To his family, it was the beginning of great darkness.

As the family prepared for their son's funeral at my former church, a thought came to me. I wonder what spiritual name I had given him four years before. I prayed it might have been a name celebrating his life in such a way that it might give a little solace to this grief-stricken family.

Searching through my notebooks, I found the actual sheet I had held at his confirmation retreat campfire, with all the names of his classmates. I looked down the list for his name and then glanced to the right column to see what name I had pronounced for him. I was astounded and thankful. It said, *My Faithful Follower.* Here was a spiritual name that depicted directly and powerfully this young's man heartfelt commitment to Christ when he was just a fourteen-year-old.

Then I realized something more. There was something unusual about this name. Unlike almost any other name I have given, this was a name that I had visualized as Christ saying directly to this young man: *My Faithful Follower.* Here was an appellation that was accolade. Here was one young Christian face to face with his Redeemer hearing a holy affirmation. I was moved to tears when I realized this. I was so thankful that this name had been given to me to give four years before it would be so desperately needed.

I told the family. And I put in writing my reflections of their son and my sympathies for all of them. I hoped it was, in some small degree, the peace that passes all understanding.

Recalling their names for the future

Seven years after their confirmation, I usually send these young adults an 8 ½ x 11" certificate of their original naming, which they may have been forgotten over time. At the certificate's top is a quote from (Isaiah 43:1 NRSV): "Do not fear, for I have redeemed you; I have called you by name, you are mine." At the bottom of the certificate is the verse from Genesis 32:28 about Jacob being named Israel.

In the middle of the certificate, I write their spiritual name in calligraphy. Beneath it the texts reads:

Dear _____,
On the Confirmation Retreat of _____, *I gave you this spiritual name as I strived to express the special gifts God has created within you. May your name continue to inspire and challenge you to grow closer to Christ and to courageously show his love to all the world.*

Amnesia recovery: "Remember who you are"

A minister friend of mine, when she was putting her kids on the school bus each morning, always sent them forth with an

I-love-you hug and the words, "Remember who you are!" They knew who they were, and how to spell it, but they knew she meant something deeper. Their understanding would grow with each passing day and year, until at last they would say it to their children: "Remember who you are."

What do I hope it means for my children and grandchildren to *Remember who you are?*

Remember our family's ways of speaking to each other, even during angry conflicts, when we use caring code words to signal our willingness to stop and start over, to try again to listen, to forgive, to cherish.

Remember our family's tradition of special days — in addition to birthdays — when each family member is given one day each year to be affirmed and to receive rejoicing.

Remember our family's adventures in mission trips and volunteer projects, as we discover the joy of service, and find our Savior in our neighbor.

Remember who you are.

"Without my name...I have no life"

In the movie *Sommersby*, a Confederate soldier named Jack Sommersby, played by Richard Gere, returns to his southern farm after four years away during the war. He looked a little different than people remembered, and his dog barked at him as if a stranger, but he called them all by name and recalled things only Jack could have known. His wife, Laurel, played by Jodie Foster, suspected something was amiss but said nothing. She welcomed him as her husband.

Soon Jack noticed the newly freed slaves were struggling to survive, they were landless and unemployed. At the same time many of the town's white farmers were also barely scratching by. So Jack decided to divide up his large tract of land and sell it to each of the struggling farmers, African American and white alike, signing a note to that effect. Then he convinced them all to form a cooperative and convert to tobacco farming in order to make significantly more money for all the families to prosper. They agreed.

From each person he received a large sum from their savings

or a large quantity of brass or jewelry. With these, he left town on a long trip to buy the highest grade of tobacco seed that money could buy. Weeks later, just when Laurel and the townspeople began to fear he had absconded with the funds, Jack returned with the priceless tobacco seeds. Zealously they planted, nurtured, and later harvested a crop that brought in the unheard-of profit of $10,000.

But then tragedy struck. Jack Sommersby was arrested. There had been a murder in the area and the authorities charged him with it. If he was found guilty, he would be hung. Nearly every townsperson traveled down to the county seat for the trial.

In order to save him, Jack's defense attorney called Laurel to the stand to prove that this "Jack" is *not* her original husband. And she testified that, in fact, he was not the true Jack Sommersby, that "a woman would know."

Then the defense called another witness who testified that he recognized this defendant not as Jack but as a man named Horace Townsend, a former school teacher down in his county, who got the townspeople there to shell out all their savings to buy materials to build a new school and then was never seen again, that he had impregnated a woman and left her, and that as a soldier he had run away during battle and was imprisoned by the Yankees in a cell with a man who looked like he could have been his brother.

After hearing this testimony, the judge began to declare a mistrial on the basis of mistaken identity and to set free this Horace Townsend. But the defendant, "Jack," dismissed his own defense attorney and declared that he himself would prove his true identity. The judge warned: "Do you know what you are doing? You have just won your life!" The man replied, "Without my name... I have no life."

First, the man calling himself Jack Sommersby cross-examined the last witness, exposing him as one of the Knights of the White Race who had recently burned a cross in front of Jack's house. And Jack argued that the only reason this man was testifying that day was to nullify the sale of Jack's property to Black folks. In response, the witness burst out with self-incriminating racist remarks, resulting in the judge sentencing him for contempt of court.

Next Jack called Laurel back to the stand. She continued to deny his identity saying, "Jack Sommersby never said a kind word to me in my life; that's where *you* made your mistake." But then Jack spoke to the crowd, asking how many were from his own town, and how many had known him his whole life, and how many were willing to testify that he was the real Jack Sommersby? Every townsperson there stood up, even Laurel's nine-year-old son. But Laurel continued to deny it. He asked her how she could say that, but she would not say. He asked her again, but she would not say. He loudly demanded she answer the question, when finally, she blurted out: "Because I *never* loved Jack Sommersby the way that I love you."

Finally, Jack asked Laurel to look at something. He brought over a promissory note and held it in front of her face: "If I am *not* Jack Sommersby, then this paper is a fraud, and all these folks own nothing. If I am not Jack Sommersby, then our new one-year-old will be called a bastard. And if I am not Jack Sommersby, then I am nothing but a thief, a liar, and a deserter. Now I ask you one more time, Laurel; am I your husband?" And though her answer would mean the execution of the man she loved; she gave him — out of love — the greatest thing he desired. "Yes," she said, "You are Jack Sommersby."

Just be the one that you're called to be

I remember a time in my life when I was being tossed about by a fearsome storm. I was going through conflict in one of my previous churches. It was painful and complicated, and the way through was not clear. I needed some guidance, some help. I needed someone to say a word of faith and courage to me.

In my mailbox one day I found an envelope from my father. He rarely wrote — more often Mom would — but there it was, a handwritten note from Dad. His letter offered some supportive words of caring and wisdom but ended in a way I'll never forget: "Just be the kind of Hope that you've always been called to be." Those treasured words carried me a long way on my life's journey.

Eight or nine years later, Dad was going through a time of troubles in his own church where he was pastor. By then he had forgotten what he had once written to me, and I wrote to him with these words, "Just be the kind of Jack Harle that God has always called you to be." Later, he told me how moved and helpful those words were to him at the time. I demurred, telling him I was actually just echoing back his own pastoral voice. But he replied that he was touched that I had remembered and had given him those words when he needed them most.

Discover your spiritual name

Charles Dubois once said, "We must always be ready at any moment to give up who we are for who we may become."

I encourage you to embark on a quest to discover your spiritual name. And when you find it, ponder it, until you comprehend what this Christ-given name might mean for this moment in your faith journey — not so you can feel proud, but so you might not deny to others what God seeks to do through you.

"...Yet I will not forget you. See, I have inscribed you on the palms of my hands" (Isaiah 49:15b-16a NRSV).

Sketch #8 ...Jesus, Our Questioner:

"Do You See This Woman?"

Luke 7:36-50 — The sinful woman forgiven at Simon the Pharisee's banquet

*"Then turning toward the woman, he said to Simon, 'Do you
see this woman? I entered your house; you gave me no water for
my feet, but she has bathed my feet with her tears and dried them
with her hair. You gave me no kiss, but from the time I came in she
has not stopped kissing my feet. You did not anoint my head with
oil, but she has anointed my feet with ointment. Therefore, I tell
you, her sins, which were many, have been forgiven; hence she has
shown great love. But the one to whom little is forgiven, loves little'"*
   Luke 7:44-47 (NRSV)

> *"Care for the life of another,*
> *even material bodily care,*
> *is spiritual in essence.*
> *Bread for myself is a material question.*
> *Bread for my neighbor is a spiritual question."*
>   —Nikolai Berdyaev

Jesus the lover of questions

Christ loved questions. And he was asked many questions by
many kinds of people: by the common people, the *am ha-aretz*,
who considered him a rabbi; by the religious authorities who
considered him a threat; and by the Pharisees, who considered
him a question mark.

In debates about scriptural interpretation or the will of God,
Jesus was incomparable. He often responded to a question with a
counter-question, which often put the original questioner into an
inescapable theological corner.

Jesus' embrace of questions as a spiritual-truth path is on full
display in the following contentious encounter:

83

When he entered the temple, the chief priests and the elders of the people came to him as he was teaching, and said, "By what authority are you doing these things, and who gave you this authority?" Jesus said to them, "I will also ask you one question; if you tell me the answer, then I will also tell you by what authority I do these things. Did the baptism of John [the Baptist] come from heaven, or was it of human origin?" And they argued with one another, "If we say, 'From heaven,' he will say to us, 'Why then did you not believe him?' "But if we say, 'Of human origin,' we are afraid of the crowd; for all regard John as a prophet." So they answered Jesus, "We do not know." And he said to them, "Neither will I tell you where my authority is from" Matthew 21:23-27 (NRSV)

Jesus' questions, from age twelve to Easter

Jesus' questions span his earthly sojourn. At the age of twelve, Jesus ran away from his family to stay in the temple for three days, where he asked questions that amazed the great Jewish teachers there. When his parents finally found him and chastised him for making them worry, and he answered with two questions: "Why were you searching for me? Did you not know I must be in the house of my Father?" (Luke 2:49 NRSV).

At Golgotha on the cross, Jesus cries out with a question, expressing both his agony and his trust in his Abba, as Jesus quotes the query of desperation from Psalm 22's opening (which Mark preserves in the original Aramaic words): "'Eloi, eloi, lama sabachthani,' which means, 'My God, my God, why have you forsaken me?'" (Mark 15:34 NRSV).

At the empty tomb, the risen Christ asks Mary Magdalene two questions, as she presumes him to be the gardener, "'Woman, why are you weeping? Whom are you looking for?'" (John 20:15 NRSV).

Even at his last resurrection appearance in the gospel of John, the Risen One makes a point of asking Simon Peter three questions, to counter and forgive his three denials, and to give him all the courage he will need for the future: "Simon, son of John, do you love me more than these?" …"Simon, son of John, do you love me?" …"Simon, son of John, do you love me?" (John 21:15-17 NRSV).

Jesus' questions that challenge and provoke us

Some of Jesus' questions teach us: "Which of the three, do you think, was a neighbor to the man who fell into the hands of robbers?" (Luke 10:36 NRSV). Some of them challenge us: "Were not ten made clean? But the other nine, where are they? Was none of them found to return and give praise to God except this foreigner?" (Luke 17:17-18 NRSV). Some of his questions cut us to the bone, questioning our devotion, as when, in exasperation, he asks the Twelve **nine questions in a row**, ending in, "Do you not yet understand?" (Mark 8:21 NRSV). And some questions could determine the course of our lives: "But who do you say that I am?" (Mark 8:29 NRSV). All of these interrogatories echo down the centuries to confront us in the present.

Questions possess exceptional power to penetrate beyond our masks, beyond our formulaic answers, to confront our naked souls with stark truth. Gifted interviewers such as Christianne Amanpour, Terry Gross, Ira Glass, Anderson Cooper, Lester Holt, Scott Pelley, Lesley Stahl, Bill Whitaker, Bob Costas, and Oprah Winfrey dazzle us with their use of questions to open an interviewee beyond the pretenses to a more intimate, more vulnerable sharing of themselves, revealing someone we can connect with and understand.

One of the most intriguing questioners I've ever met was one of my college professors, a one-year visiting professor of theology named Ed Theisen, whose questions were so penetrating they were almost unnerving. He would ask me who Jesus was, and I might give a traditional kind of answer, and then he'd ask me what I meant by that, and I'd try to explain that as best I could, but then he'd ask me what I meant by that! And I began to realize how rarely I had wrestled with these sacred concepts enough to find my own metaphors of understanding, my own voice of connection and conviction. I began to realize how inadequate my religious words were in depicting or in approaching the Spirit of the living God.

Jesus' question to Simon the Pharisee

Jesus utters a profound question in the scriptural story of

Luke 7:36-50 at the home of Simon the Pharisee.

While some Pharisees were open to Jesus' insights or were friends who personally warned him about Herod's threats against him (Luke 13:31), other Pharisees were outspoken opponents or hard-hearted toward those Jesus touched, welcomed, and chose.

As the story opens, we do not know Simon's view toward Jesus. Perhaps he just wanted to impress his friends by having a banquet with this famous Galilean celebrity, or maybe he wanted to test or trap Jesus in some way. Only later do we learn that when Jesus first arrived, Simon had treated him with blatant disrespect. Simon never offered the usual signs of hospitality traditionally given any guest, not to mention a guest of great honor. He did not offer the kiss of greeting, the washing of the feet, nor the giving a drop of perfumed ointment on the head.

We only learn of this egregious slap in the face because Jesus points it out himself, as he speaks out in defense of a woman who had entered the room, weeping. With her tears she bathes Jesus' feet, and with her hair, she dries them. She then kisses his feet and anoints them with costly ointment.

Simon is scandalized by Jesus, and says to himself, "If this man were a prophet, he would have known who and what kind of woman this is who is touching him — that she is a sinner" (Luke 7:39 NRSV).

But Jesus seizes this moment to teach Simon about what it means to truly see, eyes that see not categories but cherished children of God, hearts that see what a life of gratitude looks like when lived out.

Imagine you are there. Imagine the scene. Imagine the characters. Imagine that you overhear Jesus as he engages Simon, challenging him to be blind no longer…

An experience of overhearing Jesus at Simon's:

Simon, do you see this woman?

*Do you truly see this **child of God**, this daughter of faith, forgiven and freed from a life of using and being used into a new life of unconditional hope? Or do you see only a category, a low-life tramp, detritus, expendable debris — discard after use?*

86

*Simon, do you see what **a life of gratefulness** looks like? Tears of thankfulness for a holy forgiveness... given before "I'm sorry," given before "I'm unworthy," given before "I'll earn your love." Or do you see her only in the cage of her past, defined forever by her worst mistake, her greatest regret, forever unwelcome in your house and God's?*

*Simon, do you see what **a life of redemption** looks like? Gentle hands of caring thoughtfulness, free-of-expectation touch, surprising the other with soothing tenderness. Or are you blind that you've treated me with the same contempt you have for her — intentionally insulting me, denying me common hospitality: no washing of my feet, no anointing my head with perfume, no kiss of welcome?*

*Simon, **with my back to you as I keep looking at this woman** — I say to you now, Simon:*

> *Do you see what a spirit-filled life looks like?*
> *Do you see her giving of her life with joyful abandon?*
> *Do you see her prodigal generosity?*
> *Do you see her lavishing love unabashed?*
> *Do you not know that this is what it means to lift others into God's presence?*
> *Simon, do you see this woman?*

Imagine

What if Jesus confronted us today as he confronted Simon? What might he say to us, teach us to see?

An experience of encountering Jesus today

Christians of North America:

> *Do you see **this woman***
> *walking down the street talking to herself,*
> *who everyone ignores,*
> *her inner beauty as invisible as the bruises she hides?*
>
> *Do you see **this Muslim woman** in your neighborhood*
> *who finally tells you her story — of fleeing as a refugee*
> *from Baghdad to Damascus to Buffalo —*
> *but tells you only when you took the time*

to wish her a blessed Ramadan,
took time to leave a gift on her doorstep,
and took time to take her children to the park with your
grandkids?

*Do you see **this man on the bus***
looking out the window,
weary and heavy-laden late in the day,
whose eyes meet your eyes,
heading from one low-wage job to the second?

*Do you see this **young teen in the hoodie***
walking down your street eating Skittles,
who needs a neighbor willing to care,
to care enough to know his name,
and shout out, "Hey, Jalen, how's it goin'?"

*Do you see **this prisoner***
who asks you to find someone
willing to be a pen pal for one of their block-mates,
but no one will?

*Do you see **this child of Honduras***
who you walked past when you were there,
who recently has fled San Pedro Sula's violence,
and has followed your bread crumbs back to this land,
and has appeared unannounced
at the threshold of your home,
wanting only to be held and hear the words,
"It's going to be okay now."

*Do you see **this woman at the store** who you failed to*
see this week,
who saw you smiling at a photo on your phone
with such joy that it made you glow,
and touched by your beauty,
she asked you about the weather,
wanting to connect with you for a minute,

but you never looked up,
as you replied, "Yeah, nice weather,"
and you missed the sacrament of the moment.

*Do you see **this young gay man***
bullied in high school,
now an assistant dance teacher,
so smart and articulate,
thrown out by his parents and shunned by his siblings,
until your daughter starts inviting him to dinner,
and with nowhere to go for Christmas
comes to your house,
where you discover his favorite thing in the world —

the Houston Ballet —
and later, when you hear this dance troupe
is coming to your city,
you surprise him with two tickets,
and he says to your daughter,
"Your parents can adopt me anytime,"
and she replies, "I think they already have."

*Do you see **this African American teen***
on your commuter train
frantically looking under the seats for something,
as a white security officer comes over to ask
what he's doing, demanding to see his ticket.
And he says he had money for his ticket
but dropped it somewhere and is searching,
and the officer starts yelling at him to get off the train —
"We don't want your kind around here!"
And an African American woman
at the other end of the car comes over, interrupting:
"Officer, I'm a minister; can I be of any help?"
And the officer starts yelling at her to sit down
and stay out of it,
but she reaches into her purse, pulls out a twenty,

and says to the young man, "I found this over there.
Isn't this what you were looking for?"
And the young man sheepishly nods yes,
and the officer backs down and moves on.
And the woman looks up and down the car —
noticing all the white people
who stayed in their seats as things escalated.
And as she sits down —
very tired that it had to be her again — and wonders,
"When will this world change enough
for this young man to be valued and safe?"

Jesus leaves us with these final words:
I'm sorry for these unwanted intrusions
into your overbooked, drive-thru life,
but I didn't know who else to send them to.
But I thought maybe I could break through to you,
give you the life you've always longed for,
by breaking open your heart
with their shattered hearts,
and giving both of you
new hearts,
remixing the fragments —
yours and theirs —
by intertmingling them forever by my touch,
and then restarting your hearts
with my lightning love:
To redeem the world
two hearts at a time,
to revive the earth
two hearts at a time,
to restore your souls
two hearts at a time.

Christians of North America:
Do you see the peace I bring?
Do you see this woman?

POSTSCRIPT: A RESPONSIVE READING

Questions Jesus Asks

by Hope Harle-Mould

One: Jesus loved asking questions: shocking and delighting people with new vistas of God's agapé, provoking people to turn around and enter God's movement.

All: **God, may Jesus' questions challenge and transform us anew.**

One: Jesus asks, "Why were you searching for me? Did you not know I must be in my Abba's house?" (Luke 2:49).

All: **God, teach us where to look for Christ — from sanctuary to city streets — wherever you open our minds to deeper truth and our hearts to wider compassion.**

One: Jesus asks, "Which of these three was a neighbor to the man who fell into the hands of the robbers?" (Luke 10:36).

All: **God, help us to grow beyond our prejudices and borders to embrace your grace as it comes to us in the form of the stranger.**

One: Jesus asks us, "Why are you afraid? Have you still no faith?" (Mark 4:40).

All: **When winds and waves threaten to overwhelm us, may we remember that in our boat is Christ and, in his storm-stilling voice is a peace that passes all understanding.**

One: Jesus asks us, "Do you see this woman?" (Luke 7:44).

All: **God, forgive us for being blind to the world's forsaken ones, and hard-hearted to the people you to send us to love.**

One: Jesus asks us, "What do you want me to do for you?" (Luke 18:41).

All: **God, may we dare to come inside your embracing presence, and dare to leap into your promises we can't yet see but only receive. (1)**

91

ENDNOTES

Sketch #8…Jesus, Our Questioner
"Do You See This Woman?"

    1. Hope Harle-Mould © 2018.

Sketch #9 ...Jesus, Our Captives-Redeemer

The Slave Who Redeemed His Wife

Exodus 6:2-9 — I will free you, deliver you, redeem you

Isaiah 43:1-21 — I redeemed you, called you by name

Mark 10:41-45 — To serve, to give his life as a ransom

> *"Do not fear, for I have redeemed you; I have called you by name, you are mine"* Isaiah 43:1 (NRSV)

> *"For the Son of Man came not to be served but to serve, and to give his life a ransom for many"* Mark 10:45 (NRSV)

"The ultimate weakness of violence is that it is a descending spiral, begetting the very thing it seeks to destroy. Darkness cannot drive out darkness; only light can do that. Hate cannot drive out hate; only love can do that."

— Martin Luther King Jr.

NOTE TO READER: This chapter was first preached as a sermon at Springboro United Church of Christ, Springboro, Ohio (near Dayton). Its spirit and message are best preserved and presented by retaining its original form. Please, imagine you are there.

The handcuffed pastor

This morning I preach my sermon to you as I am manacled. Why did I do this? Maybe it was because I wanted you to remember my sermon this day. I know that years from now you'll probably forget all the content of my message this morning, but I'll bet that you'll be able to say, "Remember that Sunday when Pastor Hope preached with a handcuff on? I don't remember what his point was, but I do believe he had a point. I'm not sure what it was, but I'll never forget those handcuffs!"

And here are the only keys. It's rather important that these be kept in a secure place and not lost. Is there a volunteer to keep these keys during the sermon? *[Pastor Hope's fourteen- year- old daughter Jen raises her hand and waves it wildly in the air.]* Okay, come on up, Jen. On second thought, is there someone else, anybody else? *[She takes the key away with a triumphant smile.]*

The handcuffed activist

During the civil rights movement in Wilmington, North Carolina, a young African American minister of the United Church of Christ, Reverend Ben Chavis, was arrested with nine others on false charges and unjustly imprisoned for a year and a half, simply because of their activist work for integration. They became known as the Wilmington Ten. After years of court battles, justice finally prevailed. They were exonerated on all charges. And decades later, the state of North Carolina gave them an official pardon plus an apology.

But in those early days, when Reverend Chavis and the others were imprisoned and felt forsaken, when times were darkest in the belly of the beast, God's providence sent them a sign. As Reverend Chavis was being moved from one prison cell to another, tightly handcuffed with his hands behind his back — as he walked along — he felt one handcuff fall free of its own accord. Chavis did not call attention to it but wisely continued walking. He waited until a *kairos* moment, a moment of divine decisiveness. When they reached the new cell, Chavis turned around toward the guards and the other civil rights prisoners and boldly declared: *Our God is the Justice God who hears the cry of the powerless. Our God is the Exodus God who liberates the oppressed. Even here, in the darkness of this dungeon, God's power is present.* Then he raised his arms to the heavens.

[At this moment Pastor Hope raises his arms, showing that one of his handcuffs has come free as well.]

Then Reverend Chavis dramatically called out: *No chains can bind us, no bars can imprison us, no walls can contain us. Someday we shall be free!* Many days of imprisonment awaited them, but from then on, they were certain of victory, and their hope was never extinguished.

My benediction in American Sign Language

At the end of each Sunday worship service, when I give the benediction, I perform a benediction based on 2 Corinthians 13:13, and — as you know — I perform it in American Sign Language (ASL): "May the grace of our Redeemer, Jesus the Christ, and the love of God, and the communion of the Holy Spirit be upon you now and forever. Amen." What you may not know is that I have made one significant change from Paul's version. Instead of saying and signing, "May the grace of our *Lord* Jesus Christ... be upon you," I say and sign, "May the grace of our *Redeemer*, Jesus the Christ... be upon you." Why?

Why do I say Redeemer instead of Lord?

One reason for this change is for its visual drama, the beauty of the word "Redeemer." To say "Lord" in ASL is simply done by using an "L" sweeping across your chest from upper left to lower right, as if you were wearing a sash. But to say "Redeemer" in ASL dramatically depicts what Christ's sacrificial death means for us.

Here's how to say "Redeemer" in ASL: First, cross your fingers on both hands (index and middle fingers crossed), which stands for the letter "r." Now cross both your arms across your chest so that your hands are nearly touching your shoulders. Imagine that your arms are manacled by chains. Now, suddenly open your arms upward and outward swiftly and strongly, as if breaking free from your fetters, and holding your freed hands high. That is how you say "Redeemer," for that is what our Redeemer does.

But the deeper theological reason I say Redeemer instead of Lord is that Redeemer expresses more. Lord means ruler or sovereign. And yes, Jesus is our Lord, the one whose values and priorities are to rule our daily life, the one to whom we are to pledge allegiance above political and earthly allegiances. But Jesus is Lord because he is Redeemer.

God as Redeemer in the Old Testament

Throughout the Hebrew scriptures, we hear that *Redeemer* is who God is and what God does. Psalm 19 climaxes with the psalmist calling God "my rock and my redeemer" (v. 14). In Isaiah 43 God says through the prophet, "Do not fear, for I have redeemed you; I have called you by name, you are mine" (v. 1b). In Job 19, Job replies to his tormentors: "I know that my Redeemer lives" (v. 25). But the decisive deed of the divine in the Old Testament is the Exodus.

Exodus 6:6 is often called the gospel of the Exodus, the whole book in one verse:

> *Say therefore to the Israelites, "I am the LORD, and I will free you from the burdens of the Egyptians and deliver you from slavery to them. I will redeem you with an outstretched arm and with mighty acts of judgment" (NRSV).*

Notice the active verbs: God will **free** you, **deliver** you, **redeem** you. The Jews experienced God as the great emancipator into freedom, the deliverer from oppression, the Redeemer from captivity.

Christ as Redeemer in the New Testament

In the New Testament, Jesus describes himself as the one who came to give his life as a ransom for many (Matthew 20:28). The gospel of John declares from the beginning that Jesus' death on the cross was the Passover lamb sacrificed for all: "Here is the lamb of God who takes away the sin of the world!" (John 1:29). And Hebrews 9:11-15 makes clear that Christ's blood and death emancipate us from the old covenant and bring us into the new.

(Let me make one thing clear. The cross is not the sacrificial payment God requires from Jesus in order for God to forgive us. It is the cost *we* require of *God* to reach us. The cross is how far God was willing to go and how much God was willing to suffer in order for us to be reconciled to God's own self. Think of the cross as a bridge, across which humanity and heaven could finally touch and be brought into righteous relationship.)

As B.J. Hoff wrote:

> *Christ is the bridge that reaches past today and destiny, to join the things of heaven with those of earth... He links creation's dawning with infinity's vast shore, the arch across all history is his birth... His cross of love is raised above a world where war and sin have torn God and his children far apart... It spans the centuries, to give safe*

passage to his peace — Christ is the bridge, the way to God's own heart.

The true way for us to receive this new life — to stop living as if we are dead and to start living with the Spirit's aliveness — is to open the cell door of our captivity and rush into the abiding arms of our new freedom in Christ.

The freed slave who redeemed his wife out of slavery

In 1849, a newly freed slave from the South arrived here in Springboro, Ohio, and settled here. His name was Napoleon Johnson. Eventually he became an accomplished plasterer and leading citizen of Springboro, owning five properties along South Main Street in addition to his home on East Mill Street, just three blocks from where you sit — currently the taxidermy shop. But at first the only work he found was as a handy man on the Janney farm.

He scraped and saved every nickel and penny until he had enough. Enough for what? His goal was to buy his wife, Celia, for she was still in slavery. The slave owner who had freed Napoleon had refused to emancipate his wife at that time, so they were forced to separate, fearing it might be forever. But Napoleon was determined to be the redeemer of his wife. As soon as he had enough, he made the perilous journey back into the slave-holding South.

Napoleon met the slave owner face to face and paid him the price of redemption for his beloved. Celia was now free forever. And as Springboro historian, Don Ross, points out — just to show you what a good soul Napoleon possessed — he also paid the price of redemption for his *mother-in-law*, and permitted her to live with them in their Springboro home the rest of her days!

But there's more. Napoleon didn't hoard his family's new-found freedom for themselves but risked it again and again on behalf of redeeming others, as their home became a station on the Underground Railroad. And later, during the Civil War, Napoleon left Springboro to join the Union troops, and at age 44 marched into battle, as together they sang of a Redeemer who "died to make men holy," whose "truth is marching on!"

Sin = Captivity

Why do we need a Redeemer? Because of sin. Now I'm not talking about sins with a lower case "s" but Sin with a capital "S." Sometimes we focus on our little sins, the private indiscretions we've grown accustomed to. These may be significant, and may hurt ourselves and others, even hurting God as well, but there is a more ominous kind of sin. It is when we participate in the incivility, callousness, non-constructiveness, violence, evil, and death of our institutions and culture.

Sometimes God calls us to *be* the answer for some impoverished village or family, but we do not hear the call, for we're out acquiring additional possessions. Sometimes our family or friends cry out for healing, but we do not hear the cry, for we are occupied accumulating merit badges of social status and career recognition. Sometimes when prisoners — despite the dehumanizing conditions of prisons — are reformed and ready to contribute good, we keep them behind bars or execute vengeance upon them. Sometimes when our darkened world needs our insights and inspiration, our conviction, our compassion, we withhold them, keeping them inside, depriving others of the light only we might give.

That is *sin*. And we live in a state of captivity to it. So we need more than a forgiver. We need someone to unshackle our lives, to open the barred doors into our new beginning, to lead us to the gates of our maximum-security block and teach us that all we need to do is walk out into the sun. We need a someone to face *The Powers That Be* with the power of the cross, a someone to lift up the downtrodden and to love them into chosen ones, a someone to out-suffer evil's worst until new hope is born.

The great news is that it's already been done, once and for all. The principalities and powers are powerless before the cross. Whether we feel it or not, it's true. The shackles are unlocked. The chains are broken. All we need to do is take the first step out of our captivity and into the new light of a new day.

"How will I know who to thank?"

Imagine that there was a man thrown into a dark dungeon for no just reason. And none of his family or friends knew he was there. Imagine that he had been there a long time and had no idea how much longer he would languish there. Imagine that he had given up, had lost his hope. But suddenly one day a guard opened his cell door and said, "You are free to go." The man was flabbergasted. "How could this be?" "Someone has paid your bail," the guard replied. "Who?" "They wish to remain anonymous." The prisoner asked, "But how will I know who to thank when I walk down the streets of my new life? It could have been anybody out there!" The guard made no answer.

That *was* the answer. Yes, it could have been anybody. But we know in whose name that unknown one was acting: in the name of the One who once posted *our* bond to free *us* from bondage, the one who anonymously chose to free *us* for life, the One who simply says, "If you want to thank me, become a redeemer for others."

The church that put up its building as bond

The church that Linda and I belonged to while we were in seminary — and the church we were married in after graduation — was a small congregation in a big yellow brick sanctuary on the west side of Manhattan: Good Shepherd/Faith Presbyterian Church. While we were involved there, we found out what made that church's mission outreach so mustard-seed mighty. It was something in its DNA.

In the late 1960s, after years of sacrifice, Good Shepherd-Faith had finally paid off the mortgage on their building. But then they heard of a need. Several community activists, members of the Black Panther Party, had just been arrested. They did a lot of good work in the neighborhood, but their politics had made them suspect. Some church members were seriously concerned: "Will these men receive a fair trial? They should be freed on bail. Would it be possible for the church to put up the building as bond to free them?" Other church members thought that while this might be a grand prophetic gesture, there was simply no guarantee for the church; the Panthers could jump bail, skip town, and leave the church with an irrecoverable loss. The church prayed, debated, and prayed some more. Finally, Good Shepherd/Faith

Presbyterian Church made the amazing decision to risk all it had just achieved in order to ensure that justice was done for these accused ones. They offered redemption to set the prisoners free. In the end, the defendants kept the trust of the church, stayed to face trial, and received a fair trial. In the end, the church — in a time of trial and risk — had acted not as an institution but as a body of Christ.

Father Maximillian Kolbe

During World War II, Father Maximillian Kolbe was a Polish priest who dared to speak out against the Nazis and help rescue many Jews. Kolbe himself was arrested and sent to Auschwitz, the largest death camp for Jews. One day the order came down that one of the Jewish cellmates of Father Kolbe was to be executed. This man had a wife and children, who were believed to have escaped to a place of safety. The man wept, knowing he would never see them again. All the men in that cell wept with him. But Father Kolbe did more than weep. He had an idea.

He arranged to go and meet with the commandant of the concentration camp about this condemned prisoner. Kolbe said, *I want to stand in his place. I know someone is scheduled to die, but let it be me that he might live.* The commandant agreed. Father Kolbe went back and told them the good news. They all wept again. The next day, Father Kolbe was executed. The Jewish man lived. After the allies liberated the camp, the man found his way home. To everyone he met, he spoke the name of Maximillian Kolbe, his redeemer from captivity, his redeemer of great cost.

Some years ago, one of my dearest mentors, United Methodist minister Richard Deats, told me of his trip to see Auschwitz and how he was able to enter the tiny cell where Father Kolbe and his Jewish friends suffered. Today in Israel at Yad Vashem, one of the plaques honoring the "Righteous Among the Gentiles" is for Father Maximillian Kolbe.

For how many prisoners will you open the door?

How can we participate in the work of Jesus the Redeemer? One way is to work for the release of prisoners of conscience around the world through Amnesty International or Human

Rights Watch. If we do, perhaps one day we'll receive a letter in the mail like the following:

They kept seeing and hearing my name. I was lost. I was nothing to them. They had locked me away for years for no cause. They had totally forgotten me. But you wouldn't let them forget. My name! They kept hearing my name. Thank God for you, unknown friend. You kept my name alive.

When they finally released me, they said my file was two inches thick with correspondence. Most of it was from you. They simply said that the file was two inches thick, and that was too much trouble for just one prisoner.

I owe you my life. Words can never express my thanks. May every political prisoner's file become two inches thick. (1)

Sisters and brothers, for how many prisoners will *you* open the door?

"You are free to go."

In the dark dungeons of our life and world, in the locked cells of our crushed-hope wounds, Jesus comes to us, and declares to you and me: "Do not fear, for I have redeemed you; I have called you by name, you are mine" (Isaiah 43:1 NRSV). So, if I were you, I would get up, go over, and try that locked door one more time. If I were you. One more time. Maybe now.

ENDNOTES

Sketch #9 ...Jesus, Our Captives-Redeemer:
The Slave Who Redeemed His Wife

1. From Hope Harle-Mould's short story, "The Shut-In Freedom Fighter," first published in *Presbyterian Survey*, June 1987. This letter, which is quoted in the story, is based on true incidents in the life of my friend Bill Frelick, who was a young activist for Amnesty International (AI) for many years, who then served on their staff for fifteen years, and who currently works for Human Rights Watch as their Refugee Policy Director.

Sketch #10 ...Jesus, Our Forgiver:

Louie Zamperini, The Amish School Shooting, And My Father-In-Law Harry

Mark 2:1-12 — Healing, forgiving the paralytic man

Luke 23:33-34 — Jesus forgiving his crucifiers

> *"Father, forgive them; for they do not know what they are doing"*
> Luke 23:34 (NRSV)

> *"There is...a condition for receiving God's gift of forgiveness. [We] must be willing to accept it. Absurd as this may seem, there are few who will believe in and accept the forgiveness of God so completely as to... leave their sin with [God] forever. They are always re-opening the vault where they have deposited their sin,... forever asking to have it back in order to fondle it, to reconstruct it, to query, to worry over it.... Thus, their sin ties them to the past."* —Douglas Steere

No forgiveness.

What if there were no forgiveness? For anyone. Ever. What would it be like? Hannah Arendt describes it this way:

> *Without being forgiven, released from the consequences of what we have done, our capacity to act would, as it were, be confined to one single deed from which we could never recover; we would remain the victims of its consequences forever, not unlike the sorcerer's apprentice who lacked the magic formula to break the spell.* (1)

When I was in fifth grade, our teacher Mrs. Halvorson once left the room, telling us to remain totally silent and work, that we were on our honor. As soon as she was out the door, the smart-aleck next to me said loudly, "Sure, on our honor." And I replied out loud, "Yeah, on our honor." The rest of the time I was silent. When Mrs. Halvorson returned, she informed us she had been behind the door listening and she wanted each of us to tell her if we had been talking or not. I said I had not, forgetting I had blurted something out at the outset. Later a classmate confronted me: "You were talking, too." Only then did I recall I had. And I had lied.

One winter in sixth grade, our teacher Mr. Gridley once left the room, telling us to stay in our seats and work while he went down to the office. Immediately a few people got out of their seats. I got up, went over to the open window, grabbed a handful of snow from the windowsill, walked around wondering whose back I should put it down, until I decided to throw it back out the window. But for the rest of the time, I stayed at my desk. When Mr. Gridley returned and saw half the class all over the room, he flew into a fury and required us to write a log of everything we had done while he was out. I wrote that I had stayed in my seat, forgetting what I had done at the outset. Only later did I recall what I had omitted. I never admitted my lie. I shrugged it off as no big deal.

Sometime later, I had a night when I couldn't sleep. I kept tossing and turning. My conscience was bothering me. I was guilty of breaking the trust of a teacher and of covering it up with falsehoods, not once but twice. Finally, my mom woke up and asked me why I couldn't sleep. I told her the whole story. Tears came as I told her that the longer these dishonesties were hiding within me, the larger they were growing. But how could I undo the past? Those wrongs would always be there. My dear mother said, "Son, I forgive you, and if I can forgive you, God will certainly forgive you, and if God forgives you, then your past is healed. You can start with a clean slate." Mom gave me a hug, my conscience was freed, and I have slept soundly ever since. (My wife would say I have snored loudly ever since!)

The paralysis of unforgiveness

A guilty conscience can produce not only insomnia but paralysis. Such is the case in the scriptural story from Mark 2:1-12. Four friends lower a stretcher through the thatched roof of the courtyard where Jesus is preaching. On it is a man in fetal position, with fingers, arms, and legs grotesquely curled inward. Jesus immediately senses that this man's grievous sins of the past were so inescapable that his subconscious had overloaded and shut down his body. To heal the man's illness, Jesus must first heal his soul.

Jesus says to the paralytic, "Child, your sins are forgiven." He speaks to the man as if he is speaking to a child at a second story window in a burning house, paralyzed with fear from smoke and flames but too fearful to jump: *It's okay, little one, just jump and I'll catch you; I promise you, I won't miss, 'cause you're God's cherished child.* So like the child who jumps into a rescuing arms, the forgiven paralytic rises, picks up his pallet, and walks — just as Jesus commands.

Without forgiveness, there can be no new beginning. We are sentenced to repeat the past forever.

"I need a new start"

As a parent, I have found it essential not only to be quick to forgive my children but quick to ask forgiveness *of* my children. I remember once when my son Josh and daughter Jessica were not getting along in another room. I thought I overheard Josh say something mean to Jessie. In reality, it was just the opposite. Jessie had been jumping up and down near the headboard of the bed, and he said something to warn and protect his little sister. I'd listened with negativity, hearing the worst instead of the best. When I realized this, I quickly asked his forgiveness, but he was so hurt and angry that he couldn't accept my many apologies. Finally, I said, "Look, I need a new start. Can we just begin again, here and now, and start over?" And he agreed. The concept of a new start has helped me countless times as a parent in breaking through wrongs I have done, or others have done to me.

Why forgive?

What is forgiveness? It is not denying the depth of our hurt or giving into martyrdom. And it is not forgetting or excusing unjust behavior. Forgiveness means, in the words of Marjorie Thompson,

> ... to make a conscious choice to release the person who has wounded us from the sentence of our judgment, however justified that judgment may be. It represents a choice to leave behind our resentment and

desire for retribution, however fair such punishment might seem. It is in this sense that one may speak of "forgetting"; not that the actual wound is ever completely forgotten, but that its power to hold us trapped in continual replay of the event, with all the resentment each remembrance makes fresh, is broken. (2)

We need to forgive those who have harmed us grievously, not for only for our *spiritual* well-being but also for our *mental health* and *physical survival*. Some hurts inhabit our minds, replaying the injury again and again, until our insides are torn to shreds. That is why we need to forgive our parents for what they did to us when we were growing up, or for what they did *not* give to us or were incapable of giving to us as children. That is why the group, *Families of Murder Victims Against the Death Penalty*, forgives: to free the forgiver from the inner ravages of continual vengeance.

Let me share with you three images of the holiness of forgiveness.

Holy Forgiveness #1: Louie Zamperini

Every night, Louie Zamperini had the same nightmare: his hands around the neck of the man who had once tortured him, the man he wanted more than anything to strangle to death.

The son of Italian immigrants, Louie Zamperini grew up in the rough neighborhoods of Torrence, California, where he often got in trouble. The chief of police noticed how fleet-footed he was and suggested he try out for track. By his senior year, Louie set a world record for the high school mile, made the US Olympic team, and competed at the 1936 Berlin games. He was looking forward to winning another medal at the 1940 Olympics when World War II broke out.

Louie Zamperini was trained as a bombardier and stationed at Kahufu Airbase in Hawaii. In May 1943, he was sent out in the only remaining plane to search for and rescue the crew of a downed B-29 when two of his plane's four engines failed and the plane went down in the central Pacific, exploding on impact. Of the twelve-man crew, only three were alive in the water. Louie found an inflated yellow raft and they climbed aboard, but no one back at the airbase knew whether they were alive or how to locate them.

After 33 days, one of the three died from exposure and lack of food. Then for seven days running there was no rain, so they had no fresh water to drink. On the edge of death, the next day brought a great rainstorm. On day 47 they finally spotted land. It was an island. They had drifted 2,000 miles to the Marshall Islands. The only problem was the Japanese were already there. As the two crawled ashore, they were taken prisoner, thrown into a dark cell, and fed one small ball of rice three times a day.

They were constantly threatened with execution until one day they were blindfolded and taken to the officers' headquarters where a Japanese doctor injected them with disease-causing agents and asked them to report everything it did to them. After 43 days of captivity, the two were taken by boat to Japan and placed in separate prisoner-of-war camps. Zamperini was imprisoned in Tokyo Bay at Omori Prison where he met the most terrifying person of his life: Sergeant Motsuhiro Watanabe. The prisoners considered him a sadistic psychopath. The other Japanese officers considered him — well, a sadistic psychopath. The prisoners nicknamed him *The Bird*. The Bird had such demonic eyes that Louie would not look into them — even when punished for not doing so. For ten days Watanabe beat Zamperini senseless.

On November 18, 1944, Tokyo officials allowed Zamperini to make a radio broadcast in his own words. It was heard in Torrence, California, where two and a half weeks before the newspaper had declared him dead, and a memorial track meet in his name had been run. A few months later he was told he had to make another broadcast using a propaganda script or else he would be sent north to punishment camp. He refused. Besides, anything would be better than staying in the claws of The Bird.

Zamperini was sent by train up into the Alps-like mountains forty miles past Nagano (site of the future 1998 Winter Olympics), to the town of Noetsu. In the cold of that prison camp, they were made to stand at attention for an endless period of time, waiting for someone. Out of a door came none other than The Bird. Louie was ready to give up then and there, but somehow, he clung to life, despite the lack of food there and in all of Japan. In the summer of 1945, they were taken down to a river and for the first time allowed to wash. Just then, flying right overhead, came an American plane signaling to them in Morse Code: "The war is over!"

Not in the movie — the rest of the story (and best part)

The movie about Louie Zamperini, "Unbroken," ends soon after his return to America. But there is something even more astonishing in his story than survival.

Louie returned home to be reunited with his parents and family. It was as if he had died and come back to life. In 1947, he got married, but his past haunted him. Every night he had the same nightmare: his hands around the throat of The Bird, choking the breath of life out of him. But Louie was actually strangling himself, drinking heavily and drifting aimlessly.

In 1949, Louie's life was transformed when he heard the sermon of a young preacher named Billy Graham, and he committed his life to Christ. Graham told him that there was one place he had to go: back to Japan to preach the Good News and face his personal demons. In 1950, he did so, and with the spirit of Christ he met many of his former guards in the war criminals' prison and forgave them face to face. His nightmares ended. He was free.

But where was The Bird? No one knew. Louie wrote him a letter and hoped it would somehow get to him.

Forty-eight years later, just a few weeks before the 1998 Winter Olympics in Nagano, 81-year-old Louie Zamperini returned to Japan to try to meet with Watanabe. He refused to see him.

So, Louie went on to Naoetsu, now called Joetsu, site of his prison camp. There he saw a monument like none other in Japan — two descending angels in flight, a memorial to the American and Australian POWs who suffered and died there. Louie was deeply touched that the Japanese people would care enough to remember enemy soldiers such as him. He laid a bouquet of flowers there.

Then something astonishing happened. Louie was chosen by the people of Naoetsu to be their representative to bear the Olympic torch when it came to their city on its way to Nagano.

When the day arrived, Louie was handed the burning Olympic torch and began to run, holding it high. First, he ran through a line of one hundred twenty Japanese soldiers formed in two columns, parting to let him run through in honor. Then he ran through crowded streets lined with Japanese, old and young, men, women, and children calling out his name, cheering him on, cheers that were prayers of forgiveness, cheers that were embraces of friendship.

At the edge of town, Louie passed the torch on to the next runner. Afterwards Louie would say, "The graciousness and compassion of Naoetsu's thousands more than compensates for the depravity of a few a half century ago." (3)

Holy Forgiveness #2: The West Nickel Mines Amish School

On October 2, 2006, a young white man with a 9mm handgun entered the Amish one-room schoolhouse at West Nickel Mines, in Lancaster County, Pennsylvania. The teacher escaped to run for help as the man took all the girls hostage, forced the boys to help carry in more guns and equipment, and barricaded himself inside.

State troopers surrounded the school and attempted to negotiate. When the young man decided to start shooting, the oldest two girls, Marian and Barbara Fisher, ages thirteen and eleven, requested they be shot first in order to spare the younger ones. They were indeed shot first, with Marian dying and Barbara surviving. The state troopers moved in at the sound of the first shots. The young man killed five girls, ages seven to thirteen, and wounded five other girls, before killing himself.

What transpired next stunned the nation as much or more than the shooting itself, shocking even many fellow Christians, who, like the Amish, are taught to forgive.

The parents of the dead children sobbed with broken hearts as any parent would, but something else immediately began to emerge. The grandfather of the attacker's wife went to the farmhouse of two of the girls who had been shot. He was greeted there by the father of the girls who extended his hand to shake in understanding. Then it was the grieving father who reached his arm around the shoulder of the sorrowful grandfather, telling him that they held no animosity toward his family, no grudge, nothing against them. They only had forgiveness.

News reports began to discover many other acts of forgiving compassion, such as the many Amish reaching out to show caring for the attacker's widow, who was devastated.

Reporters who had come from across the country to cover the grisly attack became amazed at an entirely different storyline from what they had expected. They discovered mourning without rage, an utter lack of bitterness, and a disinterest in any press coverage. In the face of this shooting's hell, the reporters began to witness unimaginable grace, glimpses of God's face.

There was nothing unusual about this for the Amish. It had long been their Christian spiritual practice that when someone in their own family was injured or killed by someone else in a traffic accident, they would go to the family of the guilty person who was responsible for the accident and express their forgiveness first before it was even asked for.

The attacker was buried near a small Methodist church in a grave next to the pink, heart-shaped gravestone for the infant daughter whose death had apparently driven this father into a deranged killing spree. At the burial service, half of the mourners were Amish neighbors. The attacker's widow poured out words of gratitude for all her Amish neighbors whom she's always loved and would continue to love, that there would be many difficult days of grief ahead for all the families whose loved ones were gone, "so we must continue to put our hope and trust in the God of all comfort, as we seek to rebuild our lives." (5)

The freedom that comes with forgiveness

The media was mystified and mesmerized by the radical forgiveness that flowed so freely from the entire, brokenhearted Amish community. Ann Taylor Fleming of the PBS News Hour described what she found in the grieving Amish families:

...not revenge or anger, but a gentle, heart-stricken insistence on forgiveness; forgiveness, that is of the shooter himself. The widow of the shooter was actually invited to one of the funerals, and it was

said she would be welcome to stay in the community...

This, the Amish said...was Jesus' way, and they had Jesus in them, not for a day, an hour, not just in good times, but even in the very worst...

We have seldom seen this in action.... So many tribes and sects in a froth of revenge, from Darfur to Baghdad. So many victims and victims' families crying out in our courthouses for revenge.

To this, the Amish have offered a stunning example of the freedom that comes with forgiveness, a reminder that religion need not turn lethal or combative. I, for one, as this week ends, stand in awe of their almost unfathomable grace in grief. (6)

Within six months, the old school has been torn down and returned to pastureland, a new school was built at a new location and named New Hope School, and a baby was born to the pregnant woman the attacker had released from inside the school (along with the boys), and she named her baby Naomi Rose, after a six-year-old martyr of that shooting.

Holy Forgiveness #3: My father-in-law's greatest moment

My father-in-law, Harry Mould, was one of the most talented and intriguing people I've ever met. In college, he played piano with the Glenn Miller band whenever they toured through Indiana. In World War II, he designed the engine cooling systems for planes as well as the amphibious vehicles known as Ducks. As a mechanical engineer, he helped design the first window air conditioners in Buffalo, New York, — but refused to own one of his own his whole life long! His avocation was performing as Uncle Harry the Magician, making doves appear out of nowhere. In retirement, he learned leather-tooling and scroll-sawing and created amazing works of crafted art. But his greatest moment may have come in one small deed of mercy when no words were spoken.

At the peak of his career, Harry had started his own engineering business, along with a partner, and it had evolved into a thriving, successful company, bringing him growing recognition and affluence. But one day his partner suddenly disappeared, and with him vanished all the company's wealth, having flown to a Caribbean Island out of the law's reach. Harry was devastated and in debt. He had to start all over, deciding to work for someone else's company.

A number of years later, his partner's daughter, who still lived in western New York, suddenly died of a tragic drug overdose. She had been like a big sister to Harry's daughter, Linda, my wife- to-be.

Harry's former partner flew back to Buffalo for the funeral. At the funeral home, the broken-hearted father was sitting in a chair. Harry went up to him — this man who once had stolen everything he had — put his arms on his shoulders, and just stood there in caring sympathy. Without a word, Harry just stood there in utter forgiveness and in utter compassion for this man who had lost far more of life's true treasures. Without a word, Harry just stood there as the man sobbed for all that he had squandered and lost, as the man wept for the grandeur of a pardon he knew he did not deserve and never thought he'd receive. It was a moment of coming face to face with the holy ground of forgiveness.

Close your eyes

To be able to forgive as freely as the Amish, as finally as Louie Zamperini, or as fully as Harry Mould, we need to open our arms to receive the forgiveness we have been offered.

I invite you to take time now… or at a quiet moment later … for the following guided meditation.

Close your eyes. Center yourself. Bring to mind your faults and failures, the things you have done and the things you have not done, which have wounded God, your neighbors, and even your very self. Picture your greatest betrayals of Christ and of the people Christ has given you to love.

Now picture Jesus on the cross, suffering the betrayals of all, liberating you from sin, redeeming you to be a new creation.

Now hear his words from the cross — spoken *not* to the historic people surrounding him at Golgotha but spoken directly, personally to *you*, here and now:

Abba [Father], forgive her.
Abba, forgive him.
They know not what they do.
They know not.
Abba, forgive them.
Please, forgive them.
Forgive.
Now.
Amen.

ENDNOTES

Sketch #10 ...Jesus, Our Forgiver:
Louie Zamperini, the Amish School Shooting, and My Father-in-Law

1. Hannah Arendt, The Human Condition, (Chicago: University of Chicago Press), 213.

2. Marjorie J. Thompson, "Moving Toward Forgiveness," *Weavings*, vol. 7, no. 2, March/April 1992, p. 19.

3. Laura Hillenbrand, *Unbroken: A World War II Story of Survival, Resilience, and Redemption* (New York: Random House, 2010), 397-398.

4. From a CBS news special on Louie Zamperini with Bob Simon.

5. John L. Ruth, *Forgiveness: A Legacy of the West Nickel Mines Amish School* (Harrisonburg, VA: Herald Press, 2007, 2011), 37.

6. Ibid, 43-44.

Sketch #11 ...Jesus, Our Overturner Of Tables:

Prophet Of The Liberated Zone

Luke 4:16-30 — Jesus at the Nazareth synagogue

Luke 13:31-34 — A prophet killed outside Jerusalem?

Luke 19:41-44 — Jesus weeps over Jerusalem

> *"Prayer is meaningless unless it is subversive, unless it seeks to overthrow and to ruin the pyramids of callousness, hatred, opportunism, falsehoods. The liturgical movement must become a revolutionary movement, seeking to overthrow the forces that continue to destroy the promise, the hope, the vision."*
> — Rabbi Abraham Joshua Heschel

> *"Prophets were not predictors of future events. They were those who had the eyes to discern the presence of the holy God in the living moments of history, and they spoke to that insight, opening the eyes of the people of their generation to the realization that God was active in their lives. Security for the Hebrews did not reside in an unchanging tradition. It resided only in the holy God who was always in front of his people calling them to step boldly into the future."* — John Shelby Spong (1)

No longer a threat to anyone?

Non-Christians often view Jesus as a great prophet. But many Christians have lost sight of the prophetic identity of Jesus. We've so *spiritualized* Jesus that, while he comforts the afflicted, he no longer afflicts the comfortable! We've edited the sting out of his words. We emphasize, "My yoke is easy and my burden is light," but we ignore, "Take up your cross and follow me."

We've so *universalized* Jesus that we take him out of the particularity of his time and nation so that he no longer criticizes the religious or political powers that be, so that he is no longer a threat to anyone, but only "gentle Jesus, meek and mild," a law-abiding citizen who would never get into trouble with the authorities and would certainly never end up on a cross.

Standing in the line of the great prophets?

Was Jesus a prophet? Did Jesus ever see himself as a messenger of God sent to his nation with a message of warning and hope? Did Jesus ever identify himself as a prophet, or is the author just making this up? Did Jesus see himself as standing in the line of the great social justice prophets — Amos and Hosea, Isaiah and Jeremiah — who condemned injustice against orphans, widows, foreigners, and the poor, who condemned the nation's failure to worship and trust only the ways of Yahweh?

Always quoting the prophets

One way we know Jesus considered himself a prophet is how often he quotes from the prophets in his teachings.

When the Pharisees criticize him for eating at the home of tax collectors and sinners, Jesus challenges them with a remedial Bible lesson, telling them to go back and look up the prophet Hosea (6:6): "Go and learn what this means, 'I desire mercy, not sacrifice.' For I have come to call not the righteous but sinners" (Matthew 9:13 NRSV).

When Jesus is criticized for *not* following the human traditions of the elders (when his disciples failed to eat without ritually washing their hands), he responds by quoting the prophet Isaiah (29:13): "Isaiah prophesied rightly about you hypocrites, as it is written, 'This people honors me with their lips, but their hearts are far from me; in vain do they worship me, teaching human precepts as doctrines.' You abandon the commandment of God and hold to human tradition" (Mark 7:6-8 NRSV).

When the scribes demand of him a sign to prove he is the Messiah, Jesus points to the prophet Jonah, whose prophetic warning saved an entire city from destruction, saying, "...but no sign will be given to [this generation] except the sign of Jonah. For just as Jonah became a sign to the people of Nineveh, so the Son of Man will be to this generation... The people of Nineveh will rise up at the judgment with this generation and condemn it, *because they repented at the proclamation of Jonah,* and see, something greater than Jonah is here!" (Luke 11:29-32 NRSV).

At Jesus' triumphant entry into Jerusalem, when the people greet him with palms laid down before his path and shouts of "Hosanna," Jesus is clearly orchestrating a public demonstration with a prophetic message. In fact, he is enacting a prophetic parable straight from words of the prophet Zechariah (9:9), showing through provocative action what kind of Messiah he is, and what kind he is not: "This took place to fulfill what had been spoken through the prophet, saying, 'Tell the daughter of Zion, Look, your king is coming to you, humble, and mounted on a donkey, and on a colt, the foal of a donkey'" (Matthew 21:5 NRSV).

And what did the crowds say about who this man was? "This is the prophet Jesus from Nazareth in Galilee" (Matthew 21:11 NRSV).

When Jesus clears the moneychangers and those selling things from the temple, he does so as he quotes from both the prophet Isaiah (56:7) and the prophet Jeremiah (7:11): "He said to them, 'It is written, "My house shall be called a house of prayer"; but you are making it a den of robbers'" (Matthew 21:13 NRSV).

Referring to himself as a prophet

But even more compelling are the times that Jesus specifically refers to himself as a prophet.

When Jesus inaugurates his ministry, he turns to the scroll of the prophet Isaiah and reads from Isaiah 61:1-2a: "The Spirit of the Lord is upon me, because he has anointed me, to bring good news to the poor. He has sent me to proclaim release to the captives and recovery of sight to the blind, to let the oppressed go free, to proclaim the year of the Lord's favor" (Luke 4:18-19 NRSV). And to make it crystal clear that he identifies himself with this prophetic word, he concludes, "Today this scripture has been fulfilled in your hearing" (Luke 4:21 NRSV). When the congregation responds with outrage and anger, Jesus remarks, "Truly I tell you, no prophet is accepted in the prophet's hometown" (Luke 4:24 NRSV). Then he directly speaks about two prophets who were sent to foreigners: the prophet Elijah who stayed with widow at Zarephath in Sidon and the prophet Elisha who healed Naaman the Syrian (Luke 4:25-27).

At the end of his Galilean ministry, Jesus receives warnings from sympathetic Pharisees that the tetrarch Herod Antipas (who had beheaded John the Baptist) is spying on Jesus and is planning to kill him. How does Jesus respond to this assassination threat? "Go and tell that fox for me, 'Listen, I am casting out demons and performing cures today and tomorrow, and on the third day I finish my work. Yet today, tomorrow, and on the third day I must be on my way, because it is impossible for a prophet to be killed outside of Jerusalem'" (Luke 13:32-33 NRSV). Then immediately Jesus starts thinking about the holy city to which he is now headed, to which he is coming as a prophet, and says in lament, "Jerusalem, Jerusalem, the city that kills the prophets and stones those who are sent to it! How often have I desired to gather your children together as a hen gathers her brood under her wings, and you were not willing!" (Luke 13:34 NRSV.)

Just say yes

How can we participate in Jesus' prophetic ministry? We can — when Christ calls us to be prophets in our time, just say yes.

In the religious cartoon strip "Pontius Puddle," a young person looks up in the heavens and says, *God, if you are really there, speak to me now and tell me what do you want me to do with my life.* Immediately a voice from heaven replies, *Feed the hungry, heal the sick, shelter the homeless, welcome the refugee, visit the prisoner.* Taken aback, the young questioner says, *Oh... well, um... just testing.* And the voice from heaven replies, *Same here.*

When the call comes to transform the world, don't hang up. When Christ calls you to be a mustard-seed agent of change, please believe you can make a difference. When the call comes... just say yes.

The Courage Prayer

How can we participate in Jesus' prophetic ministry? By praying for the courage to follow wherever Christ leads.

Perhaps you know Reinhold Neibuhr's prayer, which in its original form went like this:

117

God, grant us the serenity to accept the things that cannot be changed, courage to change the things that must be changed, and wisdom to distinguish one from the other.

Most people call this the Serenity Prayer, but I call it the Courage Prayer, because I believe we accept too many can things as unchangeable when, in reality, they not only *can* be changed but *must* be changed! Too often we don't even try. We fail to change things because we have too little courage. And our dirty little secret is this: we never ask for more. We ask for more serenity and wisdom, but not courage. We don't want to be the ones who dare to transform and transfigure our world. And so we don't have enough courage to do so.

But God understands. That's why we've been given the Courage Prayer. And that's why God nudges us and compels us to keep praying it until we have received the feeding-of-the-5,000 courage that we need to change the things that not only *can* be changed and *must* be changed but *will* be changed.

Most of the time we fail to act courageously and prophetically because we believe that the small things that we can do will make no difference. But all God asks from us is that we do the little that we can, so that the scales will be tipped just enough to change the whole edifice of justice. Anthropologist Margaret Mead once said, "Never doubt that a small group of thoughtful, committed citizens can change the world; indeed, it's the only thing that ever has."

Ambulance drivers or tunnel builders?

How can we participate in Jesus' prophetic ministry? By moving beyond charity and social service to social change.

As Christians, we are called to take up our cross — the Roman punishment for rebels — and follow Christ's example of confronting the powers that be with the ethical might of the kingdom of God.

But too often our vision is limited. We feel comfortable focusing on charity to individuals or social services to a community of people, but we draw the line there. We stop short of following Jesus all of the way to challenging the structures of injustice

118

— religious, social, or political. Too often, when Jesus leads us forward into the risk and controversy of overturning tables of wrong, we turn our backs and go the other way, fearful of where he is leading us, far out of our comfort zone.

In his book *Rich Christians in an Age of Hunger*, Ron Sider told a powerful parable for our time, a parable often titled "Ambulance Drivers or Tunnel Builders."

The parable begins by setting the scene. A group of devoted Christians lived in a quaint town in the foothills of a mountain. Winding up and down the mountain side was a slippery road with sharp curves and steep drop-offs with no guard rails. Car crashes were frequent and often fatal.

Heart-broken by seeing so many badly injured people pulled from the wreckage, the three churches in town decided to take action. Pooling their donations, they purchased an ambulance to speed the accident victims to the hospital in the nearest city. In addition, church members volunteered to drive the ambulance 24 hours a day, sacrificially giving their time and talent. Many lives were saved, though many suffered life-altering injuries.

One day a young visitor came to the village and was perplexed. Why, he wondered, did they not close the road over the mountain and in its place build a tunnel? The ambulance volunteers were shocked at his question. They immediately pointed out that although this was technically possible, it was not really feasible or advisable. They explained that he didn't understand that this mountain road was a beloved and scenic pathway. And that the mayor would vehemently oppose the idea. (After all, he was the owner of a gas station and popular restaurant halfway up the mountainside.):

The visitor was shocked that the mayor's economic interested mattered more to these Christians than the many human casualties. Somewhat hesitantly, he suggested that perhaps the churches ought to speak to the mayor. After all, he was an elder in the oldest church in town. Perhaps they should even elect a different mayor if he proved stubborn and unconcerned. Now the Christians were shocked. With rising indignation and righteous conviction they informed the young radical that the church dare not become involved in politics.

The church is called to preach the gospel and give a cup of cold water. Its mission is not to dabble in worldly things like social and political structures.

Perplexed and bitter, the visitor left… Is it really more spiritual, he wondered, to operate the ambulances which pick up the bloody victims of destructive social structures than to try to change the structures themselves? (2)

Live into the Liberated Zone

How can we participate in Jesus' prophetic ministry? By not only *proclaiming* the promises of God, but by living *inside* the promises, as if they've already come true — like living inside a liberated zone, where the kingdom of God is already in effect, where God's will is being done, on earth as it is in heaven.

During the movement against apartheid in South Africa, Archbishop Desmond Tutu organized many marches, nonviolent campaigns, and international boycotts. Many chided him, telling him only violence could overcome the power of South Africa's oppressive laws and police brutality. But Tutu believed in something more — the power of God's promised time. It might take a long time in coming, but it was coming. And it could not be stopped — because God had promised it.

At one dark moment, during the time Nelson Mandela was in prison over two decades, Desmond Tutu came to Washington, DC to lead a nonviolent protest outside the South African embassy. He spoke these words of truth:

Those of you inside, are you listening? Do you hear me? You have already been defeated. Do you understand that? You have already lost and we on the outside have won. Out there, we know how this struggle for Black freedom and liberation will turn out, for God is on the side of the oppressed. It's not 'We shall win.' Oh no! We have already won! Only you on the inside have not yet realized it. We outsiders have, and we know the future. We are the future."

Be pastoral in the way we are prophetic

How can we join Jesus in his prophetic ministry? By being pastoral in the way we are prophetic and prophetic in the way we are pastoral.

Jesus didn't just confront the rich and speak truth to the powerful; he also loved them into the truth and invited them into a new relationship.

Jesus didn't use force to tear down old injustices or take up arms to defeat oppressive enemies; he drew together old enemies into an alternative society, a beloved community, and showed by example how a new world could be built on the vacant lots of the old. Jesus transcended party lines, bridged national boundaries, and gave birth to a multi-ethnic organism, a living body that could not be killed.

Weeping with Jesus

How can we join Jesus in his prophetic ministry? By learning to see the world through Jesus' eyes and weeping with him.

I've never seen it on a Sunday school poster, but it is a stunning image from scripture — our Savior sobbing over Jerusalem, tears streaming down his face. Can you see him in your mind's eye, his head bowing as his shoulders quiver with sobs, then looking up with eyes brimming to gaze again at the holy city? The tears of Jesus are something we must never forget.

What did Jesus see that made him cry? He saw where his nation was heading. He saw that they would choose not *his* way of peacebuilding but *Barabbas'* way of warfare. In 66 AD the people of Judah rose up with the sword to drive out the Roman occupiers from their land and become free and independent once again. But the end result was that the nation was defeated, the holy temple razed, and the holy city set ablaze in 70 AD.

"If you, even you, had only recognized on this day the things that make for peace! But now they are hidden from your eyes" (Luke 19:42 NRSV).

What would Jesus see... through weeping eyes?

If Jesus stood at a hill overlooking my city of Buffalo, or your city of Main Street USA, what would Jesus see through weeping eyes? Perhaps what a child does.

Sometimes children ask questions that cut through to the bone: "Why do rich people have so much and don't share with all the poor people?" Or "Why can't I play with my friend of a different color?" Or "Why don't they just stop the war?" Children ask us questions that haunt us, questions we cannot answer.

What if this question-asking child was Jesus, at perhaps the age of seven, whom we had to take on a tour of our nation and explain why things are the way they are. How could we answer little Jesus' questions? How would we respond if we saw little Jesus looking at a slum and starting to weep, and then uncontrollably sobbing? Would we be reduced to tears at the tears of our young Savior? Would we finally be moved to action, to change our world enough that we might stop Jesus' tears?

"Forgive us, O God, for looking at your world through dry eyes." This prayer of missionary Frank Laubach should be ours as well.

Eleven-year-old Trevor of Philadelphia

One child whose tears moved his parents and transformed his community was eleven-year-old Trevor Ferrell of suburban Philadelphia.

One evening Trevor burst in on his parents saying, "Quick, turn on the TV!" He had just seen TV pictures in the other room of people living on Philly's streets. "I thought they lived like that in India...but not here — I mean America."

His father said, "Yes, Trevor, people sure do live like that, right in center city." Trevor replied, "You mean they're out there in the cold and snow right now? Tonight?" His father replied, "Trevor, not everyone lives the way we do here in Gladwyne."

Trevor's questions continued: "How do they stay alive without a bed or blanket when they sleep outside in the winter?" The parents' answers evaded the question. But Trevor would not be put off: "Well, can we go downtown and help them?" His dad answered, "Sure, sometime." "Why not tonight?" "Not tonight." He explained what an awful day he had had at his electronics store, and his mom said they could talk about going downtown another time. When Trevor continued to persist, his dad said, "That's enough, Trevor!" Crestfallen, the boy went off to bed.

Mr. and Mrs. Ferrell stayed up to talk. They had always hoped Trevor would develop a soul sensitive to the needy and neglected; that's why they had always taken him to church school. But now they wondered, *Are we sending him a contrary message about what is really important?*

The parents had a change of heart. They called Trevor in, told him to grab an old blanket to give away, and jump in the car. Trevor was elated. He grabbed not only a blanket but also his pillow, the one he still needed to fall asleep each night.

At 15th and Moravian, they saw a shoeless man huddled on a steam grate. Trevor got out alone and walked over the man, offering the blanket and his pillow. The man mumbled, "Thank you very much; God bless you." "God bless you," Trevor replied. Circling around the block to see how the man responded, they could see him snuggled up and sound asleep. On the way home, Mr. Ferrell said, "Did you see that man's smile?" Trevor's face beamed as he replied, "Yeah, it was great!"

The very next evening, they headed downtown with two more blankets Trevor had dug up. In the weeks that followed, he gave out donated blankets from neighbors and new blankets they purchased. In the years that followed, Trevor's compassion became a non-profit organization, Trevor's Campaign, a daily program to feed, clothe, and shelter Philadelphia's homeless — a cause that became the center of their family life. (3)

"Don't just do something; stand there!"

Jesus — the one who called himself prophet — calls us to be prophets following him. He calls us to go forth in courage, holding fast to that which is good. He calls to stand with the meek and welcome the outcast, to love the enemy and overcome evil with good. He calls us to go "where there is wrong and try to right it, where there is suffering and try to heal it, where there is war and try to stop it." (4)

One day, folksinger and songwriter Michael Stern went to the post office in his hometown and stood in line. In front of him was a very tall and husky man. Behind him into line came a little girl with her father, a very short man wearing a colorful cap on his head, a distinctive sign of his ethnicity and religion. The short man needed some kind of form to finish preparing his package, so he moved forward and reached onto the shelves in the line next to the big guy. Suddenly out of the blue, from hard-hearted prejudice, the big guy started yelling and swearing at the short man. He moved closer and leaned down in his face, saying, "I don't like you coming in here and getting in my way." The short man said, "I was just getting something, and please stop swearing in front of my little girl," but the big guy started yelling louder and appeared ready to start slugging the man.

Michael didn't know what to do. He was in a rush and really didn't want to get involved. But despite being quite scared, he thought he should do something. Without any more time to think, he quickly squeezed between the two of them and simply said, "I'm just going to stand here."

The big guy was quite surprised but immediately began yelling at Michael, starting to threaten him. Suddenly, something unexpected happened. The first guy in line turned around and spoke to the big guy in a very calm tone, "Why don't you just be quiet? Nobody did anything to you." This totally confused the big guy, not knowing which of the three of them he wanted to bully the most. Then the most astonishing thing happened. Instead of yelling and swearing at any of them, the big guy just started mumbling and cursing to himself, and suddenly walked out of the post office.

Michael thought about this event for a long time, saddened by how wide the little girl's eyes were as she watched this ugliness, shocked at how much bigotry existed below the surface in his town. He later wrote a song about this titled, "Stand Up," hoping that if, one day, he was ever attacked in such a way, someone else might be there to get in the way of hate. (5)

"Christians belong where things are out of joint"

Jesus, the prophet of the Liberated Zone, calls us to go and be prophets where things are out of joint. My father, Presbyterian minister Jack Harle, put it this way in one of his sermons when I was growing up, which I believe has influenced me to this day:

Christians belong where things are out of joint... Amending the defective is the high calling of the follower of Christ... The more we are in touch with the spirit of Christ, the more we are aware of and troubled by the gulf between what is and what ought to be... He stirs us with "divine discontent" that is an impetus to action...

[This] is not to imply that we can change the big things which are wrong in the world all by ourselves.... The world is not changed by big events and mighty issues so much as it is altered by the small events and unimportant people in everyday life.... Our task is to do what we can in our own small way to set things right....

We were put here to use up our lives in His service. We will be bruised and beaten, but we will know an inner satisfaction which comes only when one seeks to do God's will and by His power helps to make this world a better place to live in.

Prophet Jesus, our overturner of tables, calls you and me to go where things are out of joint and amend the defective. May we respond with a daring *Yes!* and pray for the courage to follow wherever Christ leads.

ENDNOTES

Sketch #11 ...Jesus, Our Overturner of Tables:
Prophet of the Liberated Zone

1. John Shelby Spong, The Continuing Christian Need for Judaism, *The Christian Century*, September 26, 1979), 919.

2. Ronald J. Sider, *Rich Christians in an Age of Hunger: Moving from Affluence to Generosity* (W. Publishing Group, 1997, 2015).

3. Frank Terrell, *Trevor's Place: The Story of the Boy Who Brings Hope to the Homeless* (New York: Harper Collins, 1990).

4. From the ending of Senator Theodore Kennedy's eulogy for his brother, Robert F. Kennedy.

5. *Chicken Soup for the Soul: Stories for a Better World* (Deerfield Beach, Florida: Health Communications, Inc.), 230-231.

Sketch #12 ...Jesus, Our Teacher-Rabbouni:

The True Story Of The Praying Hands

Mark 10:17-22 — A rich young man's question to Jesus

> *"Jesus said to her, 'Mary!' She turned and said to him in Hebrew, 'Rabbouni!' (which means Teacher)"* John 20:16

"I Need a Teacher," by Hope Harle-Mould

> *I am a child of God.*
> *I am young.*
> *I am growing.*
> *I am curious about all things.*
> *I have heard there is a mountain*
> *where you can see God face to face.*
> *And I have heard that this mountain*
> *is always there in your journey*
> *when you need it most.*
> *I have heard you cannot find this mountain*
> *unless a teacher guides you where to go,*
> *unless a teacher shows you how to see with the heart,*
> *unless a teacher trains you how to scale the heights,*
> *unless a teacher dares you to dare.*
> *I am a child of God.*
> *I have heard there is a mountain.*
> *I need a teacher.*
> *Will you be mine?*

"Teacher, tell my son to give up sugar"

There is a story told about Mohandas K. Gandhi in which a mother brings her son to the Mahatma, this "great soul," and says, "Teacher, this may seem a minor problem, but I'm worried about my son's nutrition. He consumes much sugar but resists the vegetables and fruits he needs to grow strong. If only you would tell him to give up sugar, he'd do it. He'll listen to you." The Mahatma replied, "Come back in a week and make the same request." Patiently the woman did so. One week later she asked, "Teacher, please tell my son to give up sugar." Gandhi replied, "Come back in a week and make the same request." Perplexed the woman did so. One week later she asked, "Teacher, please tell my son to give up sugar." He replied, "Yes, I will. Let me talk to your son." "Thank you, so much," the mother said, "But I'm curious. Why didn't you grant my request the first or second time? Why did I have to come back a third time?" Gandhi replied, "I did not realize how difficult it would be to give up sugar."

That is a true teacher — one who gives no counsel which he himself does not exemplify, one who teaches only what she herself practices. Jesus was that kind of teacher.

My most beloved title for Jesus

Of all the sacred titles of Jesus — Risen One, Promised One, Anointed One, Christ, Messiah, Master, Lord, Redeemer, Savior, Son of David, Son of Man, Son of God, Lamb of God, Word of God — my favorite, the title which connects most to my life and faith, is Teacher.

Jesus is my teacher par excellence. He opens my eyes to a God wider than my religious imaginings, vaster than my cultural blindfolds, deeper than my truest feelings. Like any good teacher, Jesus comforts me when I'm afflicted and afflicts me when I'm comfortable. He goads me into new modes of thought and invites me to walk into unnoticed beauty.

But Jesus teaches best because he exemplifies the truth he teaches. To me, Jesus is the one teacher who shows me most clearly what God is like and what human beings are meant to be.

Even though he had no formal rabbinical training (John 7:15), Jesus was often called Rabbi, as he widely recognized for his religious teachings and spiritual wisdom. The twelve called him Teacher or Master almost exclusively, which are two meanings of the title, rabbi. And when Mary Magdalene at the empty tomb recognizes the risen Christ, what does she say? "Rabbouni!" — My teacher!

Looking for apprentices

Like other rabbis, Jesus began his public teaching ministry at age thirty, the youngest age that a new rabbi was traditionally allowed to gather students and teach. But unlike other great rabbis who taught in one place and attracted a large school of students, Jesus went out in search of students. He called people to follow him, but he didn't treat them like students. Jesus sought disciples, which in Aramaic literally means "apprentices." He was looking for apprentices of his trade, to come with him, to follow him around, to see how he lived, to watch what he did, to learn by osmosis his way of ministry. Through this mobile school on the Galilean roads, through this laboratory of learning through communal living, Jesus transformed ordinary peasants into extraordinary apostles.

A rabbi to solve disputes and answer questions

People were amazed at the way Jesus taught. "They were astounded at his teaching, for he taught them as one having authority, and not as the scribes" (Mark 1:22 NRSV).

People came to him as to a rabbi with disputes to be resolved, such as the case of the woman caught in adultery (John 8:1-11). Learned scholars came to him with controversial questions of theology such as the resurrection (Luke 20:27-40), or questions of ethics such as paying taxes to Rome (Matthew 22:15-22). Seekers of religious truth came to him to ask which commandment was greatest (Mark 12:28-31), or "And who is my neighbor?" (Luke 10:25-37).

The rich young ruler's question

One of those seekers was a rich young ruler who sought out Jesus and asked him a question.

This encounter is preserved in all three synoptic gospels: Mark (10:17-22), written about 70 AD, Matthew (19:16-30), written about 80 AD, and Luke (18:18-30), written about 90 AD. But there are significant variations between the three as to what the young man asked and what Jesus replied. But Mark, seems to preserve historical details that make the scene pulse with life and breath.

First, notice how each narrative begins. Matthew's account begins, "Someone asked Jesus...." Luke begins, "A certain ruler asked Jesus...." But Mark paints a more vivid scene that reveals something about the questioner and his motives: "As Jesus was setting out on a journey, a man ran up and knelt before him, and asked...." Here we picture a wealthy man who clearly has already heard about Jesus, who wants to meet this famous man, and who is so caught up in the emotion of the moment that he breathlessly runs up to Jesus and throws himself at his feet. The man asks his question while on his knees, humbling himself before this holy man.

In the accounts in both Mark and Luke, the young man asks, "Good Teacher, what must I do to inherit eternal life?" This is the kind of question one often asked a great rabbi in those days, a question about the key to life's purpose, the secret of finding holiness. But notice how Jesus responds. In both Mark and Luke, Jesus retorts, "Why do you call me good? No one is good but God alone" (Mark 10:18 NRSV).

Even the most skeptical of biblical scholars consider this to be one of the most clearly authentic sayings of the historical Jesus, for it is such a surprising statement. No one in the early church would have imagined or passed on this kind of statement unless it was authentic, for it shows Jesus pointing away from himself and toward God. In fact, Matthew appears so scandalized by Jesus' original words that he moved the word "good" in the young man's question from describing Jesus to describing a deed: "Teacher, what good deed must I do to inherit eternal life?" And according to Matthew, Jesus responds, "Why do you ask me about what is good?" But I believe Mark and Luke preserve the original.

Jesus will not accept the effusive flattery of this pious, prosperous person: No one is good but God alone! Jesus will not allow this man to adulate him so highly that he loses sight of what Jesus is teaching. And Jesus will not allow us to put him on such a high pedestal to worship that we will fail to follow him in our lives, or to sing so many praise songs to him that we fail to "go and do likewise" (Luke 10:37 NRSV).

The forgotten Beatitude: "Blessed are those who hear the word of God and perform it"

Jesus was constantly concerned about our temptation to worship the messenger rather than follow the message. In one revealing encounter, Jesus is being lauded by the crowd when suddenly a woman cries out, "Blessed is the womb that bore you and the breasts that nursed you!" (Luke 11:27 NRSV). But Jesus turns the question away from idolizing his mother or even himself toward what truly matters: "Blessed rather are those who hear the word of God and obey it!" (Luke 11:28 NRSV.) The crux of the issue is our own in-breathing and incarnating of the message.

This is one of Jesus' forgotten Beatitudes, but I use it every Sunday in worship after the reading of scripture, as I say, *Blessed are those who hear the word of God and perform it.* The more contemporary term, "perform," captures the multiple meanings of the biblical word translated "keep," "obey," or "do." To perform something not only means to preserve the meaning of something but also to express it, to pass it on, to enact it into being. For Christians, to perform the word of God suggests that each of us have a unique and critical role to play in the drama of God's redeeming love.

Worshiping the messenger or living out the message?

Worshiping the messenger rather than living out the holy one's message is epidemic in our age.

Some preachers on TV gather huge followings despite living a brashly materialistic lifestyle of luxurious cars and homes, despite having committed (and asked forgiveness for) sexual sins, despite preaching fear of immigrants and condemnation toward LGBTQ Christians — all the while claiming that they have all the answers. Too often large crowds glorify these types of messengers despite the fact that their life and message contradict the life and message of Jesus Christ.

Is there something more?

In our scriptural story, notice how Jesus turns the questioner's question back on the asker, catching him off guard, telling the rich young man: "You know the commandments: 'You shall not murder; You shall not commit adultery; You shall not steal; You shall not bear false witness; You shall not defraud; Honor your father and mother" (Mark 10:19 NRSV). According to Mark and Luke, the young man replies, "Teacher, I have kept all these since my youth" (Mark 10:20 NRSV), but he wonders, is that enough or is there something more?

Yes, there is. It is not enough *not* to do evil. One must *do* the good. William Barclay comments on this passage:

> *Respectability is not enough... In effect the man was saying, "I never in my life did anyone harm." That was perfectly true. But the real question is, "What good have you done?" And the question to this man was even more pointed, "With all your possessions, with your wealth, with all that you could give away, what positive good have you done to others? How much have you gone out of your way to help and comfort and strengthen others as you might have done?"* (1)

Many times, people came to Jesus eager to follow, wanting to join the praise-the-Lord parade, but Jesus discouraged them, as when he rejected three potential followers (Luke 9:51-56). He forced them to count the cost. He challenged them to make a complete commitment, or none at all. Jesus didn't want them to put him on a pedestal to worship. He wanted them to put a poor person on a pedestal to serve.

One detail: Jesus sees something in him and loves him

Then Mark adds one touching detail that Matthew and Luke omit: "Jesus, looking at the rich young man, loved him" (Mark 10:21). Gazing into the eyes of this eager follower, Jesus saw something: perhaps a charisma that might attract others, or the spirit of a deep holiness, or the potential for a powerful commitment. More than anything, Jesus wanted this young man to attain his ultimate calling as a child of God. So, Jesus revealed the secret of his quest: Sell all, give to the poor, come, follow me!

This man had the chance of a lifetime — something we would die for — the chance to meet Jesus' face to face and hear him invite us to be his disciples. And this man couldn't do it. Why? Because there was a catch. You couldn't hold anything back. You couldn't love with half a heart. You couldn't serve two masters. You couldn't do it part-time. He had to give up that final thing keeping him from harmony with God and neighbor. And so do we.

Now notice the young man's reaction to Jesus in the end: "When he heard this, he was shocked and he went away grieving, for he had many possessions" (Mark 10:22 NRSV). He was thunderstruck. The young man had wanted more than anything to be an apprentice of Christ — more than anything in his life — except his wealth, of course.

Liberated from possessions, freed to find our calling

What does it mean for Jesus to be our Teacher-Rabbouni? It means we are called to be liberated from our possessions so that we can be freed to find our calling.

Let me tell you about an American rich young man. By age twenty-nine, this successful businessman had reached his first million, but was unhappy, discontented, and his marriage was in crisis. Was there nothing more to life than riches? He and his wife decided to find out. They sold all they had, gave the proceeds to charity, and moved to the Koinonia Community in Americus, Georgia, not knowing what God wanted them to do with the rest of their lives.

There they met Reverend Clarence Jordan and other Christians building low-income housing in partnership with the poor of that community — Blacks and whites together, against great opposition from their segregationist neighbors. This couple joined them and learned the miracle of community-built housing with zero-interest financing.

Next, the man and wife moved to Zaire to try to do such homebuilding for the poor on a large scale. It worked. A few years later, they returned home to replicate this project in US inner cities. It worked. Soon thousands of people were inspired to do what they were doing across America. It was called Habitat for Humanity. And the founder's name was Millard Fuller, a rich young man liberated from his possessions, whose marriage to his beloved Linda was not only saved but fulfilled. Together they were freed to discover their true calling.

When Jesus calls us to sell all, give to the poor, and follow him, perhaps we are being called to give up the glory of our individual potential and become the wind beneath someone else's wings — for our family, for our church, or for the children of the world.

To give up our greatness to make others great

What does it mean for Jesus to be our Teacher-Rabbouni? It means we are challenged to give up our greatness to make others great.

Son of a Hungarian goldsmith, Albrecht Durer was born in Nuremberg, Germany, on May 21, 1471. By the time of his death at age fifty-seven, he had become the most influential German artist of the Reformation period. He was lauded not only for his paintings but his wood cuts and cooper engravings, which were widely distributed through the new communication medium, the printing press.

At age fifteen, after years of studying under his father, Durer became an apprentice to painter and printmaker Michael Wolgemut. Three years later, in 1490, he went off on his own to see if he could establish himself as an artist.

Durer soon found that working low-paying jobs to support himself was stealing his time and strangling his creativity. His friend Franz Knigstein was in the same predicament, unable to advance as an artist while struggling to make ends meet. Albrecht concocted a plan. He would go to work to support them both while Franz would be free to study and pursue his art unfettered; then when Franz became successful, he could support Albrecht while he developed his talents. Franz was delighted with the plan, but insisted he be the first to work while Albrecht continue his art. And so, Franz went off to hard manual labor while Albrecht went off to Basel and Strasbourg.

Four years later, his talent recognized as genius, Albrecht returned as promised to Nuremberg to assume the burden of support and free Franz for art. Only then did Albrecht discover the costly sacrifice his friend had made on his behalf. Physical labor had twisted and stiffened Franz's fingers. There was no hope of him ever holding a paintbrush and performing the delicate brushstrokes necessary for a great canvas. Albrecht was saddened but also amazed, for Franz expressed no bitterness, was filled with no resentment, but openly rejoiced that his friend, Albrecht, was achieving his dream.

Sometime later Albrecht happened to walk in on his friend unexpectedly as Franz was kneeling with head bowed, gnarled hands brought together in reverence to his God, praying in whispered thanks for the success of his friend, accepting that he himself would never be an artist. Albrecht was so touched by that scene that he immediately sat down and sketched those faith-filled hands, to show his gratitude and fondness for his faithful friend.

Today, the stature of artist Albrecht Durer is widely applauded in textbooks and galleries the world over, but the name Franz Knigstein has long been forgotten. But Durer ensured that we would never forget the selfless servanthood of his friend. Durer's drawing became a woodcut, and that woodcut has been printed and painted, sculpted in wood and fired in ceramic — in every nation in all the world, so that now, over 500 years later, the hands of **Franz Knigstein** have become the most famous hands in the world, and that woodcut is known today simply as "The Praying Hands."

A society like no other

> **What does it mean for Jesus to be our Teacher-Rabbouni? It means we are called to join Jesus as he intentionally and systematically subverts the established order to bring in God's new era.**

In his book, *The Original Revolution*, John Howard Yoder describes the way Jesus sought to bring in the kingdom of God: by creating a society like none other in human history. First, Jesus' society was a voluntary society, not one you could be born into but one you had to choose to enter, through repentance and freely pledging allegiance to its ruler. Second, it was mixed racially, composed of Jews and Gentiles; it was mixed religiously, with both strict keepers of the law and advocates of freedom from the law; and it was mixed economically, bringing together rich and poor.

Yoder continues with a third point:

When he called his society together Jesus gave its members a new

way of life to live. He gave them a new way to deal with offenders —
by forgiving them. He gave them a new way to deal with violence
— by suffering. He gave them a new way to deal with money —
by sharing it. He gave them a new way to deal with problems of
leadership — by drawing upon the gift of every member, even the
most humble. He gave them a new way to deal with a corrupt society
— by building a new order, not smashing the old. He gave them
a new pattern of relationships: between man and woman, between
parent and child, between master and slave, in which was made
concrete a radical new vision of what it means to be a human person.
(2)

The church is called to be a teacher like Jesus, a subversive
teacher. In a culture of materialistic greed, we can be a place
where people have fun making up games for giving away as
much as possible. In a culture of random violence, we can be
a place where the young are taught the courageous tools of
nonviolent intervention and conflict mediation. In a culture
of too much sex and too little commitment, we can be a place
where friends receive *agapé* hugs from friends and where long-
term commitment in marriage is modeled and celebrated. In a
culture where the young disrespect the old, we can be a place of
multigenerational bonds, where children are adopted by a host
of grandparents, and teenagers interview the elderly in depth to
learn the pearls of wisdom that must never be lost.

"Who I Am Makes a Difference"

**What does it mean for Jesus to be our Teacher-
Rabbouni? It means we are catalyzed to make a
difference, even when we have no idea the difference
we are making.**

There was once a high school teacher in New York City
who gave her students an unusual assignment. She gave each
of them three blue ribbons with gold lettering that read, "Who I
Am Makes a Difference." They were told to go to someone who
had made a difference in their lives and to present a ribbon to
that special person. That person was also to receive the two other
ribbons with instructions to pass them on to someone else in the
same manner. One week later, the students were to follow up

with each of the three persons to see what happened and report it to the class.

One of the boys in the class went to see a junior executive in a nearby company who had been a mentor and friend to him. The student pinned the ribbon on this man and asked him to pass on the remaining two.

The junior executive, much to his own surprise, decided that the person who most made a difference to him was his boss. Yes, the boss was cantankerous and overbearing, but the young executive respected his creativity and his ability to move the company toward excellence. He went up to his boss' office and pinned a ribbon on his lapel. The boss was equally surprised. Then he gave his boss the final blue ribbon to pass on to someone else.

On his way home, the boss realized whom he had to honor with this ribbon. He went up to his fourteen-year-old son's room and sat down with him. He told his son he knew he was often away at the office too many hours and when he came home, he often yelled at him about grades or his messy room or crazy clothes, but what he usually didn't get around to telling him was how proud he was of him, that he knew he tried hard and was a fine human being. He handed his son the special ribbon. "Besides your mother, you are the most important person in my life. You're a great kid and I love you."

The astounded boy began to weep. Then the weeping turned to uncontrollable sobs. The father didn't know what was wrong. Finally, the son was able to pause and say through the tears, "I was planning on committing suicide tomorrow, Dad, because I didn't think you loved me. Now, I don't have to." (3)

Do we dare become apprentice to such a teacher?

Jesus is the master teacher who calls you and me to be liberated from our possessions, to make others great, to welcome God's new era, and to make a difference. Do we dare to become apprentice to such a teacher? Let us dare. So when the risen Teacher calls our name — even if we don't recognize him at first through our tears — may we respond by turning our face toward him, throw our hands in the air, and shout for all to hear: "Rabbouni!"

ENDNOTES

Sketch #12 ...Jesus, Our Teacher-Rabbouni:
The True Story of the Praying Hands

1. William Barclay, *The Gospel of Mark: The Daily Study Bible*, Revised Edition (Philadelphia: Westminster Press, 1975), 244-5.

2. John Howard Yoder, *The Original Revolution* (Scottdale, PA: Herald Press, 1971, 1977, 2003), 29.

3. A true story told by Helice Bridges, from Jack Canfield and Mark Victor Hansen's book, *Chicken Soup for the Soul* (Deerfield Beach, FL: Health Communications, Inc., 1993), 19-21.

Sketch #13 …Jesus, Our Foreigner-Lover:

Refugees Who Taught Me Christ's Ways

Leviticus 19:33-34 — Love the alien as yourself.

Matthew 8:5-13 — A Roman centurion's servant healed.

Luke 17:11-19 — Only the foreigner returned in thanks.

> *No one leaves home unless home is the mouth of a shark…*
> *You only leave home when home won't let you stay…*
> *No one leaves home unless home chases you*
> *Fire under feet…*
> *Until the blade burnt threats into your neck…*
> *No one puts their children on a boat*
> *unless the water is safer than the land.*
> — *Warsan Shire, Somali refugee/UK citizen*

"[Immigration] isn't so much a policy debate. It's a battle for America's identity. Are we the people already here, or are we a set of ideas and ideals that are universal — such that the people who come here and subscribe to these ideals are American? You can never become a German if you weren't born in Germany. But you can become American. America is permanently evolving. That's what scares people, but that is what we're all about."
— Frank Sharry, Executive Director, National Immigration Forum

Jesus' fixation on foreigners

Jesus was fixated on foreigners. Time and time again throughout the gospels, we see Jesus noticing foreigners in a positive way. We see him pointing to foreigners as people of faith worthy of emulation. And we see him going out of his way to travel through foreign territory to connect with people: to heal, to teach, and to be a presence of good news wherever he went.

At the outset of his ministry, in his first sermon at Nazareth

(Luke 4:25-27), Jesus points out that God often chooses to work through foreigners: as when the prophet Elijah was sent to a widow in Zarephath, to receive from her and to provide for her (1 Kings 17:1-16); and as when the prophet Elisha was sent to the Syrian commander Naaman, to heal him from leprosy — thanks to the suggestion of his Israeli servant, a foreigner in their land, who had compassion on Naaman (2 Kings 5:1-14).

At the end of his ministry, the day after Palm Sunday, Jesus clears the moneychangers (Matthew 21:13) from the only part of the temple where foreigners were allowed to worship, the court of the Gentiles, so they too could open their hearts in prayer, a symbolic action Jesus used to enact what the prophet Isaiah taught:

> *And the foreigners who join themselves to the LORD...these I will bring to my holy mountain, and make them joyful in my house of prayer; their burnt offerings and their sacrifices will be accepted on my altar; for my house shall be called a house of prayer for all peoples.*
> Isaiah 56:6-7 (NRSV)

"Where are the other nine?"

Throughout Jesus' ministry, Jesus points to foreigners who surprise people with their exemplary faith.

On one such occasion, Jesus pronounces healing words to ten lepers and then tells them to go and show themselves to their local priest to prove their healing and their ritual cleanness. It is only as they begin to walk away from Jesus toward their hometowns that their dreaded skin disease disappears. Nine of them, when they see their miraculous wholeness, rush off in amazement and joy to reunite with their families. But one of them, the only Samaritan, turns back in the direction of thanksgiving, back to the source of his healing, back to Jesus, to fall on his knees rejoicing in the new beginning he has been given. Looking at the man, Jesus is fascinated that this foreigner felt a greater gratitude than the people of his own land, and wonders out loud, "Were not ten made clean? But the other nine, where are they? Was none of them found to return and give praise to God except this foreigner?" (Luke 17:17)

A Roman centurion's servant healed

In another encounter with a foreigner, Jesus is approached by a Roman centurion, an officer in the occupying army, seeking healing for his favorite servant. Jesus offers to go to his home to see the sick one, but the centurion demurs, perhaps feeling unworthy as a Gentile to have a great rabbi enter the home of an outsider. Instead, the centurion says, "Lord, I am not worthy to have you come under my roof; but only speak the word, and my servant will be healed" (Matthew 8:8 NRSV). The centurion says that just as he gives orders to his soldiers and slaves and they do it, so he believes that Jesus can utter a command and the healing will be accomplished.

Deeply touched at the conviction and hope in this foreigner, Jesus turns to those following him and declares: "Truly I tell you, in no one in Israel have I found such faith" (Matthew 8:10 NRSV).

Because Jesus pointed to this faith-filled foreigner, we continue to hear the echo of his words preserved to this day in the Roman Catholic Mass: "Lord, I am not worthy for you to enter under my roof, but only say the word and my soul shall be healed." How beautiful that we are taught to believe by the believing of a foreigner!

Love your foreigner-neighbor as yourself

When Jesus taught his Great Commandment about loving God and neighbor, he took the second part of his commandment from the Torah's teaching at Leviticus 19:18b: "…you shall love your neighbor as yourself." But in Jesus' mind and ministry, the neighbor included and embraced the foreigner, for also in Leviticus 19, just fifteen verses later, the Torah teaches:

> When an alien resides with you in your land, you shall not oppress the alien. The alien who resides with you shall be to you as the citizen among you; you shall love the alien as yourself, for you were aliens in the land of Egypt: I am the LORD your God"
>
> Leviticus 19:33-34 (NRSV)

This is an astonishing passage. It not only commands us *not* to mistreat foreigners in our country, but to treat them as compassionately and justly as if they were citizens! We rarely live up to this divine imperative. Perhaps our Bibles have a hole in this page, where these two verses have been excised so as not to disturb our complacency. (I'll wait while you check.)

We have yet to live up to these holy words. But Jesus did. He went as far as to incarnate this command. But we have yet to catch up to Jesus.

Abraham and Sarah as aliens

Long before Moses, the story of the Hebrew people was one of being economic refugees.

Not long after first arriving in Canaan, Abram and Sarai had to flee from their home in Hebron because of a famine: "Now there was a famine in the land. So, Abram went down to Egypt to reside there as an alien, for the famine was severe in the land" (Genesis. 12:10 NRSV).

Many years later, when the promised son Isaac was finally born to them, where was he born? Not at home by the Oaks of Mamre in Hebron. No, he was born in the land of Gerar, for once again they had had to flee a famine: "While residing in Gerar as an alien..." (Genesis 20:1b NRSV), Isaac is born (Genesis 21:2).

Joseph the Dreamer

Becoming economic refugees is also at the heart of the story of Joseph and the other eleven sons of Jacob (Israel). When Joseph's brothers sell Joseph into slavery in Egypt, Joseph ends up being chosen by Pharaoh to prepare for the coming great famine, which Pharaoh had dreamed about but could not understand until Joseph had interpreted it. When famine finally strikes, Joseph's brothers travel from Canaan to Egypt seeking food, and eventually Jacob's entire family migrates to Egypt, where they are saved from starvation and where they settle as immigrants. All of Egypt is also saved by Joseph, the dreamer, the foreigner in Egypt. (Genesis 37-50)

Ruth and Naomi in Moab

In yet another story of fleeing famine, Naomi, her husband, and two sons are forced to leave Bethlehem as economic refugees. They move to Moab. Tragically, all of Naomi's family dies there, except her two Moabite daughters-in-law. One of them, Ruth, chooses to migrate back to Bethlehem with Naomi, even though Ruth will be a foreigner there with an uncertain future. Today, Ruth's loving connection to her mother-in-law is admired as so noble that many wedding services feature Ruth's words of commitment to Naomi (Ruth 1:16-17), two grieving women maintaining family bonds across border lines, as foreigners in one land or another.

Do not oppress the sojourner and other at-risk people

In the prophets there are many warnings not to mistreat the poor and vulnerable, including the sojourner in the land: "If you truly act justly one with another, if you do not oppress the alien, the orphan, and the widow... then I will dwell with you in this place" (Jeremiah 7:5-7 NRSV).

Jeremiah is rescued by a foreigner, an Ethiopian eunuch.

But there are also instances in the Prophets when a foreigner is an instrument of God's purposes. One of the most dramatic instances was when Jeremiah was imprisoned in a deep cistern, sinking in the mud, with no bread to survive. An Ethiopian eunuch in the king's house leaps into action. He dares to approach the king, plead for Jeremiah's life, and receives permission to rescue him. The Ethiopian gathers ropes and friends and pulls Jeremiah to safety, allowing this voice-of-God to continue his prophetic work. We should all remember the name of this foreigner: Ebed-melech (Jeremiah 38:7-13).

Isaiah: Be a refuge for the refugees from war.

In Isaiah 15 and 16, the people of Judah see the cities of its neighbor Moab (just east of the Dead Sea) being laid waste by "the Destroyer," the armies of Assyria. Refugees are streaming toward Judah seeking shelter, and Moabite leaders offer lambs as tribute-gifts in return for refuge. Though Moab had been Judah's enemy in the past, God commands the people of Judah to give safe sanctuary to these suffering families coming across the border.

This is a stunning appeal to magnanimity, sent to us today from God, if only we would take it to heart: "Hide the outcasts, do not betray the fugitive. Let the outcasts of Moab settle among you; be a refuge to them from the destroyer" (Isaiah 16:3-4 NRSV). Do we believe the Bible? Do we live this out?

The Good Samaritan

Jesus made clear that the neighbor includes the foreigner by his parable, The Good Samaritan (Luke 10:25-37), as Jesus responds to the lawyer seeking to limit and set boundaries on his caring: "And who is my neighbor?" (Luke 10:29 NRSV)

In this story, Jesus breaks the border walls of our own truncated compassion. He weaves a story in which two citizens fail to stop and care for a bleeding fellow citizen, but a foreigner, of mixed race and mixed religion, a Samaritan, cares enough to stop and save a life with practical compassion.

Refugees: God's spiritual question for us today

Nikolai Berdyaev once said, "The question of bread for myself is a material question, but the question of bread for my neighbor, for everybody, is a spiritual and religious question." In our time, I believe that *refuge for myself* is a material question, but *refuge for the refugee* is a spiritual question. Welcoming the refugee is not a partisan, political issue. It is a question of faith. It is an ethical calling. It is a moral imperative.

Vietnamese refugees right before Christmas? Really?

A telephone call came to me one day at church. It was from Interfaith Refugee Services of Ohio (who were state-wide partners with our national denomination in refugee resettlement). It was late November 1992, and I was an Associate Pastor at Dublin Community UCC, Dublin, Ohio, (the Columbus area).

The caller said there was a Vietnamese family of five who had the chance to leave Vietnam now that the father, a former officer in the South Vietnamese Army, had been released from the re-education camps there. They desperately needed a church to sponsor them so that they could be approved for coming here. I replied that it was almost Christmas and that our Mission Committee was already booked with projects, but I promised I would try.

After talking to the senior pastor and the mission chair, it was clear that the only way we could take on such a vast task at such an inopportune time was if many new volunteers came forward willing to work. I said I was willing to ask.

So ten days later, on a Sunday morning, I stood up front at the end of the 9:00 am service after having made my appeal and waited to see if anyone would volunteer. To my utter amazement, six people came and signed up as willing to help in any way they could. At the end of the 11:00 am service, I stood up front and waited again, and to my astonishment six more people came and signed up. I never expected such a response, and no one else did either. Just think if I had not tried, if I had not asked. It was a lesson I would take with me for the rest of my ministry.

One of the women who came forward that day was Dawn Hornung, who had just moved into a new condominium but still had to pay for her old apartment for six months. She had cursed her bad luck, but now, she said, she knew why. She immediately and joyfully offered this as the home for our Vietnamese family.

We were told the family would probably arrive in late January, so we had a few weeks to get everything ready. But then a call came saying they were arriving three weeks early, on December 21!

We leaped into overdrive. Somehow, we furnished an entire apartment for five just in time and headed to the airport with balloons and signs written in Vietnamese to welcome them. It was a moment I'll always treasure.

Just two years later, both parents had good jobs, their daughter had graduated from high school and entered a major university in pharmacology, and their two boys continued to thrive and love that community. But what if, in our Christmas busyness, we had said there was no room in the inn?

Xenophobia or xenophilia?

In our world and time, xenophobia is becoming epidemic. But Scripture calls us to different priorities on a different path. Jesus calls you and me to... *xenizo* the *xenos* with *xenia*. If that's Greek to you, well, it is Greek! So let me translate. Jesus calls us to welcome (*xenizo*) the stranger (the *xenos*) with hospitality (*xenia*). Christ is prodding us to show the opposite of xenophobia, to show *xenophilia*, the love of the stranger, to embrace the alien.

Welcoming Christmas into our lives: A Bosnian family

During the war in Bosnia, when I was Senior Pastor of Springboro United Church of Christ, Springboro, Ohio, we welcomed into our midst a refugee family from that war-torn land, the Redzepagic family.

The father, Sasha, would later tell me what a frightening moment it was arriving in America that November night at the Dayton International Airport, having no idea if anyone at all would be there to greet or help his family. A stranger in a strange land, homeless and friendless with $50 in his pocket, he had no way to provide for his wife and daughters. They had barely survived the war's bloodshed. Their five-year- old daughter, Ena, never remembered a night without mortar fire. But what would happen to them here?

Sasha told his family to stay back on the plane while he went out to see what awaited them. He told them everything would be fine, but he was petrified. So, he went out and peeked round the corner of the gateway, seeing 25 people from our church with flowers, balloons, teddy bears, and cameras. Yet it was only when he saw one of our signs that simply read *Redzepagic* that he knew that everything would be more than fine.

After an hour of welcoming them and orienting them to what we had prepared, we finally headed out down the long airport corridors. I was walking with Sasha while his eight-year-old daughter, Anja, was walking behind us with others in the group. Suddenly Anja raced around us and ran to catch up to others in the group walking ahead of us, her balloons trailing behind her, her new teddy bear snugly in hand. Seeing this, Sasha turned to me and said, "Look! She no more scared. She no more scared."

Nine months later, Sasha was working in a job in his field, a machinist and mechanical engineer, and Francika had started studies to become a pharmacy tech. To this day, they continue working in their fields, and are still close friends and beloved by the church people there.

One year after their arrival, Sasha revealed something to me that was surprising and beautiful. Sasha said he wanted me to know what Francika's maiden name was. He said it was Bordzič (bor-ZHEECH), which in Serbo-Croatian means… "Christmas." The mother of our family was Francika Christmas!

When our church sponsored this family to come to America for a new life, we knew we were doing a good thing, but we had no idea we were doing a holy thing. Little did we know that when we welcomed these strangers into our midst, we were allowing Christmas to come and reside with us, allowing Christmas to come and abide with us, changing our church and community, day by day, forever.

The refugee who appeared in our time of greatest grief

When I moved to the Buffalo area, I challenged my new church to welcome a refugee family from Sierra Leone, West Africa. On Mother's Day Sunday, 2001, our new family was welcomed into our sanctuary at St. Peter's UCC (West Seneca, New York): Phebian, the mother, Braima, the father, the children Martha, Ruth, and Emmanuel, and their niece Kumba.

Four years later, Phebian was already well along in her training to become an LPN nurse and working at area nursing homes and clinics.

Then one day, my father-in-law, Harry, who had been at a hospice facility for a couple of weeks, suddenly passed away in the middle of the night. We got the phone call at home and rushed over to hospice to see his body and to say our final goodbyes. We sat in the room distraught and in tears. Suddenly into our room came a familiar face to console us. It was Phebian! She had recently started working there on the night shift. We had no idea. Her caring presence was so comforting to us. She offered a prayer with us when it was hard for us to pray. To have her there at 3:00 am in the morning was an experience of being held in God's hands when we needed it most.

Phebian's vision: mobile medical miracles

By 2009, Phebian had graduated as an RN and had been working on the staff of the Jericho Road Family Health Center (JRFHC) for several years when God sent her a vision.

When Phebian had left war-torn Sierra Leone, she vowed she would never return to "that God-forsaken land" where so many died, and she had so narrowly escaped. But then came the vision. She sensed the suffering of the people in her birthplace at Koidu Town, where there was only one hospital with a dearth of doctors, basic equipment, and antibiotics. And she sensed the cry of all the people in the outlying villages in the Kono District where there was no medical care at all. And she saw the face of her mother Martha, who had been a nurse and midwife traveling to those villages on her own, trying to do what she could to relieve suffering, until she too died during the war from lack of medical care. Phebian felt God was calling her to go back and find a way to bring a mobile medical clinic to the people of those villages.

One day Phebian shared this with Dr. Myron Glick, the founder of Jericho Road. He told Phebian that he also had had a vision: of a refugee-now-citizen going back to their homeland to start a medical clinic, with direct connection to and full support of JRFHC. And he believed the country they should start with was Sierra Leone, because of her, because of her courage and deep conviction.

So Phebian and Dr. Glick began to sketch out plans and prepare for Phebian's first trip back to Sierra Leone to meet leaders, to find people excited by her vision, and to make connections in each of the villages.

On the Sunday before she left, I gave her symbolic gifts of Christ's love for her, our church's love for her, as well as gifts to give away to the children she would meet. And I spoke these words about Phebian and her family:

> *They came here from Sierra Leone as strangers.*
> *They return to Sierra Leone as...us.*
> *They came with nothing but fear in their eyes.*
> *They return with the perfect love that casts out fear.*
> *They came with complete trust in God's providing,*
> *presence, and purpose.*
> *And they return with complete trust in God's*
> *providing, presence, and purpose.*

"We thought we had lost our Martha"

Over the course of three years and many trips, Phebian succeeded in organizing community support, obtaining land, and preparing to lay the foundations of a clinic. But Phebian did not want to wait until the money was raised and all the building complete before beginning medical care in those villages. She planned a three-month trip to prepare for doctors to come from Buffalo and provide medical care in each of the four outlying villages during a two-week period.

When she returned, she spoke at our church. It was another Mother's Day Sunday, May 12, 2013:

> We were able to "sit clinic" [see patients all day] in all of the four villages, including [the district capital] Koidu — which was not [even] in our plan! A group of people [were] already there before our door in Koidu, asking, What about us? What are you going to do for us? This is where the [clinic] center is going to be, the headquarters; why are you leaving us out? And we eventually decided to help them, so instead of four villages, now we have five!
>
> And guess what? After all those five sittings, we have other villages coming, pleading for them to be adopted, because conditions, health care is very deplorable out there. And we have just limited resources now; we are fighting to get support and sponsors and everything. So, what I told them is… I'll go back and take your cries to them and take your pleas to them…
>
> But I'm trusting God for them, that he will send more support, he will give more provision, and he'll open the doors for help to come. This is not just one person's journey; this is not just one person's mission; it is the Lord's.

Then Phebian shared about one village where people still remembered her mother Martha's courageous work:

> For me, personally, it was amazing to see my mother's dream and vision come to pass — [of village clinics for the common people], which was the top-most thing that really touched my heart.
>
> And it was amazing: all the places that [my mother and I had] walked together — to see myself going to those places again, doing what she was doing [as a nurse like her]. It touches my heart.

*In one of the villages, the leaders said, "**We thought we had lost our Martha, but we got her back.** Martha really left behind the love she had for mankind, the love she had for people. She left it behind, and that's the footstep you're walking in, and we thank God for that."*

In January 2015, Phebian opened her new clinic in Koidu Town, named after her mother and grandmother: The Adama Martha Memorial Community Health Center. In the spring of 2015, *The Buffalo News* chose Phebian as a Citizen of the Year. And to this day, Phebian works eight or nine months of the year in Sierra Leone and returns to be with her family in Western New York the remaining time. *(Note: For an inspiring video about Phebian Abdulai and the opening of her clinic, please check out the film by Hans Glick on Vimeo, "Adamamartha.")*

A potluck greater than ourselves.

I believe more of our churches can do a beautiful thing by giving hospitality to refugee families. Maybe your church is called to do so.

Is your church famous for putting on joyous potluck dinners where, like the loaves and fishes, there's always more than enough for an additional family to be included? Is your church adept at running rummage sales where you have enough left over to furnish a small apartment? Does your church identify its greatest strength as being a warm and caring fellowship of people who, when a neighbor has gone through great tragedy or illness, will surround the suffering one with support, encouragement, and love?

God may now be sending you a suffering neighbor from a part of your community you didn't realize was part of your community. God may be connecting to you one refugee family in need, one family you will grow to love, one family in whom you'll see the face of God.

A calling to galvanize and revitalize your church

But God may also be calling you to this new mission because your church needs it most. First, refugee resettlement can spark a whole church to work together in a divine endeavor that will galvanize and revitalize your whole congregation. People will come out of the woodwork to help embrace a family from afar: inactive members, friends of the church, youth, as well as members looking for a new role.

Second, refugee resettlement can attract individuals and groups in the community who will see the media coverage of your family's dramatic story and your church's open-arms welcome.

People without a church will come forward to donate cash and household goods, as well as volunteer to tutor, teach English, or host a baby shower. Service clubs — like the Rotary Club, which co-sponsored one of our families — will get involved in everything from giving driving lessons to finding them jobs.

Third, refugee resettlement can foster a new depth of spiritual understanding as you hear the family describe how they trusted God in their harrowing journey through violence and evil, how God consoled and strengthened them in dismal refugee camps, and how God delivered them by choosing your church to open your hearts.

The Holy Refugee family

If you had been in Egypt when Mary, Joseph, and the Christ Child arrived as refugees, would you have opened your doors to them? We'll never know. You weren't there, but you are here. And today there are frightened families who stand outside our churches' doors and knock.

But why, you ask, do we not hear them knock? All the families coming through your denomination's refugee program must be adopted by a local church before they are approved to come.

And so, they stand outside America's gates waiting, waiting for you, knocking at the entrance but unable to come through the doorway, until you are willing to go to that door yourself and open it, and let them in, and take them home to their new home. *For I was a stranger and you welcomed me… Enter into the joy of your master.*

Sketch #14 ...Jesus, Our Dark-Side's Deliverer:

My Perfect Plan To Commit Adultery

Luke 10:17-20 — The return of the seventy

Colossians 2:13-15 — Disarming the powers

> *"The seventy returned with joy, saying, 'Lord, in your name even the demons submit to us!' He said to them, 'I watched Satan fall from heaven like a flash of lightning'"* Luke 10:17-18 (NRSV)

> *"Jesus' strategy was simple but profound: celebrate God's presence now in the messianic banquet, prior to the destruction of evil, and evil will be transformed by the celebration itself. The incredible effect of this strategy is visible in stories like the conversion of Zacchaeus, a tax collector hated by his fellow countrymen (Luke 19:1-9). Rather than denouncing Zacchaeus or supporting the Zealot campaign of ritual assassination for him and his family, Jesus invited himself into the rich man's house for the messianic banquet."*
> — Robert Jewett, *Jesus Against the Rapture: Seven Unexpected Prophecies*

The return of the seventy

At the beginning of Luke 10, Jesus sends forth the seventy disciples in 35 pairs to go into all the villages where he intended to go and commissions them to cure the sick and declare that the kingdom of God is dawning in their midst. The number 70 symbolizes the 70 non-Jewish nations of the world, the future mission depicted in the Acts of the Apostles, also written by the author of Luke.

In verse 17, the seventy return and joyously tell Jesus that not only had they healed and preached with great success, but something more had happened, something not promised — the casting out of evil spirits: "Lord, in your name even the demons submit to us!" (Luke 10:17 NRSV). They were astonished at the power flowing through them. Mere fisherfolk they were, but fearsome dark forces were bowing down before them through the name of Jesus.

Sent out by Jesus, they had done Jesus-deeds. Living and acting in the *name* — in Jesus' purpose, personhood, and power — they had done miracles wherever they went.

The finger of God

What were these demons? In the first century world, it was commonly believed that many physical and mental illnesses, such as epilepsy, were caused by possession by evil spirits. In order to heal these people, one needed to drive the demons out of their bodies. Mary Magdalene may have had severe schizophrenia, for Luke's gospel describes her as possessed by seven demons, which Jesus drove out of her (Luke 8:1-3).

These demons were believed to be under the command of Satan. Satan was the personal name for the evil one. In Genesis, evil is personified by a serpent, one of God's created creatures, who is punished by losing his legs and becoming a slithering snake. In the Hebrew scriptures, Old Testament evil was named "the satan," with a small "s," meaning "the adversary." Similarly, in verse 19 we see Jesus refer to evil as "the enemy." In the Lord's Prayer, Jesus speaks of "evil" or "the evil one." In Matthew 13:39 evil is called the devil.

In Luke 11, the crowds accused Jesus of casting out demons by the ruler of the demons, whom they named not Satan but Beelzebul. Jesus replies, "Now if I cast out the demons by Beelzebul, by whom do your exorcists cast them out? Therefore, they will be your judges. But if it is by the finger of God that I cast out the demons, then the kingdom of God has come to you" (Luke 11:19-20 NRSV).

A rare look inside Jesus' mind

After the seventy share what their experience has been out in the villages, Jesus shares an experience he has had while they were away. He says something so astonishing, so unbelievable, that not only do we skip over this gospel passage, but we simply can't bring ourselves to believe it.

Jesus shares with them a vision he has had, something only he has seen. Here we get a rare private look inside Jesus' mind. He tells them, "I watched Satan fall from heaven like lightning." In the modern, popular image of evil, we picture Satan living not in heaven but in hell. But for the Jews — who emphasized that there is not a good god and an evil god but only one true God — the satan was seen as residing in the courts of heaven.

What had Jesus seen? A vision that Satan's throne had crashed, his rule terminated, his power destroyed. Jesus proclaims that at a certain moment, when his disciples were out on their ministerial travels, he had received a revelation that the Adversary's time was over. Satan had been defeated.

This viewpoint of Jesus was very unpopular, for most Jews of his time — including the Dead Sea Scroll community known as the Essenes — preferred the apocalyptic belief that Satan would be defeated at the end of history, and then only after a great war in heaven. But for Jesus, Satan was already defeated. All that was required was mopping up operations.

In his book, *Jesus Against the Rapture: Seven Unexpected Prophecies*, Robert Jewett said:

> What others had expected as a result of a future Battle of Armageddon, Jesus saw as already having occurred. Since Satan's power has already been broken, the kingdom is available here and now. When this message was accepted by those who formerly assumed that Satan was in control of the world, the kingdom's triumph would be complete...
>
> ...Since the fall had already occurred, the exorcisms were to be viewed as the joyous freeing of prisoners after an evil adversary had collapsed...
>
> ...Jesus constantly emphasized faith as the key to successful exorcisms. It was not a matter of magical belief or superstitious power. To have faith in Jesus' sense was to believe in the power of God as manifest in his kingdom, and to know that a fallen Satan could no longer prevail in the lives of God's children.... Faith the size of a mustard seed would suffice. (1)

The time of the demonic is over

Jesus is not surprised the disciples have such success against the demons, for he has seen that the time of the demonic is over. Like a house of cards, one person with the faith of a mustard seed can triumph over an evil spirit.

The Acts of the Apostles, the sequel to Luke's gospel, describes many examples of the demise of the demons: exorcisms, deceitful believers within the church exposed, the defeat of the magician Stephen, the punishment of the persecutor Herod Agrippa, and more. Evil had always tried to keep the Gentiles divided, separated, and antagonistic toward the Jews. The apostles' mission to the Gentile nations destroys evil's strategy.

Paul's letter of the Colossians is one of the strongest voices proclaiming that Christ's triumph over evil has already occurred. In the cross, the forces of evil have been dethroned: "He disarmed the rulers and authorities and made a public example of them, triumphing over them in it" (Colossians 2:15 NRSV).

The problem is…we don't believe this, and when we don't believe this, we become allies of the Adversary.

The demonic has no form until we give it form

In Jesus' ministry, Satan fell from heaven, and in Christ's cross the powers of evil were exposed and dethroned — although evil does continue in our time. As a comedian once observed, "The good book says that rain falls on the just and the unjust, but as far as I can tell rain falls more on the just, because the unjust have stolen the *umbrellas* of the just!"

The demonic is real, but it has no form until we give it form. It cannot exist until we allow it to take shape inside of us, in our relationships with others, and in our institutions and systems. Once the demonic gains a foothold, it takes on a life of its own. It runs roughshod over human beings. It cannot easily be stopped by those who started it.

The experiment

A notorious research experiment was once conducted to determine how likely it was for common people to go along with evil simply because they were told to follow instructions by some authority figure.

In a room divided by a wall with a large window in the center, the experiment involved three people: the researcher and the volunteer assistant, who were on one side of the window, and the experimental subject on the other side. The researcher informed the volunteer assistant that the purpose of the experiment was to test the ability of the mind to learn and memorize at higher speeds by applying low-level electrical impulses to the skin of the subject when an incorrect answer was given. The assistant's job was to push the button to apply the mild shocks and to increase the voltage in small increments to see whether slight pain increased the curve of learning.

After a period of time, the severity of the shock had been increased to such a degree that through the window the assistant could see the subject was in pain. The assistant questioned the researcher, but he replied, "The voltage is within acceptable parameters; it's all part of the experiment; increase the levels." When the assistant saw that subject was suffering severe pain, he complained to the researcher, but he replied, "The voltage is within acceptable parameters; it's all part of the experiment; increase the levels." When the assistant saw the subject crying and begging for him to stop, he told the researcher it should stop, but he replied, "The voltage is within acceptable parameters; it's all part of the experiment; increase the levels."

Unbeknownst to the assistant, the researcher and subject were both actors and the real experiment was to see how far the assistant would go. To the horror of the experimenters, a majority of the assistants went all the way, despite their ambivalence and protests. Most of the assistants increased the levels to whatever level the researcher said, despite the apparent harm they were inflicting, following whatever orders they were given. Only a few of the assistants that were tested refused to cooperate early in the experiment at the first signs of torture.

The conclusion? In a structured situation under an official authority, common people — you and me — are probably willing to inflict severe suffering on complete strangers for no reason.

That is how official torture happens, how military massacres of civilians happen, how policies of ethnic cleansing happen, how crimes against humanity become holocaust.

How can you and I become possessed?

How can you and I become possessed by the demonic?

It's simple. It's all about choices. And we can go about it very deliberately. We can even create a strategy to become extremely possessed!

If we increase our self-centeredness in systematic ways, we will run roughshod over others. If we have emotional problems from childhood or adult traumas and we avoid counseling, bury these deep within, and deny they are there, we will treat others unfairly and inflict terrible anger and manipulation on others. If we suffer addictions and do not seek medical treatment, counseling, or twelve-step programs, we will act in out-of-control ways. If we increase our fears and prejudice, increase our desire for control and accumulation of power, increase our extremist views and de-humanize anyone with differing views, we will become more demonic. These are the moral consequences of our moral universe.

This is what the New Testament calls *the principalities and powers*, demonic realities such as the Roman Empire.

Many multinational corporations today act like invisible realities which seek only to maximize profit, which will downsize people out of jobs despite years of loyal service, which will strip the environment and make governments pay, and which will oppose the policies of their nation of origin because they are a nation unto themselves.

John Newton: Possessed by the demonic and freed

John Newton was once possessed by the demonic forces in his time. We memorialize and lionize him as the composer of "Amazing Grace," but we often forget how he struggled to allow Christ to transform the entirety of his life.

As a young man, John Newton worked as a slave trader, first on the islands off the coast of West Africa where he helped collect human beings to be sold to visiting slave ships, eventually becoming the captain of his own slave ship. But on March 10, 1748, returning to England from Africa during a storm when he feared the ship would be lost, John began reading Thomas a Kempis's book, *Imitation of Christ*. Soon after, Newton surrendered his life to Christ, his redeemer.

But he did not surrender all of his life. For several years he continued to buy and sell slaves, justifying his profit by improving the conditions of the slaves and leading Sunday worship for his hard-tack crew of thirty. Newton could not yet surrender his business dealings and his colonialist worldview to Christ.

Finally the day came when John's conversion to Christ became also a conversion to the neighbor. He gave up slave trading, became a clerk, and then studied and was ordained as an Anglican priest. Part of the good news he proclaimed was abolition, to free both the slave and the slaveholder from such cruel inhumanity and sin against God. Newton preached far and wide in advocating and organizing to end Great Britain's international slave trade. And with the decades-long moral leadership of William Wilberforce, parliament finally outlawed slave trading throughout the British empire in 1807.

John Newton knew that he had allowed the demonic to take shape and find a place inside his Christian lifestyle for far too long. He always recognized his wretchedness and God's unmerited grace.

Once late in his life, with his health, eyesight, and memory failing, he was urged to give up the ministry. He replied, "What, shall the old Africa blasphemer stop while he can still speak?" And on another occasion, when he was preaching and totally lost his train of thought, he stopped and declared, "My memory is nearly gone, but I remember two things: 'That I am a great sinner, and that Christ is a great Savior!'"

For his tombstone, John Newton wrote this epitaph:

"John Newton, clerk, once an infidel and Libertine, a servant of slavers in Africa, was, by the rich mercy of our Lord and Savior Jesus Christ, preserved, restored, pardoned, and appointed to preach the Faith he had long labored to destroy."

Casting out demons in Jesus' name: Andre and Magda Trocme

How can we cast out demons in Jesus' name? We can do it by risking our lives to overcome evil with good.

After Adolf Hitler had conquered and occupied the nation of France, in the village of Le Chambon in southwestern France, a minister named Andre Trocme of the Presbyterian-related Huguenot church, and his wife Magda, began to hide Jews from the Nazi and Vichy authorities. When Jews knocked on their parsonage door, they could not turn them away, even though by doing so they both risked death for these outcast strangers. The Trocmes welcomed them to live with them until every room was filled. Magda organized them to help cook and clean and do chores. They became part of the family.

On Sundays, Reverend Trocme would preach about Jesus the Jew, our Messiah and Redeemer, and Christ's call to love our neighbor, welcome the stranger, and to overcome evil with good. Everyone in the village knew what was happening. Gradually, every family in the entire village either took in Jews to hide or helped those who did. During the war, over two thousand Jews were protected and eventually smuggled into Spain.

Whenever the authorities were about to raid the village with a surprise inspection, an anonymous phone call would warn them. They never found out who it was. Eventually, the Nazis arrested Reverend Trocme anyway, but Magda and the villagers continued their peaceful resistance.

The rest of the Trocme story

Oftentimes we never find out if our small acts of resistance lead to any lasting change. We may resist violence with nonviolence — believing that in the end good will overcome evil — but we really do not know if it will. We act in courageous love, hoping and trusting that God will somehow, in some way, bring miracles of change to the souls of our enemies. But once in a while — sometimes by amazing coincidence — we find out what a decisive difference our nonviolent action has made.

Such is the case with Andre and Magda Trocme. After the war, in the spirit of Christ's forgiving love, Reverend Trocme visited German prisoners-of-war in prison. One of these was a high-ranking commandant. He said he had always suspected Le Chambon was hiding Jews, but he could never catch the people responsible. He also knew that these people were different than the *Maquis* (the French resistance), for they had no weapons, had a peaceful spirit, and still outwitted the SS.

As the Germans were retreating, the German high command gave orders to burn and destroy Le Chambon. The commandant said that even though he didn't understand these gentle people, he would not kill them. He refused to carry out his orders. Le Chambon was saved, to continue its saving work.

Casting out demons in our personal lives: "Blest be the tie that binds."

How can we cast out demons in Jesus' name? By resisting temptation and choosing instead to preserve the precious moral bonds between people in our common life together.

Let me illustrate this with a story I've written, "My Perfect Plan To Commit Adultery." (*Note to my wife*: This is *not* autobiographical, Honey!)

Story: "My Perfect Plan To Commit Adultery"

I couldn't believe how easy it was to set everything up. Restaurant reservations in a different town. Motel prepaid in cash. Roses delivered to her door with the details. Cover story that I was going out with the new guy at work for a movie marathon. All was going as plotted. Soon I'd have a well-deserved break from monogamy's long monotony, and escape into the young arms of excitation.

From the kitchen I could see my wife sitting at a card table in the living room working on the family finances. "I'm leaving now," I called out. "Okay, Honey," she said without turning around, "Have a good time."

I walked out the door.

Heading down the sidewalk toward my car at the curb, I looked down the street to my left — noticed old Rudy sitting on the porch with his wife who suffers from Alzheimer's, and I marveled at how cheerful he always is toward her. How does he do it?

And across the street at the corner house, I noticed the two cars in the driveway of the young professional couple — having endured two miscarriages and, who, hoping against hope, are expecting again.

Circling my car and opening the driver's door, I noticed the single woman from the gray house walking her dog, and I wondered why, when she smiles her friendliness, such deep sadness hides inside.

Climbing into the seat and putting my key in the ignition, I noticed all the toys and bikes out front down of Trent's house, a playful, patient dad to his kids, a quirky character but such a good husband to his wife of fourteen years.

And that's when I realized, I can't do this.

I thought to myself: Trent doesn't know what I'm planning to do, and he'd never find out if I didn't tell him, but somehow, he'd know, because somehow we're all connected. He'd feel a strand of the web that supports us all fall away, sense a dissolving of inner resolve. He wouldn't know where it came from, but he would sense a sadness in the air, a shredding of social fabric, his moral compass no longer able to see any reason to carry on with courage, to sacrifice for the common good.

I couldn't do that to Trent. Or to the young professional couple. Or to the single woman. Or to old Rudy. I got out of my car.

I looked down the street one more time. I couldn't destroy those invisible bonds of integrity and trust with neighbors I knew and those I didn't, our symbiotic community, each of us dependent on the good deeds and ideals of the other to survive and thrive.

I went back in the house.

"Did you forget something?" my wife asked.

"No," I replied, "I remembered something," and I gave her a kiss on the cheek.

"What's that for?"

"For what you're doing now."

"Oh. Okay. Well, you're welcome." And she turned back to the family finances.

Back in the kitchen to get a snack, I unconsciously started humming a song without realizing what it was. For a moment I wondered what it was and why it came to mind. Then I recognized it and knew. The old hymn, "Blest Be the Tie that Binds Our Hearts in Christian Love." It expresses what I know now to be true: that I am of you, and you are of me, that our hearts are connected by invisible filaments of kindness and caring, that I am a better person because you are a beautiful person.

Every day: Hold fast to what is good

In the Lord's Prayer, the last petition states: "Deliver us from evil." Or to put it another way: Liberate us from the influence, power, and dominion of evil forces. Or to paraphrase it for our lives: In our weakness, ignorance, and self-righteousness, keep

160

us from joining in the agenda of the adversary.

The spark of the glory of God in humanity is that every day hundreds of common folk in our community make heroic decisions *to go forth into the world in peace, to have courage, to hold fast to what is good, to return no one evil for evil, to strengthen the fainthearted, to support the weak, to help the afflicted, to honor all people, to love and serve the Lord, rejoicing in the power of the Holy Spirit. (3)*

Let us join them. This day.

ENDNOTES

Sketch #14 ...Jesus, Our Dark-Side's Deliverer:
"My Perfect Plan to Commit Adultery"

1. Robert Jewett, *Jesus Against the Rapture: Seven Unexpected Prophecies* (Philadelphia: The Westminster Press, 1979), 36-38.

2. Hope Harle-Mould, *My Perfect Plan to Commit Adultery,* © 2003.

3. A traditional Christian benediction.

Sketch #15 ...Jesus, Our Noticer:

Spiritual Sensing And Paying It Forward

Mark 10:46-52 — Healing a blind beggar near Jericho

"Many sternly ordered him to be quiet, but he cried out even more loudly, 'Son of David, have mercy on me!' Jesus stood still and said, 'Call him here...' So throwing off his cloak, he spring up and came to Jesus. Then Jesus said to him, 'What do you want me to do for you?' The blind man said to him, 'Rabbouni, let me see again'"
Mark 10:48-51 (NRSV)

'I am a noticer,' he said. 'It is my gift. While others may be able to sing well or run fast, I notice things that other people overlook. And, you know, most of them are in plain sight.' The old man leaned back on his hands and cocked his head. 'I notice things about situations and people that produce perspective. That's what most folks lack — perspective — a broader view. So I give them that broader view... and it allows them to regroup, take a breath, and begin their lives again.'" — Andy Andrews, *The Noticer*

Jesus always noticed things

One of the things I love about our Redeemer is the way he always noticed things. One day when Jesus was teaching in a synagogue, he saw someone who had intentionally come late, a bent-over woman who had suffered for eighteen years, and in shame she took a place in the women's section in the very back. But Jesus called her forward, and in front of everyone, said, 'Woman, you are set free from your ailment'" (Luke 13:12 NRSV). And together they drew up and stood straight and tall together.

On another day, Jesus was on his way to heal a synagogue official's daughter when, as the crowd was pressing around him, a woman with a twelve-year flow of blood who had suffered under many physicians reached out and touched the hem of his garment and was healed. And Jesus stopped and said, "Who touched me?" (Mark 5:31.) The disciples said it could've been anyone, but Jesus knew better. Finally, the woman of faith came forward and Jesus took time to look at her, converse with her, bless her, and send her on her way into her new life.

On another day, entering Jericho, Jesus sees a short, rich man in a sycamore tree, and he senses who this man is, a tax collector named Zacchaeus, and what he needs — to be accepted and loved, to be freed from his wealth and freed for a life of justice and salvation. So Jesus invites himself over for dinner at Zacchaeus' home, and by Christ's presence at a meal, Zacchaeus is transformed. "Today salvation has come to this house" (Luke 19:9 NRSV).

The blind beggar who would not shut up

Just after his encounter with Zacchaeus, Jesus and his disciples depart Jericho on their way to Jerusalem for Passover, with crowds of the curious lining the road. As Jesus walks along, he is teaching people and answering questions, as was the custom of the rabbis of the time. On this particular day, many people are walking with the Teacher, pressing in close to catch every word.

Just outside town, a blind man named of Bar-Timaeus (meaning Son of Timaeus) is sitting along the side of the road, begging from all who passed him by on their way — the only way a disabled person could earn a living at that time. From his later words, we learn that Bartimaeus had been born sighted but had lost his vision by some illness or tragedy. Now as he hears an excited commotion rippling through the road's bystanders, he asks someone near what's going on. *Jesus of Nazareth is coming this way!* So Bartimaeus cries out, "Jesus, son of David, have mercy on me!" (Mark 10:47 NRSV.) Those in front of him tried to muzzle him, telling him to shut his mouth, rebuking him for his noise, demanding he stop making a nuisance and stop bothering the master. Yet Bartimaeus shouts out all the more, with an animal cry of anguish, a cry of desperation and hope, his only chance to receive what he needs. If only Jesus might hear: "Son of David, have mercy on me!" (Mark 10:48 NRSV).

Suddenly, Jesus stops dead in his tracks. He has sensed a solitary voice, discerning one voice of desperation in a sea of chaotic sounds. Even in the midst of teaching deep theological truth with eager students and surrounded by boisterous bystanders, he interrupts this classroom of words and responds to one person with deeds of the heart. That's the kind of Redeemer we have: he notices the one among the many.

Jesus stopped and stood there unmoving. The disciples wonder why he halted. Suddenly Jesus says, "Call him here" (Mark 10:49 NRSV). People near Bartimaeus tell him, "Take heart; get up, he is calling you" (Mark 10:49). With great elation, Bartimaeus leaps up, throwing off his cloak — his most crucial possession — and gropes his way toward Jesus.

As the two of them finally come together face to face — one blind child of God staring into the gaze of God's grace — Jesus asks, "What do you want me to do for you?" (Mark 10:51 NRSV) Jesus' question does not presume. He allows the man the freedom to choose his future and the dignity to participate in this process of change and transformation. "Rabbouni, let me see again."

If Jesus was a different kind of Savior, he might have replied, "You already see more than the others, for you called me Son of David, a title of the Messiah, so just believe in me. That will be enough." But with compassion and understanding, Jesus gives him what he had asked for: "Go; your faith has made you well" (Mark 10:52 NRSV). And immediately Bartimaeus regains his sight. And his first sight is the face of Christ. And his first action? The text says he immediately began to follow Jesus, heading out from his hometown and toward Jerusalem, where his eyes would see a Palm Sunday entrance into a Holy Week.

Noticing a bumper sticker: RAOK

Some time ago, I remember seeing a car pass me in the lane to the right of me with one of my favorites the bumper stickers, "Commit Random Acts of Kindness and Senseless Deeds of Mercy." After a time, through the traffic, I finally caught up to this car again—but only because the driver had stopped to allow another car to start to turn left across two lanes of traffic! So, I, too, stopped and helped to make this happen, joining this thoughtful driver in practicing what we both were preaching.

It's time to start noticing things

How can we regain our sight like Bartimaeus, to see Christ's face and follow Christ's path in our present?

In the book, *The Noticer*, by Andy Andrews, a young homeless man with no family was living under a dark pier along the Gulf Coast, cleaning fish and selling bait to tourists, when suddenly one day an older man appeared in his dark hovel with a ragged briefcase. He introduces himself as Jones, the Noticer, who says he's been watching Andy for a long time and tells him it's time to get started. Andy wonders what he's talking about. Get started with what?

"We need to start noticing a few things. We need to check your heart. We need to gather a little perspective." (1)

Then Jones introduces himself further:

> *I am a noticer... It is my gift. While others may be able to sing well or run fast, I notice things that other people overlook. And, you know, most of them are in plain sight... I notice things about situations and people that produce perspective. That's what most folks lack — perspective — a broader view. So, I give them that broader view... and it allows them to regroup, take a breath, and begin their lives again. (2)*

Then Jones opens his suitcase and gives Andy three small, orange hardcover books titled, *Winston Churchill. Will Rodgers. George Washington Carver.* Andy is puzzled. "History books?" Jones replies:

> *Adventure stories! Success, failure, romance, intrigue, tragedy, and triumph — and the best part is that every word is true! Remember, young man, experience is not the best teacher. Other people's experience is the best teacher. By reading about the lives of great people, you can unlock the secrets to what made them great. (3)*

The young man begins to read. Over many weeks, when the young man crawls back into his home under the pier, he finds three more orange books, and three more, and three more, including *Florence Nightingale, Harriet Tubman,* and *Eleanor Roosevelt.*

But then comes the moment when Andy realizes he hasn't

seen Jones in a long time and must have moved on. And though he has disappeared, Andy discovers he has been hard at work. At Sea N Suds, Andy's favorite cheap restaurant on the beach, he has arranged with the owner to fry up any fish Andy brings in for just $1.00, including all the crackers, Hush Puppies, and iced tea he wants. And all of a sudden, many more charter boat captains begin giving him their boats to wash and their clients' fish to clean.

He would never see the Noticer again — not until years later when Andy had married and had children — but he had already learned to see his life and his world through new eyes.

Who am I supposed to notice today?

What if we noticed as acutely as Jesus? What if we listened as deeply as Jesus?

On a recent Saturday, I went out of the house several times, each time reminding myself to try to notice people. I kept wondering and asking myself, *Who am I supposed to notice and encounter? Who does God want me to learn from and care for?*

In the late afternoon, I was out walking our new dog when one of our neighbors came over to see our new family member. After we chatted for a while and I was getting ready to go on, he suddenly told me something surprising. He said he wanted to thank me for doing his relative's funeral a few months back — at a certain church that I chose — because at the funeral he had noticed that that particular church had an AA meeting, and he really needed one. He had tried to stay sober on his own, but after a year he had relapsed and knew he needed something more. He wanted to tell me that he was now part of the AA group there and was very thankful.

This was the first time in our thirteen years in the neighborhood he had confided in me in such a way. This was a significant breakthrough in our relationship as neighbors. He was vulnerable enough to allow me to truly care for him. Now I can pray for him and be a supportive friend at a whole new level.

Listening between the lines

What if we noticed as acutely as Jesus? What if we listened as deeply as Jesus?

Did you ever have a time when one of your loved ones mentioned something that they'd really love to have or some event they'd really love to see someday, and you were moved to remember it, to write it down, and to plan for a future moment when you would make it happen? Once in a while, we do give such perfect gifts — whether free or very costly — and the recipient says, *You really know me; you really heard me; you've really lifted my spirits; thank you!*

We all do this from time to time—not nearly enough, in my case — and when we do, we feel the joy and experience the fulfillment of surprising people with generosity and thoughtfulness. But what if we did this frequently and more extravagantly, not just for friends but for acquaintances or even strangers? What would the world look like? It might begin to resemble the world in Catherine Hyde's novel, *Pay It Forward*.

Surprising strangers with extravagance: Pay It Forward

Perhaps you've seen the film version of *Pay It Forward*, starring Helen Hunt, Kevin Spacey, and Haley Joel Osment, one of the most compelling and uplifting movies I've ever seen. But I also urge you to read the book as well, which is not only deeper but has a different ending!

One of the fascinating things which the book fleshes out is how Trevor, a thirteen-year-old from Atascadero, California, — who tries so sincerely to carry out his pay-it-forward project when obstacles and setbacks come — comes to believe that he has *failed*, that he has to *start all over*, that maybe the cynical adults were right after all: *idealistic generosity will never work.* But what he didn't know was that he had already unleashed something astonishing and irreversible into the world!

Trevor's story begins when a new junior high teacher moves into town and gives his students an assignment for extra credit, writing on the blackboard: "Come up with a plan for world change and put it into practice."

In response, Trevor invents a simple idea with profound potential: *Pay It Forward*. He must choose three people for whom he will do three very big things and then ask each of them to pay it forward, to do three big things for three others, and those nine

167

would do three big things and ask them each to pay it forward, and so on.

Trevor calculates that this would spread very quickly, exponentially reaching a host of others: from 3 to 9 to 27 to 81 to 243, and by step #10 over 20,000 people would be touched. By step #19, the entire population of the United States would be touched, and by step #21, the entire planet, changing the world.

Trevor chooses his three people: 1) one stranger, a homeless man named Jerry, to whom he gives all his newspaper-route money, 2) an old lady on his route named Mrs. Greenberg, for whom he does lawn and garden work, and 3) his own single-again mom, Arlene, whom he sets up with a date with this new, favorite teacher to try to make her happy again — since her alcoholic husband had disappeared a year ago.

Not long after he gives his three big gifts to each of the three, Trevor discovers that Jerry's drug habit has landed him in jail again. Then he hears that Mrs. Greenberg has suddenly died before she has had a chance to pay it forward. And then his mom breaks up with his new favorite teacher. All three efforts have failed. Downcast and discouraged, Trevor realizes he has to start all over, not having any idea what to do next, wondering if his next efforts might suffer the same calamity, wondering whether people will always break the chain.

What Trevor has no way of knowing is that Jerry, after he is released from confinement has moved to a Midwestern city, where he comes across a young woman named Charlotte on a high bridge in the middle of the night. He urges her not to commit suicide, pleads with her to think it over, because, as he tells her, *I have to pay it forward, and I can't explain it all to you right now, but if we could go get some coffee, I could tell you.* And not only does Charlotte agree, but very she soon she pays it forward to three others in three extravagant ways.

Trevor also doesn't know that before Mrs. Greenberg died, she had already paid it forward to three people, three acquaintances in the neighborhood — amazing them with her out-of-the-blue, extravagant gift — giving them each one-third of her matured life insurance.

One of the three, her favorite cashier at her local grocery store, buys his dream motorcycle with Mrs. Greenberg's phenomenal generosity. And while riding his bike in a big city, he witnesses a stranger being cornered at gunpoint by gang members. Catching the aggressors unawares, the young man accelerates his cycle into fray, motions for the threatened man to jump on the back of his bike, and off they zoom to safety.

This threatened stranger, Sidney Gee, turns out to be a gang member of a rival gang, but still he intentionally pays it forward to three other gang-related guys in California, claiming he had invented this pay-it-forward concept.

When one of these tough guys moves to New York City, he talks about pay-it-forward to everyone he meets. It spreads like wildfire. People there call it, "The Movement." Police start noticing an unusual decrease in gang deaths.

Other inexplicable events begin to happen. Curious about these baffling occurrences, a young East Coast reporter named Chris begins to investigate. On his way to yet another interview, his old car dies, and when a passing stranger sees his despondency, the stranger gets out of his Lamborghini, hands Chris the keys, says he'll send him the title next week, and walks away, saying, "Just pay it forward to three people."

Now Chris is determined to try and trace back where this branching movement of gift-giving first originated. His breakthrough comes when he tracks down the gang member who explains that it all started with Sidney Gee back in California. Finally meeting Sidney Gee, Chris is quite dubious Sidney started all this, so when Sidney mentions the stranger who once rescued him on a motorcycle, Christ follows that lead. The cyclist/cashier leads him directly to Mrs. Greenberg's old house, but suddenly, it's a dead end. He cannot talk to the dead. But one day, returning to Mrs. Greenberg's place, as Chris sits in his car thinking, he sees a boy who shows up unsupervised and starts to work in her garden, though she has been dead for over a year. Chris asks him his name. "My name is Trevor." (5)

Is this story too good to be true? Perhaps, but consider how the phrase, *Pay it forward*, has become part of the American lexicon ever since. (How many times have you heard it or said it?) Or consider all the remarkable happenings that have occurred since Catherine Hyde's book and movie came out — directly inspired by them. Go to her website and see for yourself: www. PayItForwardFoundation. You'll be amazed.

The ears and eyes and sensitivity of Christ

When Jesus noticed the bent-over woman who came in late and unnoticed in the back, he called her forward and said, 'Woman, you are set free from your ailment'" (Luke 13:12 NRSV). And together — maybe you can picture it — they drew up and stood straight and tall, as one.

As we go forward into a new day in our lives, may we develop *the ears of Christ*, to hear what others do not hear — the cries of the Bartimaeus-es along the roads of our world.

May we develop *the eyes of Christ*, to see what others do not see — the Zacchaeus-es in the trees of our community.

May we develop *the sensitivity of Christ*, to feel what others do not feel — the touch of those wounded ones who reach out to us... in hope of healing.

And as we do so, may we grow into the image and likeness of Jesus, Our Noticer.

POSTSCRIPT: A PRAYER OF CONFESSION

You Gave Us Eyes to See, by Hope Harle-Mould
> *God of Improbable Possibilities,*
> *You gave us eyes to see but we do not look —*
> *unwilling to see past the world's chaos and ugliness*
> *to the presence of your Presence.*
>
> *You gave us ears to hear but we do not listen —*
> *unwilling to hear what is unfamiliar yet necessary to know.*
> *You gave us a voice to speak but we remain silent —*
> *preferring to be popular instead of prophetic.*

Forgive us, O God, and help us to change.
*Give us the **eyes** of Christ*
that we may see injustices others do not.

*Give us the **ears** of Christ that we may hear within others…*
needs they can't yet name.
*And give us the **voice** of Christ*
that we may call the world to the changes you require. Amen.

ENDNOTES

Sketch #15 …Jesus, Our Noticer:
Spiritual Sensing and Paying It Forward

1. Andy Andrews, *The Noticer* (Nashville: W Publishing, 2009), 5.

2. Ibid.

3. Ibid, 8.

4. Ibid, 9.

5. Catherine Ryan Hyde, *Pay It Forward* (New York: Simon and Schuster Audio, 2000).

Sketch #16 ...Jesus, Our Jewish Christ:

The Miracle Of The Menorahs

Deuteronomy 6:1-9 — Write it on your doorposts

Luke 4:16-30 — The Spirit of the Lord is upon me

> *"When he came to Nazareth, where he had been brought up, he went to the synagogue on the sabbath day, as was his custom. He stood up to read, and the scroll of the prophet Isaiah was given to him. He unrolled the scroll and found the place where it was written: 'The Spirit of the Lord is upon me, because he has anointed me to bring good news to the poor...'"* Luke 4:16-18a (NRSV)

> *"If Judaism were to cease to be, if Christianity were to lose that peculiar Jewish witness and these insights were to lose their power or have their distinctiveness blunted, then Christianity would be poorer, more open to distortion. I as a Christian need Judaism to be Judaism lest the ultimate truth of God be compromised or even lost in the shallowness of a rootless Christianity."* — John Shelby Spong

Meeting Jesus again for the first time

In his intriguing book, *Meeting Jesus Again for the First Time*, Jesus-scholar Marcus Borg shares some of the tantalizing results of research into the quest for the historical Jesus. Scholars have been able to peel back the layers of the early church's post-Easter picture of Jesus in scripture to attempt to see what the pre-Easter Jesus may have actually been like. As they have done so, we have come several steps closer to being able to meet the historical Jesus face to face for the first time.

At the outset of his book, Borg says this:

Jesus was deeply Jewish. It is important to emphasize this obvious fact. Not only was he Jewish by birth and socialization, but he

172

remained a Jew all of his life. His Scripture was the Jewish Bible. He did not intend to establish a new religion but saw himself as having a mission within Judaism. He spoke as a Jew to other Jews. His early followers were Jewish. All of the authors of the New Testament (with the possible exception of the author of Luke-Acts) were Jewish. (1)

This reminds me a cartoon I once saw based on the classic TV game show, "What's My Line?" Three contestants sign in saying, "My name is Jesus Christ." The first contestant, labeled "The Catholic Christ," looks tall, gaunt, and other-worldly, as if already suffering crucifixion. The second contestant, labeled "The Protestant Christ," looks dashing, with beautiful flowing hair and beard, with charisma and charm, as if ready to appear on TV and move women to follow him anywhere. The third contestant, labeled "The Jewish Jesus," looks short and stocky, has a prominent Middle Eastern nose and a rugged appearance, is more homely than handsome, and might be voted least likely to succeed. And the cartoon ends with this caption: "Will the real historical Jesus Christ, please stand up?"

What was the historical Jesus truly like? Probably more like contestant #3 than the others.

Growing up as a religious Jew

Jesus grew up as a religious Jew. Mary and Joseph would have taught their young son to pray the *Shema* at rising and retiring: "Hear, O Israel: the LORD is our God, the LORD alone. You shall love the LORD your God with all your heart, with all your soul, and with all your might" (Deuteronomy 6:4-5 NRSV). On the doorposts of their home would have been a *mezuzah*, a small slender box containing the *Shema* and other scriptures on a tiny parchment, which Jesus would have touched whenever he went in or out.

From age six to twelve, he would have gone to school at the synagogue in Nazareth to learn reading and writing, using the Torah as the primer. His parents would have taught him to observe the Sabbath, to keep God's day holy, by doing no work and by going to synagogue for study and prayer. At age twelve, he would have become *bar mitzvah*, a Son of the Law, permitting him to read the holy scriptures in worship and to go on the thrice-yearly pilgrimages to Jerusalem for the festivals of the Passover, Pentecost, and Tabernacles.

During his ministry, Jesus often spoke about *the Law and the Prophets*, which was how first century Jews would refer to the Jewish scriptures, consisting of the Torah or Law (Genesis, Exodus, Leviticus, Numbers, and Deuteronomy), and the Prophets (the prophetic books of books of Isaiah, Jeremiah, Ezekiel, Daniel, Hosea, Amos, Micah, and many more). There was also a third part of the Jewish Bible called the Writings (including 1 and 2 Samuel, 1 and 2 Kings, Psalms, Proverbs, and many others).

In the present day, the Jewish faithful refer to their Bible as the TaNaKh, an acronym of three Hebrew letters, referring to all three sections of their scripture: Ta for Torah (Law), Na for Nevi'im (Prophets), and Kh for Ketuvim (the Writings). TaNaKh.

But in Jesus' time, to say *the Law and the Prophets* often meant one was referring to the whole of the Jewish scriptures. That's what Jesus does as he declares his Greatest Commandment — loving God and loving neighbor — then concludes by saying, "On these two commandments hang all the law and the prophets" (Matthew 22:40 NRSV).

In a related event, during Jesus' Transfiguration experience, when Peter, James, and John see Jesus transfigured — glowing in light — they also see Moses on one side of him and Elijah on the other, symbolizing Jesus as the fulfillment of the Law (Moses) and the Prophets (Elijah). (See Matthew 17:1-8.)

Rediscover the Old Testament and treasure its treasures

What does it mean for us today to follow Jesus, Our Jewish Christ? **First, it means to rediscover the Old Testament and to treasure its treasures of faith.**

Too often we have become truncated Christians, one-Testament believers. We've gotten fixated on the New Testament and forgotten the Old. In some churches I've worshiped in, the clergy plan the worship service with two readings from the New Testament and none from the Old Testament. I believe in always including at least one reading from the Hebrew scriptures. Sometimes I use two from the Old and one from the New, in

174

addition to a reading from the Psalms for a Call to Worship!

One of the first heresies confronting the early church was the Marcionites, who wanted to jettison the entire Old Testament and genuflect to the New Testament alone. In the second and third century AD, the church declared Marcionism a heresy, embraced the 39 books of the Hebrew scriptures and recognized 27 new books of Christian scripture to form our Holy Bible. (The books of the Apocrypha were also accepted as canon at that time but were later rejected by Protestants during the Reformation, because the Hebrew Bible does not include those books as canonical.)

By taking this action — by choosing to incorporate the Hebrew scriptures into our Christian Bible — the church officially affirmed that, spiritually, all of us are part Jewish. One might even argue that all Christians today, therefore, are Jewish Christians.

Understanding Jesus

Without the Old Testament, we wouldn't understand why Jesus said what he said or did what he did. How does Jesus inaugurate his public ministry? At the synagogue in Nazareth, as he unrolls the Isaiah scroll (to chapter 61:1) and proclaims, "The Spirit of the LORD is upon me, because he has anointed me to bring good news to the poor" (Luke 4:18a NRSV).

How does Jesus climax his ministry? By going to Jerusalem for Passover, the annual celebration of God's liberating the Jews from slavery during the Exodus from Egypt. And how does Jesus enter Jerusalem on Palm Sunday? By riding a donkey, an enacted parable of the peacemaking king of Zechariah 9.

And what does Jesus do the next day? He clears the moneychangers from the temple by quoting the prophet Jeremiah, where it says, "Has this house, which is called by my name, become a den of robbers in my sight?" (Jeremiah 7:11 NRSV)

Three days later, what does Jesus do at the Last Supper? He points to the wine-cup of his sacrificial blood as a new covenant, connecting himself with the holy metaphor of Jeremiah 31: "But this is the covenant that I will make with the house of Israel after those days, says the Lord: I will put my law within them, and I will write it on their hearts; and I will be their God, and they shall be my people" (Jeremiah 31:33 NRSV).

The next day on Good Friday, even as he is dying on the cross, he quotes the Hebrew Scriptures: "My God, my God, why have you forsaken me?" (Psalm 22:1 NRSV).

Jesus lived and breathed the Old Testament

Jesus lived and breathed the Old Testament. You could even say he died for the Old Testament, so that we might find in these holy writings something deeper, something more spiritual, something more liberating. Jesus was indeed the Word made flesh.

At this time in our life and world, I urge us to rediscover the Old Testament. There we will encounter the Israelites, who — even in darkest historical times — met the living redeemer God face-to-face.

As John Shelby Spong reminds us:

> *There can be no escape into otherworldly piety if one is to worship Yahweh, for this is the God who brought his people out of Egypt and for whom bondage and slavery are an abomination. This is the God who parted the waters, who led his people by cloud and fire, who covenanted with them at Mt. Sinai, who guided them in their homeless wanderings in the wilderness, who established them beyond the Jordan, who was known in victory and in defeat...who worked even through Israel's historic enemies to purge his people. This God the Hebrews encountered, even when their nation was destroyed, and they were exiled. For even in Babylon — a captive people once again — they discovered that Yahweh was still the God of history and that they could still sing the Lord's song in a strange land. The same God, said Jeremiah, ...will also bring you out. (2)*

Our creeds must become deeds

What does it mean for us today to believe in Jesus, Our Jewish Christ? **The second thing it means is to remember that our creeds must become deeds, and that our religion's most holy ground is the place where our compassion touches the world.**

Jesus persistently insisted that faith — trusting God — must be incarnated, that faith means acting-in-trust in God throughout our life and world. This was one of Jesus' most Jewish characteristics.

To do justice and righteousness, *tzedek*, to do acts of loving

176

kindness, *gemilut chasadim*, to carry out the repairing of the world, *tikkun olam* — these are the holiest things that a Jew can do to love God with all one's heart and soul and strength.

Jesus emphasized such faith-in-action when he told the compelling parable in which one brother said to his father, *No, I refuse to help you*, but changed his mind and did, while the other brother said, *Yes, sir, I will help you*, but failed to do so. Then Jesus keenly asked, "Which of the two did the will of his father?" (Matthew 21:31 NRSV)

At another time, Jesus said, "Go and do likewise" (Luke 10:37 NRSV). And at another, "Blessed are those who hear the word of God and keep it" (Luke 11:28 NRSV).

At the Last Supper, Jesus said, "the one who believes in me will also do the works that I do and, in fact, will do greater works than these" (John 14:12 NRSV).

In all his teachings, Our Jewish Christ demanded — in the spirit of the prophet Micah — that we go translate our creeds of faith into deeds of mercy: "And what does the LORD require of you but to do justice, and to love kindness, and to walk humbly with your God" (Micah 6:8 NRSV).

God still chooses the Jews

What does it mean for us today to follow Jesus, Our Jewish Christ? **The third thing it means is for the church to confess its anti-Semitic past, both in history and in theology, and to open ourselves to the new ways God may be teaching us through God's still-in-effect covenant with the Jewish people.**

In 1987, the General Synod of the United Church of Christ made history when it became the first denominational body to publicly declare that God's covenant with the Jews is still in effect:

The church's frequent portrayal of the Jews as blind, recalcitrant, evil, and rejected by God has found expression in much Christian theology, liturgy, and education. Such a negative portrayal of the Jewish people and of Judaism has been a factor in the shaping of anti-Jewish attitudes of societies and the policies of governments. The most devastating... occurred in our own century during the Holocaust....

177

*THEREFORE, the Sixteenth General Synod of the United Church of Christ affirms its recognition **that God's covenant with the Jewish people has not been rescinded or abrogated by God, but remains in full force,** inasmuch as "the gifts and the promise of God are irrevocable" (Romans 11:29).*

FURTHER, the Sixteenth General Synod of the United Church of Christ expresses its determination to seek out and to affirm the consequences of this understanding of the continuing divine covenant with the Jewish people in the Church's theological statements, its liturgical practices, its hymnody, its educational work, and its witness before the world. (3)

To stand with the poor, oppressed, and outcast

What does it mean for us today to believe in Jesus, Our Jewish Christ? **The fourth thing it means is to stand with the poor, oppressed, and outcasts of our day as he did in his day.**

In Nazi Germany in the 1930's, Pastor Martin Niemoeller was one of the silent majority of Christians who waited too long to speak out against Hitler's Holocaust. Niemoeller later said:

First, they came for the communists, but I did not speak out, for I was not a communist. Then they came for the Jews, but I did not speak out, for I was not a Jew. Then they came for the trade unionists, but I did not speak out, for I was not a trade unionist. Then they came for the Catholics, but I did not speak out, for I was not a Catholic. Finally, they came for me, and there was no one left to speak out.

Billings, Montana: "Are all these people Jewish?"

In the fall of 1993, in Billings, Montana, a white supremacist hate group began a reign of terror on the town's small Jewish community. Swastikas were painted on the synagogue door of the Beth Aaron Congregation. On *Rosh Hashanah*, the Jewish New Year, a bomb threat was called in just before the children's service began. In the Jewish cemetery, nineteen of the 32 graves were desecrated. In early December, just before *Hanukkah*, two homes were attacked while parents were out, and babysitters were watching the children. At the home of the Israeli-born conductor of the Billings symphony orchestra, a beer bottle was thrown through the front door while he was out conducting *The Nutcracker*.

On the third day of Hanukkah, at the home of human rights activists Mr. and Mrs. Schnitzer, a cinderblock was thrown through the bedroom window of five-year-old Isaac Schnitzer, whose window had been adorned with a paper *Menorah*, the eight-candle Jewish holy symbol of God's miraculous providence. The rock had smashed glass everywhere and landed right on his bed, but fortunately Isaac had been in the den working on math homework.

Reading the Billings newspaper's report of this latest incident, Margaret MacDonald was outraged. Although not Jewish, she was a member of First Congregational United Church of Christ [the author's denomination]. She had an idea. Picking up the phone, she called her pastor and asked if during the children's sermon they could pass out paper *Menorahs* and invite every family to display them in their windows at home — just as, she recalled, Danish Christians during World War II had worn a yellow Star of David to save Jews from Nazi persecution. The pastor agreed. He also enlisted several other churches to prepare to do the same that Sunday morning.

Their actions made the front page of the *Billings Gazette* Sunday. (2)

Later that week neo-Nazi vandals struck several churches, several homes, and one school — all of which had taped paper *Menorahs* to their windows. But these attacks drew the whole community into greater unity. Businesses got involved, and the *Gazette* printed a full-page picture of a Menorah for citizens to put in their windows.

Christmas finally came. It had been only three weeks since that first cinderblock had crashed through his bedroom window. One night, little Isaac Schnitzer was out walking with his mom around the neighborhood. Everywhere he looked, *Menorahs* were in the windows. He turned and asked his mother, "Mama, are all these people Jewish?" She replied, "No, son, all these people are our friends." (4)

The bigotry stops here

Whether it's an anti-Semitic politician or a next door neighbor, whether a TV evangelist or a relative in one's family...if anyone speaks in a way that diminishes a Jewish person, calls into doubt the Holocaust, or seeks to make any religion — even Christianity — dominant over others, we are called to speak out courageously and to say: *The bigotry stops here, the racism stops here, the division stops here, the hate-mongering stops here, for I am a follower of Jesus, Our Jewish Christ.*

Shema Yisrael, Adonai Elohenu, Adonai ehat. Hear, O Israel, the LORD our God, the LORD is one.

ENDNOTES

Sketch #16 ... *Jesus, Our Jewish Christ*
The Miracle Of The Menorahs

1. Marcus J. Borg, *Meeting Jesus Again for the First Time* (Harper San Francisco, 1994), 22.

2. John Shelby Spong, "The Continuing Christian Need for Judaism," *The Christian Century*, (September 26, 1977), 918-922.

3. "The Relationship between the United Church of Christ and the Jewish Community," *New Conversations*, Summer, 1990, 67.

4. Women's Week 1996 Issue, *Common Lot* magazine, 6-7. Also see the excellent children's book by Janice Cohn, *The Christmas Menorah: How a Town Fought Hate* (Morton Grove, IL: Albert Whitman and Co., 1995).

Sketch #17 …Jesus, Our Mother Hen:

"I'm Under God's Feathers!"

Exodus 19:3-6 — I bore you on eagles' wings

Isaiah 49:14-16 — I have written you on my hands

Luke 13:31-35 — Jesus' lament over Jerusalem

> *"You have seen what I did to the Egyptians, and how I bore you on eagles' wings and brought you to myself."*
>
> Exodus 19:4 (NRSV)

> *"Can a woman forget her nursing child, or show no compassion for the child of her womb? Even these may forget, yet I will not forget you. See, I have inscribed you on the palms of my hands."*
>
> Isaiah 49:15-16a (NRSV)

> *"How often I have desired to gather your children together as a hen gathers her brood under her wings, and you were not willing!"*
>
> Luke 13:34b (NRSV)

Your God is too small!

Some years ago, there was a teenage girl who grew up in the Presbyterian Church who felt called to the ministry. Since she had never heard of a woman becoming a minister, she went to her pastor to talk about it this unusual impulse. He told her that females were not meant to be ministers, that it was a high calling worthy only of men, that her feelings were misguided. He told her this, even though a decade earlier the General Assembly of the Presbyterian Church had voted to approve the ordination of women to the ministry — an event at which my father happened to be a delegate and voted yes, I'm proud to say! When this young woman heard what her pastor said, she walked away downcast but accepted her fate.

181

But then in college and again in her first career, she continued to feel God's call to be a minister of the gospel. In the end she decided she couldn't resist God any longer. Her pastor must have been wrong. Perhaps he needed to read J.B. Phillips' classic book, *Your God Is Too Small.*

The people in the young woman's home church were very proud and of her and gave her a lot of support as she went through seminary and eventually became an ordained minister, but never in all those years did that pastor invite or allow her to go into his pulpit to read God's word or preach Christ's gospel.

I was amazed at this young woman's courage and tenacity of faith. And that's one reason I married her! Her name is The Reverend Linda Marie Harle-Mould.

"Father Linda"

Linda's first pastorate was serving two Presbyterian churches in Maryland. One of them was in the small and very Roman Catholic town of Emmitsburg. One day not long after she began there, she was walking down Main Street past the fire station when suddenly she heard the wolf-whistles of the firefighters admiring her long blonde hair and attractive figure. Nonplused, Linda immediately took her clergy collar out of her pocket, placed in its proper place in her clergy blouse, turned around, went back, and introduced herself to the shocked, red-faced men. They became immediate friends.

None of the Catholic children in that town had ever met a priest who was female, of course. So, when they met Linda, they didn't know what to call her, so we were amused and tickled when they called her the only thing they could think of, "Father Linda."

The opposite experience happened to one of my former parishioners, ninety-two-year-old Phebe Harbaugh, who remembers growing up in the Quaker faith in Clinton County, Ohio, where the pastor of their Meeting was a woman. Years later, when they got a new pastor and he it was a man, young Phebe thought that this was the weirdest thing in the world: "I didn't even know they allowed men to be ministers! It took some getting used to, but eventually I got used to it."

For all of us when we were children, whatever we were taught in Sunday school or saw modeled in the life of our church would shape our perceptions and theology for a lifetime. This is true not only for our experience of women as leaders of the church but for our image of God as well. Is our image of God too small?

Yet more light

In 1620 when English Pilgrims left exile in Holland to sail for a new life in a new world, Pastor John Robinson sent them off with these words: "The Lord has yet more light and truth to break forth from his word." Robinson did not see the Bible as a rigid book of rules, but as a living document. He believed that God would illumine new dimensions of the word as people became ready to enter those new dimensions. How? Through the Holy Spirit.

It is a central tenet of Christianity that the only way we can interpret the Bible faithfully is as we open ourselves to the work of the Holy Spirit in our midst — unveiling our eyes, enlarging our hearts, opening our hands. In every age, we see new things in the Bible we never saw before, things we need to learn that we never learned before. The more each of us studies scripture, the more we see in it. The more we study scripture together, the more we see the whole of Scripture, not just our preferred portions.

Surprising images of God

The Hebrew Scriptures, our Old Testament, were written in a patriarchal society in a patriarchal religion. Therefore, one might predict that it would contain no female images of God — none, absolutely none. But because the Bible is inspired by God, the Word gets through despite human limitation and cultural bias. To our amazement, there are a number of female images of God.

This has been one of the most exciting discoveries in my own journey of faith. I had assumed I had a pretty good idea how the Bible paints and portrays God, but over the years scripture continues to surprise and delight me with the diversity of its images for the divine. The more I've studied, the more connections I've found within it. And the longer I've lived, the more mystifying, indefinable, and breathtaking God seems.

Many of the most important titles or images of God are unexpectedly inclusive of gender, such as shepherd. When we think of the good shepherd of Psalm 23, we erroneously assume a male figure, but women were shepherds as well. In fact, Rachel was shepherding sheep when Jacob met her, as seen in Genesis 29:6, 9.

Many other images of God are beyond gender, as the Psalms often depict God as refuge and rock, or as light and lamp.

But some images of God are striking in their depiction of God's motherlove for us. In Isaiah 66, God's way of caring and nurturing is portrayed to be as powerful as a mother's love: "As a mother comforts her child, so I will comfort you; you shall be comforted in Jerusalem" (Isaiah 66:13 NRSV). Or in the beloved passage of Isaiah 49, God's way of never abandoning or forgetting us is compared to a mother with a child at her breast: "Can a woman forget her nursing child, or show no compassion for the child of her womb? Even these may forget, yet I will not forget you. See, I have inscribed you on the palms of my hands" (Isaiah 49:15-16a NRSV).

God as mother eagle: "I bore you on eagle's wings"

One of most poignant images of God in scripture is that of the mother eagle, as delineated in Virginia Ramey Mollenkott's groundbreaking book, *The Divine Feminine: The Biblical Imagery of God*. Many of these passages were familiar to me, but why had I never noticed their deep significance? My gender-biased eyes were blind to seeing the richness of these metaphors in describing our experience with the holy.

In Exodus 19, when the Hebrews had arrived at Mt. Sinai, Yahweh instructs Moses to remind Israel how God had liberated them from slavery, had given them water from the rock and manna and quail from heaven, and brought them to this holy mountain: " ...You have seen what I did to the Egyptians, and how I bore you on eagles' wings and brought you to myself" (Exodus 19:4 NRSV). At this defining moment in this defining place, God's providential care is described by Godself as a mother eagle, carrying her young eaglets safely on her wings.

The eagle described here could be either a mother or father

eagle, for both eagle parents care for their young, but the female does most of the nest-sitting and most of the hunting and is both larger and stronger than the male.

In Deuteronomy 32, in the Song of Moses, God is described through the metaphor of a mother eagle, who is attentive and caring for her eaglets, who "hovers" (or "flutters," as this word could be translated) over the nest of her young — the chosen people — and who carries them upon her feathers, bearing them aloft on her wings, teaching them to fly: "As an eagle stirs up its nest, and hovers over its young; as it spreads its wings, takes them up, and bears them aloft on its pinions, the LORD alone guided [you]" (Deuteronomy 32:11-12a NRSV).

And in one of the greatest psalms, Psalm 91, God is depicted as a great bird (perhaps an eagle) who shields those in danger under God's feathers, who shelters those at risk beneath God's wings of refuge: "He will cover you with his pinions, and under his wings you will find refuge" (Psalm 91:4a).

Jesus as mother hen

Another surprising image of God in scripture is *mother hen*. And it comes to us from no less an authority than Jesus: "Jerusalem, Jerusalem, the city that kills the prophets and stones those who are sent to it! How often I have desired to gather your children together as a hen gathers her brood under her wings, and you were not willing!" (Luke 13:34 NSRV)

Where is Jesus when he compares himself to a mother hen? He is still in Galilee, having heard threats against his life by the tetrarch Herod. And so, he turns his face toward Zion and prepares for his final journey to the climatic confrontation of his ministry. He will go to the holy temple in the holy city, the center of his nation, to call his people to trust God's thoughts and God's ways. He will urge his people not to pursue rebellion for a political kingdom, for he senses that just forty years in the future, Jerusalem will be razed, and the temple destroyed because of an abortive war of independence against Rome. He will urge his people to pursue the things that make for peace — to incarnate the reign and rule of God in new relationships between diverse people.

185

Like the prophet Jeremiah before him, will Jesus' message be rejected by his own people? Jesus is willing to die to protect his young ones, but even then, will they come under his wings?

[Note: Almost all of Jesus' followers were Jewish, and all the writers of the New Testament except for Luke were Jews. So, in essence, all of us are Jewish Christians! See again Sketch #16: Jesus, Our Jewish Christ.]

Mother hen quality #1: Active, persistent, and strong in her caring

Why did Jesus compare himself to a mother hen? **First, a mother hen is active, persistent, and strong in her caring.** She knows where her young ones are and watches over them incessantly. She is not indifferent to the fate of her brood; she does not passively wait for them to come. When they get too far afield, she summons them by insistent clucking. They is no such thing as a lost or missing chick. They are always within the embrace of her care.

"I am covered by his feathers!"

In the book *Safe Passages on City Streets*, author Dorothy Samuel tells the story of an elderly woman in Philadelphia walking home after an evening prayer group at her church when a mugger began to stalk her. The woman did not notice the dark shadows nearby, for she was still basking in the glow of God's protective presence depicted in their study of Psalm 91, one of her favorites:

> *You who live in the shelter of the Most High,*
> *Who abide in the shadow of the Almighty,*
> *will say to the LORD, "My refuge and my fortress;*
> *my God in whom I trust."*
> *For he will deliver you from the snare of the fowler and*
> *from the deadly pestilence;*
> *he will cover you with his pinions,*
> *and under his wings you will find refuge...*
> *You will not fear the terror of the night...*
> Psalm 91:1-5 (NRSV)

As the mugger moved closer to the sidewalk, the woman was oblivious, still humming their parting hymn, "Under His Wings I Am Safely Abiding." Suddenly the threatening thief appeared before her, demanding her purse. The woman reacted without an ounce of fear, only utter incredulity, as spontaneously she replied, "You can't hurt me! I am covered with his feathers!" In immediate response, the stunned man ran away into the night.

Maybe he thought she was a little whack-o. Or maybe he thought that she might be telling the truth, that she was, in fact, under some kind of divine witness protection program!

This woman believed through and through in the God of sheltering wings.

Mother hen quality #2: Fiercely protective, even if she must lay down her life

A second quality of a mother hen is how fierce she is in caring and protecting her little ones, even if she must lay down her own life. When she leads her chicks to scratch for food, she clucks in a certain way, and they follow. But when danger lurks nearby, she sharply clucks in a different way to warn them. As the chicks feed, the mother hen keenly watches for predators such as snakes and hawks. If she sees a hawk, she drops flat toward the ground, spreads her wings to provide cover, and squawks a particular sound until all the stragglers come under her wings. She hovers over them as the hawk dives. As one farmer described this, "She would die right then and there rather than let that hawk have one chick."

Harriet "Moses" Tubman

Harriet Tubman — the escaped slave who risked her newly gained freedom to return to the South multiple times to free dozens of slaves as part of the Underground Railroad — exemplified all the qualities of a mother hen which Jesus embodied.

First, Harriet Tubman was incessant and indefatigable in bringing her children of God to freedom:

The Lord who told me to take care of my people meant me to do it just as long as I live, and so I did what He told me.

...I always told Him, "I trust to you. [sic] I don't know where to go or what to do, but I expect you to lead me," and He always did.

Second, Harriet Tubman was fierce and fearless in protecting her "passengers," even if she had to lay down her life:

I had reasoned this out in my mind, there was one of two things I had a right to, death or liberty; if I could not have one, I would have the other.

...I would fight for my liberty so long as my strength lasted, and if the time came for me to go, the Lord would let them take me.

Third, Harriet Tubman — the woman whom people called Moses — was an instrument of God's exodus, bringing a new birth of freedom into our land:

I was a conductor of the Underground Railroad for eight years, and I can say what most conductors can't say; I never ran my train off the track, and I never lost a passenger.

Fourth, Harriet Tubman gave guidance and encouragement that instilled courage and endurance in those risking it all:

If you hear the dogs, keep going. If you see the torches in the woods, keep going. If there's shouting after you, keep going. Don't ever stop. Keep going. If you want a taste of freedom, keep going.

Even to the end of her life, when she turned to caring for the elderly — building a two and one-half story clapboard Home for the Aged on her Auburn, New York, farm — Ms. Tubman was faithful to her Lord Jesus, the mother hen.

Mother hen quality #3: Active in bringing new life into the world

A third quality of a mother hen is that she is active in the creative act of bringing new life into the world. She doesn't just produce eggs, she warms them with her own body heat, staying with them, sitting on them for a long period until they are ready to hatch. On the nest, she is not passive but involved, constantly turning the eggs to keep them uniformly warm, which also keeps the yolk centered so it doesn't attach to the shell. And she does all this out of love… for no extra charge.

No extra charge

There was once a mother fixing dinner in the kitchen when her little boy came up to her and handed her a note. On it he had written a list of six chores he had done in the last week and the amount he thought he should be paid for each, from mowing the lawn to taking out the garbage to babysitting his little brother. At the bottom he wrote: "You owe me $14.75."

The mother looked up from the note and into her son's eyes and sighed. Then she picked up the pen and wrote:

For all the nights I sat up with you when you were sick: No charge.

For all the trying times and all the tears that you've caused through all the years: No charge.

For all the nights filled with dread, and for the worries I knew were ahead: No charge.

For the toys, food, clothes, and even wiping your nose: No charge.

When you add it all up, the cost of my love, son, is: No charge.

As the boy finished reading his mother's words, tears began to fill his eyes. He looked her in the eyes and said, "Mom, I sure do love you." Then taking the pen back, he wrote in large block letters right across his original note: PAID IN FULL. (1)

Mother hen quality #4: Not smothering, but encouraging

A fourth quality of a mother hen is that she is not smothering but encouraging. She not only allows her little ones to leave the nest but equips and encourages them to mature and be ready for life on their own. She guides them into a fright-filled world and instills in them the courage to thrive.

The Listening Post: "A place to be heard and accepted…"

One of the greatest exemplars of encouragement and one of the greatest ministries of nurturing-empowerment I have known is Reverend Linda Harle-Mould, my beloved, and her unique "Listening Post" campus ministry at Buffalo State College (BSC) as well as at the University of Buffalo (UB), in Buffalo, New York.

For over eighteen years Linda has set up her table in the Student Union covered with a handmade quilt and filled with baskets of apples, animal crackers (a student comfort-food favorite), peanuts, pretzel nuggets, and red and white peppermints. On the table is an inviting sign: "The Listening Post ...a place to be heard and accepted ...a place to talk about whatever is important to you." At one end of the table are two chairs facing each other. Linda sits in one of them, usually knitting or crocheting, and waits. She never has to wait long.

Over the years, students come to her to talk about everything from a good grade they want to celebrate to roommate problems, from addiction issues to suicidal thinking. Most of them never know that she is an ordained United Church of Christ minister and a trained counselor:

> I am just a non-threatening person who is willing to be there for them. That is the unique style of my ministry. I never try to "sell" them anything. I am simply present and loving. For some, that presence has made the difference between life and death...
>
> St. Francis held forth the idea of "preaching Christ always — when necessary, use words!" In the midst of our churches asking where the young people are...I set the Lord's Table for them, not with bread and cup, but with animal crackers and apples!

During the high-pressure exam week in the fall and spring, Linda's table expands to overflow with fruit, veggie trays and dip, cheese and crackers, chips and salsa, juice and hundreds of homemade cookies she bakes and decorates. For many it's a physical boost, for others it's the emotional support of knowing that someone cares, as Linda says, "The most important thing we can do is just be here, just be a caring presence."

When Linda noticed many students struggling with debt and hidden issues of hunger, Linda co-founded Milligan's Food Pantry on campus, to provide confidential help to anyone in need.

Sometimes Linda recommends a student to pursue further counseling through the BSC Wiegel Counseling Center, where

Linda is seen as a trusted colleague, and is part of their Critical Incidents Response Team. She has played a key role when there have been deaths, campus crises, or national tragedies.

But usually, Linda is a more informal source of support and well-being, of guidance and healing, where students can just drop in to touch base and get a smile, or open up with tears about buried pain and wounds that no one else has taken time to hear.

One day when Linda left the table briefly, she returned to find an anonymous student note addressed, "Dear Listening Lady." The student said that most weeks he stopped by to get an apple and a moment of friendly conversation. Other times he would walk by, and from a distance, smile to himself, content and encouraged just knowing that the Listening Lady was there: "In a way your table calms me. I want to thank you. I want you to know you are appreciated, because you are."

Also, every May, Linda volunteers at graduation, where she is the last person students interact with before they walk across the stage, here briefly and quietly celebrating with each person the struggle and triumph of their four-year journey.

One of the students that Linda took under her wing was a first-year Jewish student named Matt Schwartz, who was understandably leery of talking with any religious leader who might pressure him to be converted (which is not just a dark side of history but a contemporary problem). But one of his Jewish friends on campus said, *There's someone you need to meet,* and he walked Matt right over to Linda's Listening Post table. Matt shares his experience and journey in the following letter:

Matt's letter: Linda and her Listening Post

As an undergraduate, I was lost, as so many undergraduates often are so many incredible choices about who I wanted to become, family issues, personal issues, issues surrounding love, and career, and life, and small mundane and silly questions, and really large important ones...And here was this incredible woman who listened when I needed an ear the most. Here was a woman who was not afraid to hug a twenty-something when he was in tears and didn't know what to do and was so frustrated, he couldn't speak or explain...Here, at the Listening Post, was a truly safe space at last...

When I completed my undergraduate studies, I followed my heart, and with a beautiful rainbow Kippah *[yarmulke] hand-knitted by Linda herself on top of my head, I landed in Israel. My time there would be filled with the most incredible highs, and some of my darkest lows: including homelessness, and a military experience that saw me return to the United States as another veteran with Post Traumatic Stress Disorder.*

However, what got me through my darkest nights was Linda's voice: whether on the phone or in the back of my head. Knowing that she held me in her prayers was enough to keep that Sukkat Shalom, *that canopy of peace over me, like a warm blanket when bombs rocked my* Kibbutz, *and when I didn't have enough food to eat, and when I really wondered if this moment was going to be my last. It didn't matter, because Linda's ministry always reminded me of the word of G-d and sustained me. [She would often say to me] ..."G-d hasn't dropped you yet, and G-d's not going to. Matt, repeat after me [my prayer]: "G-d, you made him; you deal with him."*

...When I returned to the United States and I needed someone's hand to hold as I faced the demons I brought back with me, and the ones that were still waiting here for my return, there was no hesitancy, and it was once again in Linda's capable ministry that I was able to make some clear choices, and get help...

Anyone can get up and talk. Preachers on soapboxes are a dime a dozen, but someone who can hug an addict, who can wash away the tears of a young woman who has been considering taking her life because she's dealing with what feels like too much, or who can remind a veteran with PTSD that there's a heck of a lot more to give [even] as his family situation spirals out of control, takes a considerable more amount of work ...and strength, because it requires you to actually live *like Christ. And I have met so few who can meet that high standard.*

Reverend Linda has been my anchor, my lighthouse, and my savior more times than I can count, and she helped me answer my call to my ministry, which has taken its shape in Social Work.

The More-Wonderful God

"As an eagle stirs up its nest, and hovers over its young; as it spreads its wings, takes them up, and bears them aloft on its pinions, the LORD alone guided [you]" (Deuteronomy 32:11-12a NRSV).

We try to picture and understand what God is like. But God is not only more wonderful than we *imagine*, but more wonderful than we *can* imagine. Let us allow this more-wonderful God to love us into whatever we are meant to be, and to lead us wherever we are meant to go:

> *Now to [the One] who by the power at work within us is able to accomplish abundantly far more than all we can ask or imagine, to [God] be glory in the church and in Christ Jesus to all generations, forever and ever. Amen"* Ephesians 3:20 (NRSV)

ENDNOTES

Sketch #17...Jesus, Our Mother Hen: "I'm Under God's Feathers!"

1. Jack Canfield and Mark Victor Hansen, *A 3rd Serving of Chicken Soup for the Soul* (Deerfield, FL: Health Communications, Inc., 1996), 100-101.

2. Dorothy T. Samuel, *Safe Passage on City Streets* (Nashville: Abingdon Press, 1975), 39-47.

Sketch #18 ...Jesus, Our Wall-Spanning Reconciler:

Mother Emanuel And The Painter Of Walls

Matthew 5:21-26 — Leave altar gift, go be reconciled first

2 Corinthians 5:16-20 — In Christ...reconciling the world

Ephesians 2:14-16 — Breaking down the dividing wall

> *"...In Christ God was reconciling the world to himself, not counting their trespasses against them, and entrusting the message of reconciliation to us"* 2 Corinthians 5:19 (NRSV)

> *"For he is our peace; in his flesh he has made both groups into one and has broken down the dividing wall, that is the hostility between us. He has abolished the law with its commandments and ordinances, that he might create in himself one new humanity in place of the two, thus making peace, and might reconcile both groups to God in one body through the cross, thus putting to death that hostility through it"* Ephesians 2:14-16 (NRSV)

> ***"Christ is the Bridge*** *that reaches past today and destiny, to join the things of heaven with those of earth... He links creation's dawning with infinity's vast shore, The arch across all history is His birth... His cross of love is raised above a world where war and sin have torn God and His children far apart... It spans the centuries, to give safe passage to His peace.*
> *Christ is the Bridge, the Way to God's own heart..."*
> — B.J. Hoff

One verse that says everything

If I asked you to quote from memory one biblical verse that best describes what God has done for us and how we are to respond to God, which would you choose to recite? There are

194

many commendable passages, but there is one that is as famous as it is ubiquitous, popping up on placards at football games everywhere. In fact, the book and verse reference for this passage is as well-known as the text itself — John 3:16: "For God so loved the world that he gave his only Son, so that everyone who believes in him may not perish but may have eternal life" (NRSV).

But there is another passage equally great, and in all the years of my watching football games on TV (as an avid Green Packers fan), I've never seen it. It says everything about God's mission and everything our ministry: 2 Corinthians 5:19. Did you ever hear anyone refer to 2 Corinthians 5:19 and immediately know what they meant? Of course not! But maybe it's up to us to get it into our heart and spread the good news: "In Christ God was reconciling the world to himself, not counting their trespasses against them, and entrusting the message of reconciliation to us" (2 Corinthians 5:19 NRSV).

Fractured world

We live in a fractured world. Between nations: terrorism and war, ethnic cleansings and tribal genocide. Within our nation: road rage and cyberbullying, gun violence and mass killings, domestic abuse and sexual assault, crimes against people of color and the LGBTQ community.

Our fractured world has made us fractious people. Talk-radio has become hate-radio by the smearing of opponents with name-calling. Civility in public discourse and respect in political debate has become an endangered species. Trolling and conspiracy theories tear down public figures and private individuals.

What do we most need in our time? What do we long for in our hearts? A reconciler. And what does reconciliation mean? It means to resolve differences, to regain agreement, to rebuild unity, to renew relationship, to restore harmony, to revive friendship.

In fact, in the Good News Bible, "friendship" is the word used to translate "reconciliation" into a more simplified English construction in its rendering of 2 Corinthians 5:19: "Our message is that God was making all mankind his friends through Christ. God did not keep an account of their sins, and he has given us the message which tells how he makes them his friends" (TEV).

Reconciliation is a key ingredient of both Christian theology and Christ-like living. In the United Church of Christ's Statement of Faith, the central declaration, which centers on Jesus, contains 32 words:

> *In Jesus Christ, the Man of Nazareth, our crucified and risen Savior, you have come to us and shared our common lot, conquering sin and death, and reconciling the world to yourself.*

Here are four actions which describe what God has done in Christ: God has **come** to us, **shared** our common lot, **conquered** sin and death, and **reconciled** the world to God's self, a direct reference to 2 Corinthians 5:19.

The Confession of 1967

In 1967, one of the most significant creeds in the history of Christian faith was adopted by the Presbyterian Church (USA): "**The Confession of 1967.**" It reinterpreted all of Christian doctrine in light of one central motif: 2 Corinthians 5:19. Here's what it says of the cross:

> *God's reconciling act in Jesus Christ is a mystery which the Scriptures describe in various ways. It is called the sacrifice of a lamb, a shepherd's life given for his sheep, atonement by a priest; again, it is ransom of a slave, payment of a debt, vicarious satisfaction of a legal penalty, and victory over the powers of evil. These are expressions of a truth which remains beyond the reach of all theory in the depths of God's love for man. They reveal the gravity, cost, and sure achievement of God's reconciling work (9.09).*

Reconciliation is the center of God's work

Reconciliation is at the center of God's drama of redeeming love.

In the great drama of salvation, some people came to believe in Yahweh through seeing the divine design in creation, later through the Exodus and Mt. Sinai, later through priests and the temple, later through prophets and the Exile. But still the world remained distant from God, fractured in its relationship to both the Holy One and the human ones. So God decided to bridge the chasm with God's own self. For the first time since the Creation, the holy dimension and the human dimension crossed paths at a particular point in history. We call that intersection the Christ event. At that crossroads, everything changed. We count time as BC (Before Christ) and AD (*Anno Domini*, "in the year of our Lord") in reference to it.

In Christ, God spanned the divide between earth and heaven, forged a new covenant between humanity and the holy, linked in union our hearts with heaven's heart, renewed the vows of faithful relationship, taught us to sing with new harmony, and gave us permission to call one another friends. The cost was not cheap — a cross, borne by God for us all. If the cost *was* cheap, we would have ignored the gift. Only a sacrifice of unmerited sacrifice, of suffering love, could possibly reach us. Nothing else would work.

Mother Emanuel

On June 17, 2015, in Charleston, South Carolina, a young man with white supremacy hate in his heart and a gun in his hand shot and killed nine people, including the pastor, Reverend Clementa Pinckney, at the Emanuel AME Zion Church. He had entered the Bible Study as a stranger and had been welcomed with open arms and words of caring toward himself as a person. But he could not choose life, because he had already chosen to bring death.

With Confederate flags adorning his Facebook page, his stated intention was to start a race war. By killing a large group of Blacks, he hoped to provoke other Blacks to vengeful violence, which in turn would provoke whites to a racist crusade of murder.

But this young man's plans failed to account for one thing: This church had long been a courageous example of Jesus' love and forgiveness. This church had been a prophetic voice and witness throughout its history — despite persecution and bigotry — that Jesus' kingdom of God was possible on earth as it is in heaven.

At the Memorial Service for these martyrs, Joseph Riley Jr., former mayor of Charleston, spoke about this domestic terrorist's desire to incite a race war, and how he utterly failed in his objective:

> *He picked the wrong church, and he picked the wrong city. For these bridges that the community had built are strong and the relationships of compassion and respect that had been forged could not be destroyed by the hateful, heartbreaking act of racism and bigotry… That work of bridge building never stops. The arc of the moral universe has to be bent by human beings; it has to be bent by us.*

Another speaker that day was Congressman James Clyburn who presented an historical metaphor for this moment. He pointed out that Thomas Edison, a white man, invented the light bulb, but it was Lewis Latimer, a Black engineer — son of escaped slaves — who invented the carbon filaments that allow the bulbs to stay lit for long duration.

Pointing to the chandeliers hanging above him in the sanctuary, Mr. Clyburn said, "We enjoy the illumination here because two people put aside their individual differences and decided it was more important to light the world than to divide by their own personal prejudices. That's what leadership is all about: putting aside whatever it is that may divide you."

Passing of the peace of the Prince of Peace

To be reconciled to God, we must be reconciled with our neighbors. During worship services I lead, when we come to the Passing of the Peace, I often quote what Jesus says in the Sermon on the Mount: "So when you are offering your gift at the altar, if you remember that your brother or sister has something against you, leave your gift there before the altar and go; first be reconciled to your brother or sister, and then come and offer your gift" (Matthew 5:23-24 NRSV). Then I say, "As a sign that we are willing to *be* reconciled and to become a *reconciliers*, let us turn to those around us and offer the peace of Christ."

John McCain's final words to us

When Senator John McCain was dying from brain cancer, between treatments and bouts of weakness, he would fly to

Washington DC to cast his final votes and use his voice to spark the conscience of America. On the second to last page of his final book, *The Restless Wave,* he gave us a clarion call to reconciliation among our people in our land:

> *Before I leave, I'd like to see our politics begin to return to the purposes and practices that distinguish our history from the history of other nations. I would like to see us recover our sense that we are more alike than different... Whether we think each other right or wrong in our views of the day, we owe each other our respect, as long as our character merits respect, and as long as we share, for all our differences, for all the rancorous debates that enliven and sometimes demean our politics, a mutual devotion to the ideals our nation was conceived to uphold, that all are created equal, and liberty and equal justice are the natural rights of all... I want to urge Americans, for as long as I can, to remember that this shared devotion to human rights is our truest heritage and our most important loyalty. (1)*

"One kind of sin I just can't understand"

In one of my previous churches, there was an older gentleman in my Bible Study named Art Root, who once said to me after a class: "You know, there's one kind of sin I just can't understand. And that's prejudice."

As it says in the first letter of John: "Those who say, 'I love God,' and hate their brothers or sisters, are liars; for those who do not love a brother or sister whom they have seen, cannot love God whom they have not seen" (1 John 4:20).

When I was growing up in predominately white Wisconsin, I knew I had prejudice born and bred into me, despite my parent's open-minded views and my Christian convictions. Of the few African Americans I had come to know in college, none had become good friends.

Choosing to go to seminary in New York City, I knew I would learn and be challenged by the diversity of students and professors there, but perhaps most from the city itself, where it always felt like I was living in the whole world at once! But I also hoped to find someone opposite me in color whom I might get to know deeply as a close friend.

Every once in a while, I would specifically and sincerely pray for this. In time, my prayer was answered beyond my wildest expectations.

Charles Spain: A brother to see life through different eyes

I was interning as an assistant prison chaplain at Greenhaven Prison near Poughkeepsie, New York, when the legendary Methodist chaplain, Reverend Ed Mueller, asked me to get to know Charles and help lead their campaign to seek executive clemency for Charles.

Charles was a twenty-to-life prisoner there. He was innocent of the crime he was convicted of, though he *was* guilty of being with others who spontaneously committed a serious crime. He was only seventeen years old when it happened. It was his first time in trouble.

When I met him, Charles was already thirty and was a trusted leader and assistant in Reverend Mueller's programs. During his years behind bars, Charles had earned his GED, a college degree in criminal justice, and master's degree in theological degree. He was a trainer with the Quakers in their highly acclaimed in-prison program, Alternatives to Violence Project.

As I got to know him, from his growing up in South Carolina to all the books he now was reading, we developed a deep connection. I loved talking to him about religion, about noticing-things-in-life, as well as sharing with him about the woman I had just met, my wife-to-be, Linda.

As I got to know Charles, I was amazed at the beautiful spirit he possessed. I wondered how it could be, given all the abuse he had absorbed: Roughed up by police seeking a forced confession, taken by night to a deserted road — guns cocked behind each bush — and told to run, attacked in prison, ignored for clemency, denied early release, strip-searched as the cost of visiting with each visitor, and the daily indignities of maximum security's non-rehabilitation.

Charles became my best friend. Whenever our visitation time would come to an end, we developed a tradition: walking around the entire visiting room, again and again, arm in arm, as if he were free and we were going on a long walk. In those moments, as we talked and laughed on our walk, we felt as if the walls of incarceration had fallen away, and we were walking together into the new light of God's new day.

When I was ordained to the ministry, Charles was there, through the song Linda wrote, as she sang, "Hands are layin' on, hands of Charles, are layin' on..." When Linda and I were married, Charles was there, as we listed him as honorary best man — for he was still incarcerated, and our clemency campaign had failed. When my birthday came 'round, Charles was there, as his paintbrush sent the greeting: a dove descending from the palm-to-palm meeting of black hand and white hand.

Returning one day to visit him, Charles told me he couldn't believe I'd chosen that day to come, for he'd just had a breakthrough in his life. In the past he'd told me that while in Green Haven he had come face to face there with the murderer of his own brother. But now during the weekend spiritual workshop that had just concluded, he was finally able to do the hardest thing he'd ever done in his life: he forgave that man, and he declared that forgiveness publicly to the whole group. As Charles shared all this with me, he kept weeping and I kept weeping with him, all afternoon. I was awed by what he had done.

When Charles was finally released at age 37, he told me he would soon be on his way to visit me. And then we would walk together again, arm in arm, a long way: "Oh, how we'll walk!"

Whenever Charles introduced me to new people, he would say, "This is my brother." He would do so emphatically, and I felt so honored. People would be perplexed, wondering how we could possibly be brothers, but Charles never explained, as if to say, *But he is what a brother is.*

After incarceration, Charles felt called to work with at-risk children and troubled young adults. He achieved a master's degree in social work, studied for a doctorate, and worked as an adjunct instructor. Over his career he served as a social worker, substance abuse counselor, and director for group homes. He also served as a director of foster and adoption programs, of social services, and as a clinical social worker at various homes and in the school system. Later he worked as a school bus driver and founder of his own martial arts program for youth.

Early in his freedom, he found and fell in love with a wonderful woman. They were married, moved to South Carolina, and had three beautiful boys. Tragically, his wife died of a serious ailment, leaving Charles to raise his sons alone. By necessity, he became an even more amazing father than before.

We have continued to be friends for life. And I am grateful to keep learning how to see life through a second set of eyes, but through one heart — across the walls of difference and division.

Sent with nothing but reconciling presence

Can one person, armed with nothing but the Spirit of the living God, break down walls, forge reconciling paths, and build arches of friendship?

I once heard the true account of one American man who volunteered to go to Belfast, Northern Ireland, during the Time of Troubles to see if he could, in some humble way, be a mustard-seed influence for understanding and peace. He had no special attributes. He had no position of influence. He was simply a member of a non-profit humanitarian organization, the only one who said that — yes — he was willing to go.

He had a place he could stay, but his work was totally open-ended. He wondered if he could make any difference.

For weeks and months, all he did was talk to people, to Catholic radicals, victims, and common people, as well as to Protestant radicals, victims, and common people. But he listened deeply and empathized deeply. People on both sides began to trust him.

Four or five months after he arrived, there was an explosion in a Belfast home that killed one and injured more. It was uncertain whether this was as an accident caused by, perhaps, a natural gas line leak, or whether this was a terrorist attack by the other side. After so many years of killing, the assumption was that this was an act of terror. A retaliatory attack on an opposition home was being planned, but before carrying it out, the radicals decided to check with the American. They asked him if he could find out from his friends on the other side whether this was one of their attacks or was, in fact, an accident. They said that they would believe him either way, but they needed to know the truth.

202

The American went to his closest contacts, and they checked with others. The word came back that this was definitely not an attack by one of their groups. The American went to the people on the other side and told them. To his amazement they believed him and accepted it as a tragic accident. They called off the retaliatory bombing.

Because of this one bridge-building man, one terrorist attack was averted, and the attack in response to that attack was prevented, and the attack in response to that would never happen. And so, the spiral of violence was broken, at least for a time, in that city, in that neighborhood, a pause of calm, giving hope a chance.

Many missionaries of my own denomination have been sent into distant mission fields of great division and danger with these instructions: *See what you can do. Just go and be a reconciling presence.* I have personally known or met such missionaries just before or after they were sent into countries on the verge of ethnic violence or even civil war. The remarkable thing is that one person, armed with nothing but the Spirit of the Living God, *can* break down walls, *can* forge reconciling paths, *can* build arches of friendship.

A parable-story

If Christ came into our fractured world today as Reconciler, what might it look like? Let me illustrate with a parable-story I've written, "The Painter and the Wall."

The painter and the wall

There was once a land divided down the middle by a great wall built of great stones. Constructed long before anyone could remember, the wall separated two peoples, the Turquoise and the Aquamarine. For ages the wall had kept the peace, for the people on the right hated those of the left.

One day a vagabond artist was seen among the Turquoise, painting outrageously colorful murals on the ugly tall wall. As curious children gathered, he gave all of them small brushes and tubes of color and invited them to join his creativity. Elders of the Turquoise confronted the alien.

"You are a stranger here. What do you think you're doing, painting the hallowed gray stones of our wall by no one's authority?"

"I'm adding the colors and designs needed to prepare for the thirteenth day of the thirteenth month."

"What is the significance of that date?"

"The celebration!"

"What celebration?"

"Why, the tearing down of the wall!"

"Who is planning to tear down our wall? The evil Aquamarine?"

"No, you are," replied the painter.

"You must be mad. Why would we want to tear down our wall? It protects us from our enemies!"

"Because your enemy is the wall. It imprisons you in fear. It keeps you from seeing or knowing or embracing half of the family you were meant to have, for the people on the other side are your biological sisters and brothers. You are one people, not two."

The Turquoise replied, "No, the wall is our savior. Without it we'd be attacked and contaminated by the demonic Aquamarine. They're different than us. They're lazy and dirty, ignorant and immoral, drug-crazed and violent. We need the wall. Don't you understand, we're better than those others. Without the wall, our way of life will be destroyed."

The painter went on: "But these stones were never meant to be a wall."

"According to whom?"

"The Great Artist of All."

"So, what on earth was our wall supposed to be?"

"Why, a structure linking the Turquoise and the Aquamarine, a gathering place where people would join voices in common songs, a place to see works of art created out of the very soul of both peoples. These stones were meant to be... an arch!"

When the Turquoise heard this, they fumed in fury and drove the stranger from their land.

Soon, the painter was seen painting the wall on the other side, surrounded by delighted children splashing colors onto the rocks with him. When the Aquamarine authorities confronted the painter, they learned he was preparing for the thirteenth day of the thirteenth month when the ancient wall would be torn down to construct the Arch of the Great Artist. In fury, the Aquamarine drove him from their land.

On the thirteenth day of the thirteenth month, the painter was seen on top of the wall itself, and called out, "Today is the day of joy! The *wall will be torn down. The arch arc toward the heavens!"* A mob of the Turquoise gathered at the wall mocking him, shouting obscenities, and demanding he cease painting their wall. Without a word, he kept painting. At the same time on the other side, a mob of the Aquamarine gathered near the wall deriding him with name-calling, threatening him with weapons, and demanding he immediately cease painting their wall. Without a word, the painter kept painting.

Finally, the mobs from both sides surged upwards, boosted upon one another's shoulders, scaling the stones, until men from both sides seized the painter, threw him onto his back on the top of the wall, causing his head to start bleeding. Then men of the Turquoise grabbed the left arm of the painter, and with the blow of a hammer impaled his left arm with a spike into the wall. Then men of the Aquamarine grabbed the right arm of the painter, and with the blow of a hammer impaled his right arm with a spike into the wall. With his feet they did the same.

The danger was gone. The threat to the wall was dead. The ancient barrier was once again secured. Their way of life was safe.

Except for one thing. The children. On both sides. Who kept painting that wall.

And to this day they are painting still. Painting arches of many colors. The children. On both sides. Arches. To this very day. (2)

So go out the door of your home...

You don't need a call from your denominational mission board or be sent overseas to become a missionary of reconciliation. Your call is clear: 2 Corinthians 5:19. And your destination is near: sent to where you are.

So go out the door of your home, out the door of your church, out the door of your community and see what you can do: linking people, finding common ground, bridging differences, building arches.

And if one day you happen to be watching the Green Bay Packers play on TV, and you notice an end zone fan displaying a placard reading, *2 Corinthians 5:19,* well, I guess you'll know who it is!

ENDNOTES

Sketch #18...Jesus, Our Wall-Spanning Reconciler:
Mother Emanuel And The Painter Of Walls

1. John McCain, *The Restless Wave* (New York: Simon and Schuster, 2018), 379.

2. *The Painter and the Wall*, a story by Hope Harle-Mould, published in **Church Worship**, July 1998.

Sketch #19 ...Jesus, Our Prodigal Giver:

Proclaiming Abundance Before It Arrives

Luke 15:11-31 — Parable of the Prodigal Son

Luke 5:1-11 — Cast your net on the other side

John 21:1-14 — The Risen One at the Galilean shore

> *"And so, he set off and went to his father. But while he was still far off, his father saw him and was filled with compassion; he ran and put his arms around him and kissed him"* Luke 15:20 (NRSV)

> *"It did not begin when they understood him; it did not begin when they discovered who he was; it did not begin when they found out what he could do. It began when they stayed with him, when they left where they had been and went to where he was. That is how it all began. And ever since then, our whole life, whether alone or together, has been that simple struggle against ourselves and our world to stay with Jesus."* — Samuel Davis

The purpose of windows

Do you clean windows? I don't. I usually wait for God's precipitation to do them for me!

Windows are not meant to be seen, but to be seen through. All of us are windows. The only question is how translucent are we? How tinted or transparent or opaque are we? When people gaze through us, what do they see? Do we distort what's on the other side?

The historical Jesus was a window. When people looked through him, they saw something extraordinary. In his book, *Meeting Jesus Again for the First Time*, New Testament scholar Marcus Borg says this:

> *[Jesus] was young, his life was short, and his public activity was brief. He lived only into his early thirties, and his public activity*

lasted perhaps as little as a year (according to the synoptic gospels) or as much as three or four years (according to John). The founders of the world's other major religious traditions lived long lives and were active for decades. It is exceptional that so much came forth from such a brief life. He must have been a remarkable person. No wonder his followers are said to have exclaimed, "What manner of man is this?" (1)

Jesus was a window to God. When people looked at his life and ministry, they could see how God might have acted, what God might have said in those moments. Through Jesus they could see more clearly than ever the face of God. Through Jesus, they could feel God as near as a fingertip away (Luke 11:20). That is why Christians came to name the Christ event the Incarnation, the Word Made Flesh.

The clearest window to God

Of all Jesus' teachings, the one which I believe is the clearest window to God is the parable of the Prodigal Son. Found in Luke 15, it has been called the gospel within the gospel.

The moment Jesus chose to tell this parable

We don't know when or to whom Jesus first told the parable of the Prodigal Son, but I do believe that there must have been a dramatic moment when he chose to teach this particular lesson to particular listeners, a moment that transfigured their hearts and minds.

In the TV mini-series, *Jesus of Nazareth*, director Franco Zefferelli imagines just such an electrifying moment, in which the telling of the parable itself is the occasion of the parable happening between two people.

Andrew has already decided to follow Jesus and is trying to get his brother, Simon (whom Jesus will later rename Peter), to join them. Simon, a loud and irreligious fisherman, resists, but he does invite Jesus to his house where he hears Jesus teach and watches him heal.

But into Simon's house comes Simon's nemesis, Matthew, the hated tax collector, trying to collect the exorbitant back taxes Simon owes. Simon explodes at Matthew, shouting at this Jew who has become a Gentile by collecting taxes for Rome. Jesus intervenes by inviting himself over to Matthew's house for dinner. Simon and the others are appalled. Seeking to dissuade Jesus, they explain that to enter the house of a traitor was not only wrong but would destroy Jesus' reputation with any patriotic, religious Jew. Matthew himself is dumbfounded but says to Jesus, "Yes, you are welcome in my home."

At Matthew's house that night, into the midst of men and women cavorting, feasting, and laughing, Jesus enters. The disciples refuse to go into such a sinner's house and wait outside the open door for Jesus. But Simon had refused even to come near the house, staying behind.

Matthew is amazed Jesus had actually decided to come. He welcomes him warmly. Soon Matthew's tax collector friends ask Jesus, "Entertain us with one of your stories." At that very moment, in the corner of his eye, Jesus notices that a reluctant, confused Simon has joined the other disciples near the entrance to Matthew's home. Jesus replies to the guests, "Yes, I have a story to tell you."

Jesus begins to tell of a younger son who took his father's inheritance to a far country and squandered it in loose living. As he spins the tale, Matthew's guests become silent in introspection, recognizing their own loose living, feeling the sting of guilt. Jesus goes on to tell of the father's embrace of the prodigal, and Matthew is moved from shame to hope by this teacher's message.

Next, as Jesus begins to tell of the older brother, he turns and faces Simon at the entrance, describing how the older brother would not go into the celebration, because, while he had been a dutiful son, his brother had lived a riotous life with harlots. Then Jesus turns toward Matthew, who rises to face Jesus — mesmerized — as he knows Jesus is speaking about himself as the younger brother and Simon as the older. Jesus again faces Simon, and ends the parable saying, "Rejoice, for your brother was lost and now is found, was dead, and behold... is alive!"

At that moment, Simon stumbles into the house, comes up to Jesus, and tearfully says, "Forgive me Master... I'm just a dumb man." Then Jesus silently turns Simon's attention to Matthew.

Finally, Simon steps toward Matthew; the two come near. In silence Simon reaches up and grabs the shoulder of Matthew. And in response Matthew grabs the shoulder of Simon. As the two stand there in reconciliation, it seems the whole world has changed, all in the telling of one parable.

Question #1: Who is the younger son in you?

Let's examine this parable by exploring three questions which it poses to us.

The parable begins with the younger son — about nineteen years old, the age of marriage — making a shocking request of his father. He demands to be given his portion of the estate immediately. According to Deuteronomy 21:17, his rightful share would have been one-third of the disposable property. Now while it was not uncommon for an elderly man to divide his property between his sons before his death, it was unlawful to sell one's inheritance until the father died. Yet here the younger son takes his portion and turns it into cash. He turns his back on his family and heads out of town. He is treating his dad as if he were already dead!

The younger son goes to a far country and squanders his father's wealth in riotous living. When a famine strikes, he is so desperate that he becomes a swineherd, an occupation forbidden in Judaism. Thereby he has turned his back on his faith and become a Gentile.

Finally, his suffering is so great he considers returning home and plans to beg to become one of his father's hired servants, the lowest of the three levels of slaves.

Is this how we treat God? Like the younger son? Do we ask God for everything we think belongs to us, everything we think we deserve, everything we think we need because we want it all and we want it now? Do we treat God as if God was too distant, too old, too ignorant, or too irrelevant? Do we treat God as if we are atheists and God is dead?

Question #2: Who is the elder son in you?

The elder brother claims to have always been obedient. He was the loyal one who stayed on the farm, who always did his father's will, who never got a party in his honor. But the elder brother did not absorb the spirit of his father's unconditional love, because his self-righteousness leads to jealousy. When his brother returns home, he doesn't celebrate that his brother is alive but accuses him of profligate spending on prostitutes. And when he speaks to his father, he refers to him not as "brother" but as "this son of yours." But the father reminds him: "…This brother of yours was dead and has come to life; he was lost and now is found" (Luke 15:32 NRSV). But at the end of the parable, the elder brother is left out in the cold, imprisoned by his own inability to forgive, unable to allow his father to love without limits. He is left alone outside the walls of his own home as the sounds of the party go on.

Question #3: When have you seen God run to you?

The father had been watching for his lost son. How many times each day had he looked down that road hoping to see his son? How many years had he kept vigil? Finally, the day came. From a distance, he saw him. That was the walk of his son! And while he was still far off, the father ran to him. In those days, fathers never ran to meet anyone. You came to them. To run would be beneath their dignity. But nothing is beneath God's dignity. God will stoop to any depth to surprise us with love.

Then the father puts a robe, ring, and shoes on his son. What did these signify? The robe was the robe of honor, given only to esteemed guests. The ring was the father's own signet ring, used to seal signed documents. The shoes were something that belonged to free persons, never slaves. So, the father was declaring this lost son to be a free person, a guest of honor, and one whose authority equaled the father himself.

In Jesus' parable, the prodigal son would never forget that time, the day when he saw his father from afar — the only time he ever saw him run.

When God ran

I once heard a teenager sing the poignant song, "When God Ran," by Benny Hester and John Parenti. (Check it out on YouTube.). This young man sang it with such conviction that I felt as if this was his story, that he was the lost son the parable was portraying.

When my dad utterly astounded me

My own father once utterly astounded me with a love of this kind of holy magnitude, a love that awed me, a moment when I experienced the enfolding care of God.

First, let me explain that in the Harle family, it is a tradition that the older generation doesn't accumulate an inheritance to pass on but gives it when the younger generation needs it most. My grandparents had helped my parents with the costs of my braces, college, and seminary, saying to me, "Don't pay us back; just pass it on when your kids need it."

One day there came a time when Linda and I were being crushed with medical bills, on top of all the other bills of a family with three young children. The last thing I wanted to do was go to Dad, for they had helped us before in many small ways and didn't have much extra themselves. But finally, the pressure was too overwhelming. I really needed my dad. So, I called him.

Mom answered the phone, and I asked if I could talk to Dad. When Dad came on and said hello, I began to cry. As soon as I heard that voice, I couldn't say a word, not because I was ashamed of our situation, but because I knew that voice. Here was a voice that loved me unfathomably, a voice that would never hurt me, a voice that would do anything to save me.

Finally, I was able to describe our crisis. Dad reassured me: "When you come to Wisconsin next month, let's go over your finances and see what can be done."

When that day finally arrived, I felt like a kid going to the principal's office. I knew I was going to get some kind of lecture — and figured I deserved it. And I was worried how he'd react once he saw the extent of our suffocating debts. That's when Dad amazed me.

He began our discussion not by analyzing the detailed figures, not by lecturing me about being more frugal than we already were, not even by questioning how we had gotten into such a morass. He began by stating what he and Mom were willing to do for us, what they were ready to sacrifice on our behalf! They had spoken at length and had already decided to take a huge part of our burden off our shoulders and place it on their own. No questions asked. I was speechless.

Never had I ever expected this response. Even though I knew them so well all these years, even though I knew of their kindhearted goodness, I was dumbfounded by their generosity of spirit. The only thing Mom and Dad cared about was caring for us. They didn't judge us, make us grovel, or shame us. They responded in practical compassion, in caring action, in sacrificial love.

As I looked into Dad's eyes, I was in awe of what he had just said and done. It was a moment I'll always treasure. You might say it was the only time I ever saw him run.

Our Prodigal God

The parable of the Prodigal Son is misnamed. It should be called the parable of the Prodigal Father. Yes, "prodigal" does accurately describe the younger son's riotous lifestyle, profligate spending, and blatant disregard for his father, for this word means reckless abandon, lavish extravagance, and audaciousness not counting the cost. It is the same root from which we get the word "prodigious." Yet prodigal is also the perfect word to describe the father's love for the lost son. That is the way God loves us. It's the only way God knows how to love us. And it's the kind of love we meet in the cross.

With reckless abandon

In the cross, you and I are confronted by a God who loves us with reckless abandon, lavish extravagance, and audaciousness, not counting the cost. And that is the one and only thing that can overcome the prodigious nature of our sins and betrayals — the prodigal love of the prodigal God.

Prodigal abundance proclaimed beforehand

One of the most astonishing things about Jesus was the way he brought prodigal abundance into being by proclaiming the abundance before it arrived, while it was still on the way. As in the feeding of the five thousand, Jesus would thank his Abba for the abundance they were about to receive; then he would encourage his disciples to participate in the abundance which they would discover as they gave with joyful abandon to others.

Abundance on the other side

At the beginning of his ministry along the Galilean shore, when the crowds were pressing in on him to hear the word of God, Jesus got into the fishing boat belonging to Simon and Andrew to teach the people from just offshore. When he was finished, Jesus told Simon, "Put out into the deep water and let down your nets for a catch" (Luke 5:4 NRSV). Simon complained that they had worked all night and caught nothing, but he did as Jesus said. When they brought up their nets, they were bursting to the breaking point and needed help from their partners James and John. Then Jesus told them that from then on, they would be catching people, and all four of them left their work behind and began to follow him. In the miracle of abundance, they began to believe; they began their commitment to Christ's kingdom.

After Jesus was crucified, when the disciples were still so despondent and disbelieving, they had gone back to Galilee, gone back to fishing. One day at daybreak, as they approached the shore after a fruitless night of fishing, a man on the beach called out to them and asked how much they'd caught. Not a single fish, they answered. The man replied, "Cast the net to the right side of the boat, and you will find some" (John 21:6 NRSV). They did so, and they caught so many that they couldn't haul it all in. At that very moment, young John recognized who this stranger must be, as he recalled when this had happened before, and he realized Jesus must be doing this again to help them to see that *He is risen!* To help them believe that *He is risen, indeed!* Excitedly John told the others: "It is the Lord!" (John 21:7 NRSV) When they all made it to shore, someone counted what was in the nets: 153 fish.

In this miracle of abundance, Jesus was teaching them and us that the best way to recognize him is to see the miracles of *more* that come to us out of nowhere — when we least expect them and need them most — even before we begin to believe.

As I write this...

Five years ago, as I write this, I was in a moment of crisis, having recently and suddenly lost my job, and was the guest preacher at an area church on the third Sunday of Easter, preaching on this

214

very passage, Christ's resurrection appearance in John 21:1-14. Let me share with you how I ended my message that morning. Imagine you were there in the sanctuary...

One hundred fifty-three messages of hope.

As I speak these words this day, I am unemployed. I have no job. And I have no prospects for one yet. I have no idea what the future holds, or how my family will be provided for. It is a time of gloomy darkness, of the drear and fear before dawn.

But maybe this is precisely the time I need to learn to leap in faith, and be blessed with Jesus' final Beatitude to the Eleven: "Blessed are those have not seen and yet have come to believe" (John 20:29 NRSV).

Maybe today's resurrection fish-story is for me, too, 153 signs of hope.

After years of sacrificial service as a pastor, I suddenly find myself for the first time with no permanent position. I am left holding only emptiness in my hands.

But today, in this Easter-season moment, perhaps a stranger will appear at the shore of my perception, and beckon to me with a holy voice, and point me in a new direction: spinning me around like metanoia-repentance, calling me to cast the net of myself into the waters of a new and deep endeavor, into an about-to-be revealed adventure in serving Christ.

"Come and eat breakfast," the stranger says to you and me. And with 153 micro-miracles flopping in and out of our hands, perhaps there is a promise — not only of survival but of abundance, of a laughing joy at the profligate grace and the prodigal love that surprises us, arriving unannounced on our doorstep.

Yesterday, as I was writing these final words to share with you, an image came unbidden into my mind's eye: of a stranger's voice beckoning to you as well, to look down at your empty hands and then to look up above you, to see something cascading down from heaven for you: 153 pieces of paper fluttering down on you like doves, 153 messages of hope, and it looked like this....

[Note: The preacher walks down the center aisle, reaches into a brown bag, and tosses a handful of small papers up into the air to flutter down over the people in the front, then another handful to left, another to the right, again and again, sending more all over, as he says...]

153 moments of everyday beauty and blessing. 153 touches of healing, setting you free. 153 gifts of new-life vibrancy.

And on each piece of paper are just two words, two words from our risen redeemer, for you and for me.

Let me ask this young woman over here to read aloud what her message says: **Still alleluia!** *Let me ask this gentleman over here to read aloud what his message says:* **Still alleluia!** *And let me ask this child sitting right near me to read aloud what their message says:* **Still alleluia!**

153 messages of hope, fluttering into our empty hands. Two words for our church and our community: Still alleluia! Two words for our life and world: Still alleluia! Two words from our risen redeemer, for you and me: Still! Alleluia!

With joyful abandon

Astonishing. The way Jesus brought prodigal abundance into being by proclaiming the abundance before it arrived, while still on the way. Let us learn to thank our Abba for the abundance we are about to receive, which will only be revealed as we give to others with joyful abandon.

ENDNOTES

Sketch #19...Jesus, Our Prodigal Giver
Proclaiming Abundance Before It Arrives

1. Marcus J. Borg, *Meeting Jesus Again for the First Time* (Harper San Francisco, 1994), 31.

Sketch #20 …Jesus, Our Crucified Clown:

The Song Of The Clowns Of Freedom

Isaiah 55:8-11 — God's ways and thoughts are higher

1 Corinthians 1:18-25 — God's foolishness is wiser

> *"But God chose what is foolish in the world to shame the wise; God chose what is weak in the world to shame the strong"*

1 Corinthians 1:27 (NRSV)

> *"Jesus let us in on an astonishing secret. God has chosen to change the world through the lowly, the unassuming, and the imperceptible… That has always been God's strategy — changing the world through the conspiracy of the insignificant."*

—Tom Sine,
The Mustard Seed Conspiracy

PART 1: IMAGES OF THE CLOWN

Married to a clown?

One Sunday some years ago, when I was preaching on this very theme, I began my sermon by juggling three balls in the air, and I kept juggling them as I asked folks the following questions: "How many of you like going to the circus? Please raise your hand." [Continued juggling.] "And when you're at the circus, how many of you love to watch the clowns?" [Continued juggling.] "How many of you have ever dressed up as a clown?" [Continued juggling.] "And how many of you are married to a clown?" At this point, as everyone began to laugh, I let the three balls drop to the ground as I raised my hand high and enthusiastically waved it, saying, "Yes! I'm married to a clown, without a doubt. But Linda wouldn't mind me saying that, because she's involved in clown ministry; she even started her own clown troupe once!"

The clown is one of my favorite contemporary images of Jesus. We see it best in the musical *Godspell*, in which Jesus is depicted as a captivating clown who invites people to leave their overburdened lives and skip into new-life freedom by joining his traveling troupe of fools.

Jesus the Clown is also powerfully portrayed in the classic short film, *The Parable,* filmed on location at Circus World Museum (Baraboo, Wisconsin), in which a wandering white-faced clown comes into a county fair's games and into its circus to delight the children there and to set free its mistreated workers. In consequence, and with great anger, the circus ringmaster and owner of the show seizes this clown and hangs him from the trapeze riggings until death. But in the end, a surprising transformation happens among the people — even to the ringmaster — a resurrection visible in the ongoing show, as the ringmaster dons white face and begins to take on the work of the clown, the Fool Who Sets Others Free.

Sometimes Jesus chose to act like a clown

The Clown is one way Jesus chose to act in the gospels. He always welcomed children to come up front with him, and once when the disciples were arguing about who was most important, he invited a child to come forward and show the adults who and what was important to God, sweeping the child up into his arms as he continued to teach.

Jesus turned water into wine at a wedding — making far too much. He put on an outdoor picnic for 5,000 — with far too many leftovers. And he invited himself over for dinner more often than others invited him.

He made up fantastic stories and taught that, if you want to see the way God sees and values things in our world, you've got to stand on your head!

He made the ill feel thrilled and the disabled jump for joy. Yet when everyone was cheering and celebrating as he rode triumphantly into Jerusalem on Palm Sunday, Jesus wept — unexpectedly like a clown — because the city did not know the things that would make for peace.

Sometimes Jesus was treated like a clown

The Clown was also how others sometimes treated Jesus in the gospels.

In Matthew 9:24, the crowd laughed in his face when he said that the young girl who had just died was not dead, only sleeping; and only after ordering those who were deriding him to go away, did he bring life back into the lifeless little one.

When Jesus was arrested, the soldiers blindfolded him, mocked him, spit on him, hit him, and then asked him to identify who delivered the blows. They dressed him in a mock royal robe, jammed onto his head a mock crown of thorns, and laughingly bowed before the king of the Jews.

Sometimes Jesus' believers were treated like clowns

Believers in this Clown were often treated as clowns themselves.

Christians in the church at Corinth were often laughed at. To worship someone who died on a cross? What fools! The cross was a scandal, an embarrassment, a barrier to belief. The Greeks valued philosophical oratory and intellectual reasoning above everything. Wisdom was paramount. They might have valued Jesus as a creative, insightful teacher or a new godlike hero, except for one thing — that cross. Why would anyone choose to be a suffering servant rather than a broker of political clout? Why would anyone choose to associate with the misfits and powerless of society, much less risk dying on their behalf? This just didn't make sense to the Greeks. To them, the cross proved that Jesus was a fool and failure, not a god of wisdom.

Paul acknowledged this difficulty in his first letter to the Corinthians: "For Jews demand signs and Greeks desire wisdom, but we proclaim Christ crucified, a stumbling block to the Jews and foolishness to Gentiles, but to those who are the called, both Jews and Greeks, Christ the power of God and the wisdom of God" (1 Corinthians 1:22-24 (NRSV).

The foolish cross is the power of God

Notice the astonishing claim Paul makes about the cross both here and in verse 18. He admits the cross is foolishness to those who fail to believe, but he does not claim the opposite, that the cross is wisdom. He claims more! The cross is power, the power of God! God works in and through foolishness to break through our intellectual barriers and inner security systems which conspire to

219

keep God out. But God works in and through weakness, through foolishness, and through suffering clowns to overcome our self-centered abusiveness of neighbor and God.

Hope is not possible...

When I was in seminary, I took a class studying the writings of Auschwitz survivor Elie Wiesel, taught by my favorite professor, the Reverend Dr. Robert McAfee Brown. At the end of the semester, Dr. Brown invited the whole class to his apartment to meet Mr. Wiesel and his wife, and to hear a special, more personal lecture by Mr. Wiesel. Afterwards, I went up to Elie Wiesel and asked, "After all you've been through — in your writings, I see such hope. How is that possible?" And he replied, "In our world of such death and destruction, hope is not possible. It is necessary."

"Because I see what is soon to come"

In many of his novels, Elie Wiesel wrote of a Madman named Moshe, based on a man of his boyhood village of Sighet, Romania. Moshe was laughed at by everyone as a fool. Yes, he was a little crazy — eccentric, extreme, deviant, absurd — but what was most fascinating about Moshe was that his feelings were always out of sync with the rest of the community. When times were easy and prosperous and folks were celebrating, Moshe could be seen crying; and when asked why, he would reply, Because I see what is soon to come. In times of tragedy, senseless killings, and despair, Moshe could be seen laughing; and when asked why he would reply, "Because I see what is soon to come." (1)

Out of sync

How did Jesus show forth the foolish power of God? Jesus cried when others were laughing because he saw further ahead, and Jesus laughed when others were weeping because he saw further ahead — to the hope.

Out of sync. Maybe that's what we're supposed to be and do. To be out of sync with society. Out of sync enough so that when **others** say... "I'm in it for the money, for the recognition, for the power, and for *numero uno*" ...**we** might be foolish enough to reply... *I'm in it for the balloon animals that make sick children smile;*

I'm in it for the greasepaint that disguises who it was that left the CARE package of surprises on someone's doorstep; I'm in it to help people have such fun giving their money away that they lose count and don't care; I'm in it to bend down so low that those who were at the bottom can get a piggyback ride up to the top; I'm in it to sing a song into the face of evil for all that I'm worth, and to sing it until no one is afraid anymore; and I'm in it for the day when everyone will be free enough to be a clown for others.

Maybe that's what we're supposed to say. Maybe that's the power of being a fool for Christ.

Marcel Marceau

Marcel Marceau, the most mesmerizing mime of the twentieth century, was someone I had the honor of seeing perform live on stage several times, as well as seeing him perform as well as **speak** at a college mime workshop! When Marcel Marceau moved and mimed, you believed his stories. He kept you laughing with his visual antics, until he moved you to tears with his portrayal of the human condition and the human spirit. In his theatrical shows, the first half he'd perform as a hapless, everyday sort of character, then for the second half he'd transform himself with whiteface into Bip the Clown, the childlike experiencer of life's delights and tragedies. (See his performances online!)

Touring the world and performing in every culture and language — without a word — Marcel spoke with universal eloquence about the beauty of common moments and the wonder of human love, especially for those hungering for love.

But Marcel Marceau was not his birth name. It was Marcel Mangel, son of a Jewish kosher butcher (originally from Poland) and a Jewish mother (originally from what is now Ukraine). Born in Strasbourg, France, Marcel, the age of sixteen had to flee with his family to Limoges when Hitler invaded France. In response, Marcel decided to adopt the last name Marceau, in honor of a French Revolution general who inspired great courage.

Marcel's cousin, Georges, already a fighter in the French Resistance, invited young Marcel to join the Resistance, which he did. They saved many Jewish children from the Nazis, escorting them along escape routes to Switzerland.

This was the first time Marcel put his miming skills to use. From the age of five, when his mother had taken him to a Charlie Chaplin movie, Marcel had practiced mime and year by year developed his love for and expertise in clowning and pantomime. Now, with the children fleeing in fear, Marcel used mime to keep the children utterly silent when danger was near and lifted their weary souls with laughter as they climbed the steep terrain to cross into freedom.

Until his death in 2007 at age 84, Marcel Marceau's athletic, artistic body brought the miracle of understanding, friendship, and peace across borders into our common human soul.

Christ the Clown calls into question our perceptions

Robert McAfee Brown (mentioned above as a friend of Elie Wiesel) once wrote an article that inspired me at the outset of my ministry to keep searching for images of Christ that might surprise and provoke us: "From Clown to Fish: Contemporary Images of Jesus." (2) And one of Dr. Brown's most intriguing images that he conveys to us is Christ the Clown.

Dr. Brown begins by pointing out that several paintings by Rouault portray the face of a clown, and several others portray the face of Christ. Curiously, it is often difficult to distinguish between the two. And this is instructive:

> *If we think about the face of the clown, we discover that he is not only comic, he is also tragic. He not only makes us laugh, he makes us want to cry. The laugher he evokes from us is not far from tears.*

Dr. Brown illustrates this by describing the popular circus skit in which a clown holding a broom tries to sweep away the spot of light from a spotlight on the center-ring floor, and the light keeps eluding him, slipping away just as he is about to reach it. This amuses us to no end, of course, but we also sense the tragedy of his trouble, knowing the clown will never succeed. And so the clown demonstrates for us the gap between how he views the world and how the world truly is. The clown confronts us with the disturbing discovery that the way we see things may not be the way the world truly is. The clown interrogates and challenges our perceptions.

Dr. Brown asserts that Jesus came into our history to call into question our seeing and perceiving, to challenge us no matter what viewpoint or vantage point we look at the world from:

> If we believe that the world is an evil place, we are confronted by the fact that he embodied love within it in such a way as to suggest that love is at the very heart of things. If we believe that the world is a beautiful place, we are confronted by the fact that when Jesus gave expression to that beauty the world could not fit him in, and very quickly did away with him. There is no stance we can take about ourselves or our world that is not challenged when we confront Christ the clown. (3)

PART 2: THE CLOWN OF FREEDOM

What if Jesus appeared in our time as a clown? What might happen if Jesus appeared as a clown in a Latin American country whose government had just been overthrown by a military coup? What would it look like? I believe Christ would appear like Bobo the Clown in the powerful short film by Paulist Productions, *The Clown of Freedom*. (4) Let me retell this story for you at some length, a story I have often used in confirmation classes, and have invited the youth to act out.

A parable for our times: The clown of freedom

The government of a Latin American nation has just been overthrown by a military coup. Shootings and mass arrests have been happening all around the city. But people still needed to find something to eat, and sell what goods they have, so people came to the marketplace square as usual that morning, even as military jeeps and tanks rumbled by.

Into this tense atmosphere, Bobo the Clown and his troupe of three clowns suddenly appear, juggling and doing tricks, making jokes and painting children's faces in the crowd, as they sing this song:

> We shall all be free someday
> Free to laugh and free to play
> Free to dream and go our way
> Yes, we shall all be free

223

In my heart I know it's true
Freedom's song will ring right through
A life of peace of me and you
Yes, we shall all be free

The clowns make the people smile and laugh and feel alive again. But then a gunshot rings out nearby, freezing the marketplace people with fear. But Bobo calls out to them and urges them not to panic but to stay together, claiming the clown troupe has a remedy for repression and bullets.

Immediately he and his clown companions begin to put on a quick skit, mimicking a military firing squad. The clown named Lito pretends to arrest Bobo, bind his hands behind him, offer him a last smoke, and then gives the order. The clown named Juan pretends to fire a gun at Bobo's heart. At that moment, Bobo rips open his shirt and there on his chest is sitting a real white dove! A gasp of delight and applause fills the crowd as they watch the dove circle 'round and away.

The skit gives the people a moment of hope once again, but suddenly a detail of soldiers appears and arrests the clowns for subversive activities.

They are taken to an interrogation center along with hundreds of others. The interrogator examines a file of papers and says that these documents prove that Bobo's true identity is Ramon Gomez, and he asks if that is correct. Bobo replies that there must be some kind of error, that he is Bobo. The interrogator declares that there is no error here, that he is Ramon Gomez. Bobo insists that he is mistaken, that he is definitely Bobo the Clown! The interrogator continues, saying that he is charged with the crime of political subversion and making speeches in his street theater act that are threatening to the patriotic regime.

Suddenly Bobo jumps up on a desk and announces, *"Ladies and gentlemen, welcome to the most foolish show on earth. We are the Clowns of Freedom. We dance, we mime, we sing, we laugh, and we also tame wild animals."* (A pet goat is paraded around by one other clown, as people laugh.) *"Remember, as long as you can laugh at life, keep love in your heart, and freedom in your soul, you too can be a clown."*

Before Bobo can complete his speech, the interrogator orders his uniformed guards carry him away, as the interrogator orders them to take them all away to cell #26. Bobo quips to his fellow clowns that he told them he would get a free room.

As the clowns are thrown into prison, the sergeant punches Bobo hard in the stomach, doubling him over. As the guards leave, Lito says to Bobo that he knew his joking around would only get them deeper into trouble. Bobo answers through his pain that their captors have no laughter inside their hearts, only violence. Juan speaks with greater anger, saying that Bobo could have gotten all of them killed back in interrogation. Bobo, recovering from his injury replies, *"Don't fear those who can kill the body. Rather be frightened of those who can kill your laughter."*

Later in the day, as they are sitting in the cell, the clowns look down into the prison courtyard below and watch as four people are executed by firing squad. Seeing their lifeless bodies, Bobo sings through the bars out into the courtyard:

> *We shall all be free someday*
> *Free to laugh and free to play*
> *Free to dream and go our way*
> *Yes, we shall all be free*
>
> *In my heart I know it's true*
> *Freedom's song will ring right through*
> *A life of peace of me and you*
> *Yes, we shall all be free*

The sergeant down below yells that that song must be stopped. He orders his men to find out who is singing it.

Bobo starts playing his song on his recorder-like musical instrument, and he is still playing it when soldiers burst into his cell and, with one blow to his head with a gun, knock him unconscious. He is taken away to be interrogated by the leader of the junta. Meanwhile the sergeant threateningly asks each of the clowns, *"Are you with Bobo?"* The unnamed third clown denies knowing him. The sergeant asks Juan if he is with Bobo. Juan denies it. Finally, he asks Lito, if he is with Bobo. And Lito — Bobo's closest clown-disciple and friend — answers by shaking his head, no. The sergeant replies, *"You're all cowards. I hate clowns. And whatever we hate, we destroy."*

Bobo is brought for questioning before the junta's leader, an old schoolmate and friend of Bobo who knows him as Ramon. The leader warns Bobo that he is on a dangerous course, that he considers Bobo's pleas on behalf of the peasants to be unpatriotic and must be silenced.

Bobo is returned to the prison. Then the sergeant leads Bobo out into the courtyard where a firing squad is assembled. Bobo's hands are tied tightly behind him and then to a ring bolted to a brick wall. When the sergeant approaches Bobo to tie a blindfold on him, Bob retorts that he definitely doesn't want that, that he's scared of the dark. The sergeant sneers that he better get used to the dark. Then he calls out in an official voice to Bobo, asking if the prisoner has any last thing to say. Bobo replies that he thought he'd never ask.

Bobo looks up at all the prisoners looking out from their cells, all around and above him, stretching ten stories high, and declares, *"Ladies and gentlemen, welcome to the most foolish show on earth. Just remember, as long as you can laugh at life, keep love in your heart, and freedom in your soul, you too can be a clown."*

The sergeant interrupts, ordering the firing squad to prepare and to begin to aim. But Bobo interjects, saying he's not finished with his speech.

Bobo looks up at the cells and continues, saying that he the crowd is about to witness the most incredible and dangerous trick ever attempted. Suddenly, to everyone's amazement, Bobo raises his hands high above his head — somehow having freed himself from his bonds — and shouts, *"Ta da!"*

The stunned sergeant prepares to seize him, but Bobo assures him that he is not attempting to flee, saying confidently, *"Relax, sergeant, it's all part of the act."*

Again, addressing the prisoners in their cells, Bobo explains the trick, shouting out for all to hear, that this line of men will fire bullets into my heart exactly on cue, and these bullets will pass through and go out without doing any damage, because his heart is made of magic. But, Bobo warns, they need to aim most carefully, for as long as they shoot straight, he will live.

Addressing the firing squad, Bobo tells them to be great marksmen, and to remember: *If you miss his heart, the trick won't work*. Then Bobo says to the sergeant that he may proceed.

Bobo stands brightly and boldly with his chest out, confident of the outcome. The sergeant gives the order to the firing squad: ready, aim, fire! Six guns rip into the heart of the clown, and he crumples to the ground. Everyone is stunned — not shocked that the bullets had killed him, but heartbroken that a clown of such love had come into their midst and was now gone forever.

In a cell far above, Lito, who had watched it all, sobs openly — unable to stop looking at the body of his beloved Bobo, whom he had once denied. Then in a quavering voice, Lito begins to sing:

> *We shall all be free someday*
> *Free to laugh and free to play*
> *Free to dream and go our way*
> *Yes, we shall all be free*

At extreme risk to himself, he sings the subversive song of hope, the song of love, the song of freedom. The sergeant calls for the song to end, to find out who is singing it now that Bobo's dead. But despite the danger, Lito goes on singing it, louder and stronger. Then the other clowns join him. Then from a first-floor prison cell, a new prisoner joins in the singing, then from adjacent cell another voice, and from the next cell another, then from the second tier of cells the song is joined, and from the third and fourth and fifth tiers, the song rings out:

> *In my heart I know it's true*
> *Freedom's song will ring right through*
> *A life of peace of me and you*
> *Yes, we shall all be free*

PART 3: ARE YOU WITH JESUS?

On confirmation retreats I've led, after we dramatized the story of Bobo, the Clown of Freedom, after discussing its meaning, and after a worship service on its theme, I would call forward each confirmand and ask them, "Are you with Jesus?" And they would have to answer. And with only one exception, they always answered, "Yes, I am with Jesus."

Then I would give them a surprise we had arranged ahead of time: a large manila envelope full of letters and symbolic gifts from the church, from members they knew and didn't know, from teachers and mentors, as well as from family and relatives. And they would go off by themselves for an hour to read all the prayerful words of support and encouragement from so many unexpected people, and to reflect on the lifetime commitment they were about to make.

Finally, on Confirmation Sunday, I would ask each of them Dietrich Bonhoeffer's question: "Who is Jesus Christ for you today?" Then after they answered with a sentence or two, I would say, "As Christ is calling you to be his lifelong disciple, do you promise to follow courageously wherever Christ leads, to love God with all your heart, and your neighbor as yourself?" And to hear them answer "I do" was always an emotional moment.

But now it's your turn. For this time in your life. To answer a question. A critical question. A life-changing question: Are you with Jesus, the Clown of Freedom? Do you promise to follow courageously wherever Christ leads? Do you promise to love God with all your heart, and your neighbor as yourself? Do you dare to be foolish enough and faithful enough to sing the song of hope in the time of darkness? Will you teach others to sing as well, until all are free to laugh and free to play?

Are you with Jesus?

POSTSCRIPT: FOOLISH ENOUGH TO INTERRUPT TRAF-FIC ON GOOD FRIDAY ON MAIN STREET

Each year on Good Friday in one of my churches, children and adults from our church joined with the children and adults of another church in town, and together, in silence, we would carry a very large cross of heavy, rough-hewn beams directly down Main Street from one church to the other during the noontime rush hour, bringing traffic to a halt, causing everyone to pause and recall which day this was, what this day meant, what this day cost. Some inconvenienced motorists would curse at us. Some watched in solemn reverence. Most did not understand why we did such a thing: *These people are fools. What power is there in a cross?*

To carry a cross through the streets — or to wear a wooden cross-pendant next to your heart — these are foolish acts. They seem insignificant, even futile, in the face of the crucifixions dominating the daily news. But our cross is the cross of Christ, through which the power of God flows into you and me, beyond our doing, radiating hope in the darkness, a hope that is not possible but necessary.

So, dare to do deeds of faithfulness. You may discover you have succeeded in doing things that you were too foolish to know could never be done.

And when people say you're a fool, that the cross has no power, be as silent as Jesus at his trial. Then simply pick up your cross, face the doorway into the world, and go out into the new light of the new day. And behold. The power and wisdom of God.

ENDNOTES

Sketch #20 ...Jesus, Our Crucified Clown:
The Singing Clowns Of Freedom

1. See Elie Wiesel's memoir, *Night,* and his novels *The Gates of the Forest, The Oath,* and *The Town Beyond the Wall,* in which Wiesel writes: "To know when to cry and when to laugh, one has only to see far enough ahead" (New York: Hill & Wang, 2012), 131.

2. Robert McAfee Brown, "From Clown to Fish: Contemporary Images of Jesus," *Strategy* magazine, Vol. 5, No. 1, September-November, 1974, pp.19-21. An excerpt from Dr. Brown's book, *The Pseudonyms of God,* (The Westminster Press, 1971).

3. *The Clown of Freedom,* Paulist Productions. Orginally broadcast in 1971 on the TV show *Insight* (Season 12, Episode 15, Show #374). You can find this 26-minute video on YouTube by doing an internet search for "insight, the clown of freedom."

Sketch #21 ...Jesus, Our Incognito Christ-Alive:

Seeing With Emmaus Eyes

Luke 24:13-35 — Risen One on the road to Emmaus

Hebrews 13:2 — Entertaining angels unawares

> *"When he was at table with them, he took bread, blessed and broke it, and gave it to them. Then their eyes were opened, and they recognized him; and he vanished from their sight. They said to each other, 'Were not our hearts burning within us while he was talking to us on the road, while he was opening the scriptures to us?'"*
> Luke 24:30-32 (NRSV)

> *"Easter is not the conviction that there is a life after death; Easter is the experience that here and now there is a love that death can never diminish, that death can never extinguish."*
> — Hope Harle-Mould

Emmaus Eyes: The Stranger

To see the Risen One with Emmaus eyes is to recognize Christ Incognito in the form of the Stranger.

Two of Jesus' closest disciples, Cleopas and another who is unnamed, were walking all afternoon on that Easter Sunday the seven miles from Jerusalem to Emmaus, perhaps fleeing in fear from the authorities, perhaps numbed by the shock and despair of seeing their hoped-for Messiah beaten nearly to death then executed on a cross.

As the two walked along, trying to talk through their tears, someone walking the same direction caught up to them. Certainly, they didn't expect to see Jesus. How could they? They knew he was dead. So whom did they see? Only a Stranger.

"That man there is Harry Houdini!"

Harry Houdini, the great illusionist, and greatest escape artist of all time, occasionally surprised his audiences in a unique manner. On stage he would be shackled, wrapped in chains, suspended upside down in a water tank, and a partial curtain put in front. As the audience counted the seconds and minutes to see whether he could hold his breath long enough to break free, a stranger in dry clothes would appear in the back of the theater and ask someone what was going on. He would be told that Houdini was submerged and chained behind that curtain, trying to surpass his own escape record. The stranger would go forward a few rows and ask someone else what was going on. The spectator would answer that Houdini had been underwater for several minutes already and might be having trouble with the new locks designed by a local locksmith. The stranger would continue moving through the audience in this manner, getting closer and closer to the stage until finally someone would call out: "That man in the aisle is Harry Houdini!"

Perhaps that is why we see so many strangers

We, like the disciples walking to Emmaus, do not expect to see Jesus, even though we, unlike those disciples, already know he is risen. Yes, we try to be people of in-God-we-trust faith, but we are also very secular, skeptical, Westernized people. We don't really expect to see the risen Christ in our world, in our midst. Perhaps that is why we see so many strangers.

Could we be missing the Incognito One because we choose to stay and exist in night's darkness? The following parable hints at an answer.

A teacher was sitting around a campfire with a few dedicated students late one night. During a silent lull in the conversation, the teacher asked a question: "How can we know when the night has ended, and the day has begun?" The students pondered. Then...

Eagerly one young man answered, "You know the night is over and the day has begun when you can look off in the distance and determine which animal is your dog and which are the sheep."

232

...A second student ventured a guess on behalf of the group, "You know the night is over and the day has begun when light falls on the leaves and you can tell whether it is a palm tree or a fig tree."

Both times the teacher shook his head and gently said that while it was a good answer, it was not the answer he was seeking. Finally, the students begged him to answer his own question and he did:

The Teacher looked intently at the eager young faces before he began to speak. "When you look into the eyes of a human being and see a brother or sister, you know it is morning. If you cannot see a sister or brother, you will know that it will always be night." (1)

Emmaus Eyes: The Listener

To see the Risen One with Emmaus eyes is to recognize Christ Incognito in the form of the Listener

When the Stranger came walking up behind Cleopas and the other, what was the first thing he did? He asked them what they were talking about on the road, what was bothering them. Christ didn't begin by preaching at them or giving them a set of all-purpose answers. He began by listening. He offered compassionate ears.

The Chapel of the One Who Hears

In her classic book, *No One Hears But Him*, Taylor Caldwell describes a chapel to which people from distant lands would journey because of its reputation as a place where God speaks clearly and directly to each individual believer. But there was one strict rule: only one person was allowed to enter at a time.

Afterwards, as people began to talk and share with one another about their experience, they were stunned to discover that not one person who had been in the chapel had actually been able to hear a distinctive divine voice! But at the same time, every single person described the same amazing sensation: they felt that God was somehow listening more intensely and embracingly there, in that place, than they had ever experienced anywhere else before. And each person left with a sureness, knowing that their deepest cries had been heard by the Holy. That was what they had needed most. Somehow, they knew that this had already made their lives new and possible. It was as if the Psalm had come true:

You restore my soul (Psalm 23:3).

Receiving who you are, affirming who you're becoming.

Who is the listener in your life?

One of the best listeners I've ever known was a classmate of mine studying for the Presbyterian ministry at Carroll University (Waukesha, Wisconsin). Her name was Linda Kuhn. Whenever Linda would see a friend on campus, she would immediately give that person her full attention. She would always be the first to ask, "How are you doing?" Then she might ask, "How are you really doing?" You knew she genuinely cared about you and was interested in what was happening in your life. Most special of all, Linda had the uncanny ability to remember the last thing you told her about some upcoming event or some concern in your life, and she would ask you about it. She never failed to do so. It was a sacred gift of receiving who you were and affirming who you were becoming.

We, too, are called to become holy listeners of such healing depth for others. To do so may be the one thing that makes the crucial difference for someone at the critical time.

Emmaus Eyes: The Master Teacher

To see the Risen One with Emmaus eyes is to recognize Christ Incognito in the form of the Master Teacher

As Cleopas and the other disciple walked along, their hearts were strangely warmed as this Stranger opened the Hebrew Scriptures to them. They saw new things in the old words, and they felt new feelings, as if a whole new panorama of life had opened before them. For the first time, they saw in the words of the prophet Isaiah the fulfillment of a promise which no one had anticipated: a suffering Messiah, whose suffering would redeem and overcome.

Nonviolent peacebuilder, Richard Deats

Who has been your Master Teacher? One of the amazing teachers of my life has been Reverend Richard Deats, a United Methodist minister from Big Springs, Texas. After pastoring churches in both Texas and the Philippines — as well as teaching social ethics in a seminary there — Richard was chosen as director of interfaith activity at the Fellowship of Reconciliation (FOR). An international, nonviolent group founded at the outbreak of World War I, FOR has for 100 years has been a leader in the civil rights movement, in peacebuilding campaigns, and in human rights struggles around the world.

In his forty years at FOR, Richard led nonviolent training sessions all over the world, teaching the methods of Gandhi and King to social change leaders in many countries. He played a key role in supporting and giving voice to many courageous leaders from many faith traditions whose human rights were being crushed and working with them for peaceful change and nonviolent revolution. Richard also led delegations to many "enemy nations" such as Russia, Iran, and others in order to be a bridge preventing war and fostering cooperation.

But Richard was also an exemplar because of who he was on the inside, a faithful husband to his wife of a lifetime, a loving father and grandfather to his whole family, and a man whose heart was open to seeing the presence and power of God in traditions other than his own.

When I was in seminary, I had the honor of working closely with Richard for several years as an intern-organizer. Every so often, he would invite me to share bread and wine with him in a simple service of prayer and communion, just the two of us. It was a moving gift from my mentor, grounding my activism deep within our shared faith.

The following year, Richard preached at my ordination, giving me words of both uplift and challenge, enough to catalyze a lifetime of ministry. More than enough.

In Richard's book, *Stories of Courage, Hope and Compassion*, he gives us this prayer to empower our lives and restore the world:

> *Spirit of God, we long to mend the broken circle,*
> *To heal the fractures in the world around us and within our own souls.*
> *To learn from one another the ways of being fully alive,*
> *To transform the parts of ourselves and our world*
> *That block our making contact with our deepest reality*

And with the deepest, richest and most sacred
dimensions of all other beings.

Spirit of God, we long to see as reality
A world pulsing with justice and truth,
A society where everyone sits down at the great banquet
and eats until filled.

Spirit of God, we recommit ourselves to building the
Beloved Community
As brothers and sisters working together.

Spirit of God, we commit to mending the broken circle,
To building the Beloved Community.
Bless us, everyone. (2)

Emmaus Eyes: The Hungry Homeless One

To see the Risen One with Emmaus eyes is to recognize Christ
Incognito in the form of the Hungry Homeless One.

When Cleopas and the other disciple reached Emmaus, the Stranger appeared to be going further, so they ask him to stay. That is when they finally recognized him, the Risen Christ, not because they looked more carefully or heard more clearly but because of something the Stranger did. As they sat at table, he took bread, blessed it, broke it, and gave it to Cleopas and the other. As they stared at their piece of bread, they finally knew. And when they looked up with new eyes, Emmaus Eyes, he was gone.

In my church's tradition, whenever we celebrate the Lord's Supper, the communion liturgy declares these words from the Emmaus Road experience: *And they recognized him in the breaking of the bread.*

As these two disciples opened their home to this "One Unknown," as they included him at their table, as they welcomed him with their food, they recognized him. They had given hospitality to the Hungry Homeless One.

236

"Worldwalker" Steven Newman

Steven Newman was a young man from Bethel, Ohio, and the first person ever to walk around the world alone and without sponsor, never asking people for anything more than a drink of fresh water.

He did so as an experiment... Is the world truly as frightening as so many folk fear, as threatening as the news headlines shout in alarm? Or is the world actually full of good and generous people ready to open their hearts to a hungry, homeless stranger, full of compassionate people who would jump at the chance to play their part in one man's quixotic journey?

It took Steven four years to complete his journey, April 1, 1983, to April 1, 1987, across five continents, twenty countries, and 19,960 miles. But he arrived home safely, full of stories and the signatures of thousands of new friends from every country he passed through, who had written in his Book of Witness. Except for two situations of grave danger, one in Turkey and one in Malaysia, Steven had experienced 48 months of extraordinary hospitality, finding people everywhere who wanted to play a small part in his search for humanity's soul.

When Steven spoke at my church, he told a story from very early in his Worldwalk. He was walking down a West Virginia highway through dense fog at sunrise. He had not eaten a full meal for several days by this point. Suddenly an old woman from a window above him in the fog called out, *Have you had any breakfast yet?* He answered he hadn't. To his surprise, she invited him in.

Her name was Estaline, a diminutive poor widow who for two hours worked in a frenzy to fix and serve him a sumptuous country breakfast: pancakes, eggs, bacon, biscuits, grits, and more. Finally, he had to ask, *Why did you invite me in? I could have been anyone!* She blushed and answered: *When I was a little girl, I was taught to welcome strangers who come to your door, for you could be entertaining angels unawares. When I looked out my window this morning, I saw you walking where no one ever walks this time of day. And my eyesight isn't what it used to be, so your backpack looked sort of like wings, and after waiting eighty-eight years for an angel, I sure wasn't going to let one get by!"* (3)

Steven told us that he knew he was no angel, but he was sure that she was.

On the fourth and final Christmas night of his Worldwalk, Steven pondered what it all had meant, as his grand journey was nearing its end:

So many times, as on this Christmas night, I had paused alone with my memories of all those across the face of the earth who had done their best to make me feel like a son or a brother. Every time I had felt so proud and humble at the same time that I didn't know whether to cry or smile.

I could never again believe that we were a planet without hope and a future. The newspapers might print all they wanted, the leaders might scorn and condemn till their faces were blue, but I knew better. Love — yes, Love — was truly everywhere on this most wondrous globe. And where there was Love, I knew there was God. He was still with us as much as ever, and always would be. (4)

(Aside: In 1998, I had the honor of performing Steven's marriage to Darci near Bellefontaine, Ohio. They are still happily married!)

The gift of Emmaus Eyes

In order for us to see and recognize the Risen Jesus, we need to develop Emmaus eyes, eyes that expect to see the Risen One, eyes that can recognize Christ Incognito when he appears to us in the form of the Stranger, the Listener, the Master Teacher, and the Hungry Homeless One. I pray we receive those eyes, so we may see the glory of the Risen One and rejoice in serving him day by day.

I conclude with a poem I wrote this Easter, titled *Emmaus Eyes*.

Like the disciples we have Good Friday eyes —
eyes downcast from life's betrayals of the heart
and the tearing down of our preciousness,
eyes that have witnessed in our world
hate's violence,

evil's terror,
and death's darkness.

But the Risen One walks into our lives
like a stranger bearing a surprise,
the gift of Emmaus Eyes:

Emmaus eyes that see the Alleluia One,
alive over death
and on the loose again,

Emmaus eyes that see Christ Incognito
in the guise of the refugee —
who teaches us how to hold onto hope,
in the guise of the burn survivor —
who relights within us a flame of new courage,
and in the guise of the orphan-child —
who bids us to believe in Easter miracles
already on their way to us,
already bathing our faces
in alleluia light.

The gift of Emmaus eyes.
Behold and see. (5)

ENDNOTES

Sketch #21 ...Jesus, Our Incognito Christ-Alive:
Seeing With Emmaus Eyes

1. William R. White, *Stories for the Journey: A Sourcebook for Christian Storytellers*, (Augsburg Publishing House: Minneapolis, 1988), 97-98.

2. Richard L. Deats, *Stories of Courage, Hope and Compassion* (North Charleston, SC: CreateSpace, 2011), 61. This prayer, "Building the Beloved Community," originally appeared in Fellowship magazine, September-October 2002.

3. Steven Newman, *The Worldwalker* (New York: Avon Books, 1989), 36-40.

4. Ibid., 527.

5. Hope Harle-Mould © 2021

Sketch #22 ...Jesus, Our Still-at-Large Risen One:

Evidence Of Easter

Isaiah 25:6-9 — God destroys the shroud

John 20:24-31 — Christ helps Thomas to believe

> *"Jesus said to [Thomas], 'Have you believed because you have seen me? Blessed are those who have not seen and yet have come to believe'"* John 20:29 (NRSV)

> *"'There's no use trying,' said Alice, 'I cannot believe impossible things.' "I dare say you haven't had much practice,' said the Queen. 'When I was your age, I always did it for half an hour a day. Why, sometimes I've believed as many as six impossible things before breakfast.'"* — Lewis Carroll, *Alice in Wonderland*

Imagine

Imagine that a court of law subpoenaed you to appear before a jury of your peers and required you to give Evidence of Easter: Did Jesus of Nazareth really rise from the dead in or about the year 29 AD? What does the resurrection of Christ mean to you? What difference does it make in our world? Why do you still believe in the Risen One?

Now imagine that you were required to make a Power Point presentation of your argument, and that you had to select six photographs to demonstrate your convictions. How would you do it? What would you say? What would be your Evidence of Easter? Here is my attempt.

PHOTO #1: *A woman standing before a tomb, holding flowers, and weeping*

One of the strongest arguments for the authenticity of the Gospel accounts of Jesus' resurrection is that women were the first witnesses. This was not only a problem for the early church, it was a scandal. Women were considered worthless as eyewitnesses at that time. Jewish courts forbade women to testify. Male authorities viewed women as hysterical, emotional exaggerators of truth.

When the Eleven were told by Mary Magdalene and the other women that the tomb was empty and Jesus had appeared to them, they refused to believe them. They called it an idle tale. Only when they went and looked for themselves, and when Jesus later appeared to the Eleven, did they finally believe.

The early church would never have invented a story saying that women were the first witnesses of the Risen Christ. The fact that all four Gospels persist in stating that women were the first evangels of Easter must mean that they were. This inconvenient truth hindered many in the Jewish and Greek world from becoming believers, but nevertheless it was true.

Jesus was revolutionary in his treating women as equals: teaching them, defending them, and inviting them to be part of his itinerant ministry. He called them to be full participants in the kingdom of God. How typical it would be of Jesus that he would appear as Risen One first to the women. How typical that he would commission a woman, Mary Magdalene, to be the first preacher of Easter: *Go and tell…*

PHOTO #2: *An ancient stone slab inscribed with a message*

An empty tomb would not prove the resurrection of Jesus, but if it was *not* empty, it would definitely *disprove* it. All that the Powers That Be had to do to discredit the early Christian message of the Risen Christ was to produce Jesus' corpse. They could not. But is there any non-Christian evidence that the tomb was empty?

An amazing archeological find was unearthed in the town of Nazareth that dates from the time of emperors Tiberius or Claudius. It is a 15 x 25" marble slab written in Greek. It is an edict from the Caesar, saying:

> *It is my pleasure that graves and tombs remain perpetually undisturbed....If, however anyone [has] extracted the buried, or has maliciously transferred them to other places in order to wrong*

them, or has displaced the sealing or other stones....I desire that the offender be sentenced to capital punishment. (1)

What could possibly have happened to cause Caesar to issue an edict specifically about not disturbing the stones which sealed a tomb, specifically about not stealing a body, specifically about not moving a corpse to a different location? Why was the penalty for disturbing a grave jacked up from a minor fine? And is it a coincidence that this edict was made specifically in Palestine, and that this marble slab was unearthed in Nazareth, the hometown of Jesus of Nazareth?

PHOTO #3: A photograph of St. Peter's Basilica in Rome

When Jesus was arrested and condemned to crucifixion, the disciples fled in fear. One of them denied him. Another committed suicide. The Eleven remained in hiding behind locked doors, cowering in fright, afraid they too might be arrested and executed. The disciples did not expect Easter. They didn't even expect the cross. When it happened, they were in despair, ready to go home in defeat, to go back to fishing. Their teacher was dead. The experiment was over.

But then something astonishing happened. Even if we had no written account of Easter morning, even if we had no eyewitness records of appearances of the Risen Christ, if we could only compare the disciples before Easter to the disciples after Easter, we would have to conclude, something astonishing happened, something we can see reflected in the looking glass of the disciples' lives, something we call the resurrection.

What happened was a complete transformation of these men and women. Ordinary people from common fishing villages were transformed into extraordinary people of faith preaching with boldness in the entire world. Fearful followers were transformed into fearless apostles. People who betrayed their dying teacher were transformed into people ready to die for the Risen Lord. Cowards who hid from authorities were transformed into courageous activists who spoke openly and defiantly.

This change was not temporary. Decades later, Peter was still preaching faithfully and fearlessly, even in the city of Rome itself, even in prison, even when they took him out and nailed him upside down on a cross. Peter never denied Jesus again. The resurrection had transformed Peter into a rock of faith. And today, atop his grave, is this: the most famous church in the world, the Basilica of St. Peter in Rome.

PHOTO #4: *A two-year old girl with her arms raised as she flies down a playground slide.*

This photograph is from a time when my faltering faith failed to believe, when I couldn't believe that what was necessary was actually possible.

In one of my former churches, Springboro United Church of Christ, near Dayton, Ohio, there was a two-year-old girl named Christina Hagan. She had been born needing not only a heart transplant, but a dual lung transplant as well. We had prayed for her since infancy, but now time was drawing short. Though we had hoped and pleaded for a miracle, we knew in our rational minds that her chances were miniscule. The family was considering moving to Minneapolis to be as close as possible to the medical center with the best chance of providing a transplant for them.

But four weeks before Easter, while Christina was at the Cleveland Clinic for a scheduled heart valve replacement, suddenly a heart and two lungs became available right there in Cleveland, and the transplant was immediately made. The young donor child who had just died not only gave Christina new life, but also gave new life to an eighteen-month-old boy who needed a liver. Those anonymous, compassionate, grieving parents gave the greatest gift of all: a resurrection of hope, healing, and alleluia.

That Easter morning, I confessed to my whole congregation: How could I have been so surprised when this happened? How could I have had so little faith in God's goodness? How could I have bet against a God who prefers impossible odds and always finds a way?

PHOTO #5: *Tiananmen Square, Beijing. One single young man stands before a line of tanks, and refuses to move*

William Sloane Coffin once said, "Easter has less to do with one man's escape from the grave as it does with the victory of seemingly powerless love over loveless power."

In order to prove that Jesus' resurrection is real, I would need to prove — in this court — that it is possible for love to overcome death, for truth to overcome injustice, for healing to overcome war. And I intend to do just that. I submit into evidence these two exhibits to prove this contention.

EXHIBIT A: A fragment of the Berlin Wall

As you can see, I am holding in my hand a small chunk of gray cement, which you'll notice has hues of violet and other colors on the smooth side, as if it had come from a bleak wall spray-painted with messages of hope, before being broken apart. Given to me by a friend, it came from the Berlin Wall not long after it was torn down in November 1989 — one of my most prized possessions.

This fragment testifies to something I never thought I'd see in my lifetime: the crumbling of the Berlin Wall and an end to the Cold War. And it came about without a shot being fired.

It was sparked by the striking Polish workers of Gdansk led by Lech Welesa and the Solidarity Union, which started in 1980 and grew to represent one-third of the working population of Poland, and which was supported during the years of repression by Pope John Paul II — not only with financial support but with the secret threat (to the Soviets controlling the Warsaw Pact countries) that if necessary, he would come back to his homeland of Poland to live and march with Solidarity until democracy came. Finally, it did, when in 1989 a coalition government was formed, and a year later Lech Walesa was elected President.

The Berlin Wall's collapse happened after years of courageous demonstrations in East Germany, led from the only safe place for dissenters, the church and its supportive religious leaders, which kept growing in strength.

Some of my American clergy friends happened to be in Germany in November of 1989 as part of a delegation on a friendship tour, linking our historically German-American churches with the churches of West and East Germany. The time came on their itinerary for them to travel to Berlin and they were accidentally witnesses to one of history's most dramatic moments. They were caught up in the mass marches in East Berlin calling for an end to dictatorship and a beginning of democracy and human rights.

There was one moment my friends told me about that was quite stunning. It was when one of the anti-Communist Party organizers organizers was addressing the tens of thousands of protestors and said something remarkable: "Our freedom movement owes its greatest debt and thanks to the one place where the flame of protest was kept safe and kept burning bright: the churches of East Germany. Let us now turn in our hearts to thank the churches of Jesus Christ."

The loudest cheer that went up that day was for the church, for the courageous pastors and congregations who — during the Cold War, behind the Iron Curtain — dared to be sanctuaries of liberty and prophetic voices of justice.

EXHIBIT B: A clergy stole from South Africa

I also enter into evidence this decorative clergy stole from South Africa, a stole which an American minister wore when he met Archbishop Desmund Tutu on one of his visits to America, as Tutu was seeking to build international support for boycotts against the apartheid government of South Africa.

Archbishop Tutu was doing something no one thought possible. He was leading his church and people in nonviolent resistance to white-supremacist tyranny, at the same time he was modeling and striving to construct a new society of equality and justice. And he was doing so without the bloodbath against whites that skeptics feared was inevitable. Archbishop Tutu helped create and lead the Truth and Reconciliation Commissions, which fostered and formed the conditions for the apartheid government to finally release Nelson Mandela from prison in 1990, and under a new constitution for Mandela to be elected president in 1994 — a leader who had evolved into a great forgiver and a great reconciler of all races in his newly freed country.

OTHER EXHIBITS

I could submit many more recent pieces of evidence to prove my case: from the election of America's first African American president in 2008… to Tunisia sparking the Arab Spring in December 2010/January 2011 and continuing to be a democracy to this day; from the 2015 Supreme Court allowing our LGBT family members to marry in the United States… to the 2018 Valentine's Day when students of Marjory Stoneman Douglas High School in Parkland, Florida, became the conscience of America and sparked a movement to come together in nonpartisan ways to prevent gun violence.

But the most powerful example of nonviolent love overcoming evil is Malala Yousefzai, surviving a Taliban shooting in 2012, becoming the youngest ever (at age seventeen) to win the Nobel Peace Prize in 2014, and continuing to be the foremost voice and catalyst in the world for girls' education, women's rights, and the caring for refugees fleeing tyranny and violence. (On a personal note, I heard Malala speak in 2017 in Buffalo, New York, and I felt more hope for our world in that packed auditorium than anywhere else in a long time.)

All these historical events are things we never could have predicted. Some we thought were impossible. Or if they did happen, we assumed they would occur only after great bloodshed and suffering. Never did we think they might happen so rapidly and so nonviolently. But if these things are possible, then anything is possible, not because evil is weak but because even when death does its worst, God brings Easter out of the ashes. The power of resurrection is real.

Martin Luther King Jr. often said that the arc of the moral universe is long, but it bends toward justice. As followers of the Still-at-Large Risen One, we are called to look for places where we can join him in bending the arc, where walls of subjugation and separation are being broken down, where arches and bridges of reconciliation are being constructed in hope, where there are communities building up one another in love (1 Corinthians 8:1 and 1 Thessalonians 5:11).

PHOTO #6: A bride and groom at their church wedding

When my wife and I were serving in ministry in Maryland, there was a United Church of Christ pastor down the road named Reverend John Mingus. He once shared with us the story of two couples in his church.

The first couple, Andy and Priscilla, had moved into town to begin their dream. Andy had finished law school, passed the bar, and was ready to start a law practice. Andy and Priscilla put down roots. The practice grew. The two became four. They were happy.

The second couple, Carole and Greg, moved in next door to Pastor Mingus and became good friends. But on the day Greg inspected the new house, he hit his head and soon developed seizures. Tests revealed a brain tumor. Before he died, Greg stood in the pulpit of their church one Sunday and spoke of life and death. The church grieved with them.

Andy and Priscilla's dream shattered when Andy came home from work one day and discovered his wife and children had been brutally and senselessly murdered. The church was there for him throughout the months of court trial and the continuing pain.

The murderer was put in prison, and Andy's life went on. Carole buried Greg and her life went on. For both of them, the church was a place where they found people who would hold them and weep with them, people who helped each other forge a faith that could weather any storm, people who taught one another how to create meaning out of meaninglessness.

Reverend Mingus tells the rest of the story:

*On a New Year's Day, **Andy** and **Carole** were married. The church was full. There was a sense not only of celebration, but also **of resurrection.** Together we learned that there is always hope for new life. In the church we discover again and again that Easter is not an old tale. Easter is a present reality.*

PHOTO #7: *The open sanctuary doors of my home church*

One Easter morning at my home church, the pews filled with joyful families in worship, I concluded my Sunday sermon that day by saying this:

For centuries the Jewish people worshiped God on the Sabbath, Saturday, the seventh day of the week. In fact, this is one of the Ten Commandments, the fourth.

But something remarkable happened at dawn one Sunday morning. Beginning that day onward, the Eleven and the women and those who had seen and heard the good news of the Risen One gathered together once each week to pray and sing, to share bread and wine, and to remember. They called it, "The Lord's Day."

Two millennia later, believers in the Risen Christ continue to gather once a week in a community of worship and servanthood. And these people choose to gather not on the last day of the week but on the first — the Lord's Day — to pray and sing and remember.

Now look around you at all those who are here with you this day. Look around you! You are evidence of Easter.

ENDNOTES

Sketch #22 ...Jesus, Our Still-at-Large Risen One:
Evidence Of Easter

1. Paul L. Maier, *In the Fullness of Time: A Historian Looks at Christmas, Easter, and the Early Church* (Harper San Francisco, 1991), 202.

Epilogue:

Resources For *Your* Sketches Of Jesus!

RESOURCE #1: Transients At The Backdoor: A true story from the life of Joseph Girzone.

Growing up during the Great Depression, **Joseph Girzone** (author of such bestsellers as *Joshua, Joshua in the City, The Shepherd,* and *Never Alone*) was then a child in a large family. It was not unusual for transients to show up at their back door looking for a meal. His father invariably invited them in, gave them his place at table, and served them — even though the family barely had enough for themselves.

One winter day, there came a knock at the back door. They were surprised anyone would be out on such a day. A snowstorm had blanketed the ground earlier, and the temperature had turned quite chilly. At the door stood a man in ragged clothes and a hat. Before he could ask for anything, the father ushered him to the table and asked if he'd like some soup. "No," he replied, "Save it for the children. Some coffee would be just fine."

When the steaming cup was placed in front of him, he bowed his head for a moment in silence. As the children sat watching him drink his coffee, Joseph's sister piped up: "Are you a kidnapper?" "No," he said, "I love children." As the man finished, he got up, said, "God bless you all," and left by the back door.

The children scrambled to the side windows to watch the stranger go on his way. When he didn't pass, they rushed to the back porch and looked out. The fallen snow that had earlier drifted in near the door was still undisturbed. Even more puzzling, there were no footprints in the snow outside the house. Bouncing back to the table, the children breathlessly reported the amazing occurrence to their father. Without moving or looking up, he simply said, "We must always show compassion for the needy. God visits us in the form of the poor." (1)

RESOURCE #2: Seeing Jesus' Face: A Responsive Reading by Hope Harle-Mould

We want to grow close to God, to feel God's presence, to hear the guidance of God's voice, to see the glory of God's face. But how can we do so?

Jesus says: "Whoever has seen me, has seen the Father, for I am in the Father and the Father is in me."

When Jesus was walking on water and invited Peter to join him, Peter's eyes looked away from Jesus, saw the threatening waves and he began to sink.

But Jesus reached out his arm and pulled him to safety, and Peter looked into the eyes of his Savior — the Love That Will Not Let Me Go.

Like the man born blind who didn't want to change, Jesus confronts us, "Do you want to be healed?" And we must dare to risk and accept the changes of new life in the kingdom of God.

As Jesus opened the eyes of the man born blind and his first sight was Christ's face, let us allow Christ to change us so that we may live always seeing the face of Christ.

Sometimes there comes one moment when we finally see Christ's glory, radiance streaming from his face, his transfigured presence illuminating our darkness, and we want to stay with him there in that moment forever.

But Jesus commands us: "Leave this mountaintop. Go where you are called to go. Start doing the work you are called to do."

We do not want to leave Christ's side, to go out alone into the hurting world without being able to see our teacher's comforting face whenever questions come, or crisis strikes.

But Jesus says, "As you give yourself away in love to the poor, the oppressed, the outcast, the disabled, the forgotten — in their faces, you will see mine." (2)

RESOURCE #3: The Alleluia Affair, excerpt of Part I, the book's opening **by Malcolm Boyd**

Jesus pulled his legs free.

The rusty nails that had held his feet captive fell clanking below the cross.

It was not difficult now to free his left hand, then the right one. He slid easily down from the full-size wooden cross in the sanctuary of an inner-city church in Indianapolis... and left the building, walking toward the city's hub...

It was a hot day, so he felt okay in his loincloth...

A new sense of compassion was felt...for the poor, the downtrodden... the sick, the prisoners...

The thousands of Jesuses who had come down from crosses and leapt out of church windows all over the world now stayed at YMCAs while they sought temporary employment as laborers.

All the crosses in all of the churches were empty.

Thousands of stained-glass windows were shattered.

The church preached the resurrection," said an old priest. "Now it is confronted by it." (3)

RESOURCE #4: *The Risen One Goes Before Us:*
An Eastertide Responsive Reading **by Hope Harle-Mould**

One: At first, we were hiding behind locked doors, fearful and in in despair from the tragic death of the One Who Loved Us as no one else has loved us, but suddenly He appeared inside our grief and breathed on us: Receive Holy Spirit.

All: The Risen One goes before us, alive and on the loose; bringing life-over-death wherever he goes; and he's still at large.

One: As with the Holy Stranger on the road to Emmaus, we are surprised in our sadness by being given new words from scripture, a warmth of hope in our hearts, and a peace that passes all understanding.

All: The Risen One goes before us, alive and on the loose; bringing life-over-death wherever he goes; and he's still at large.

One: As we welcome the Holy Homeless One into our homes, our eyes are opened... in the breaking of the bread... and we finally recognize him, and we are bathed in the light of his face.

All: **The Risen One goes before us, alive and on the loose; bringing life-over-death wherever he goes; and he's still at large.**

One: We are called to go out to the Galilees of our world, to look for him, to catch glimpses of him, and to join him; yet when we fail, he shows up and cooks breakfast for us.

All: **The Risen One goes before us, alive and on the loose; bringing life-over-death wherever he goes; and he's still at large.**

One: As we keep searching for where we might find him next, we offer our hands to the forgotten, and then in that moment we discover that together we're freed into life anew.

All: **The Risen One goes before us, alive and on the loose; bringing life-over-death wherever he goes; and he's still at large.**

One: We gather today in his name on this, the Lord's day, another little Easter, to become the Body of Christ in our time; and we're sent through these doors to illumine our world's darkest corners, with the resurrection light in our eyes.

All: **The Risen One goes before us, alive and on the loose; bringing life-over-death wherever he goes; and he's still at large. (4)**

RESOURCE #5: The Suitor, a humorous skit about Jesus as a present-day pick-up artist, trying to pick up people like you and me. Three brief excerpts by Charlotte Heeg

NOTE: The play opens as the Suitor (modern-day Jesus) approaches a young woman at a bus or train stop who's reading a book as she waits. The Suitor comes up to her and says that he couldn't help noticing that she's reading the Bible, and she makes it clear that she's reading a romance novel and that he should stay away from her. But the Suitor states that on page 223 of her book the

253

*husky lover will say to the female character that he will never
rest until "you are mine, mine, entirely mine." Then Jennifer
starts to wonder about this Suitor...*

JENNIFER: You mean you're trying to pick me up?

SUITOR: Yes, is it working?

JENNIFER: No!...

SUITOR: Because I want you to be mine.

JENNIFER: But you don't even know me!

SUITOR: Yes, I do. I've been watching you...

JENNIFER: Get away from me... You creep!

SUITOR: I know your whole family... Did you know your brother
Ed is feeling pretty depressed? ...If you could just sort of
stop by, for coffee...

JENNIFER: I've been meaning to...

SUITOR: Jennifer, please say you'll be mine. I could change your
whole life. I could give you everything you're dreamed of.

*As they continue to talk, and Jennifer starts to trust what he has to say
about her family and her own struggles, the Suitor gives her
something to show everyone that she belongs to him, a locket.
Jennifer begins to read the inscription:*

JENNIFER: "To Jennifer, with all my love, forever yours, "J.E.S.U.
— "Are you—are you Mexican?

*The play goes on with Jennifer realizing who the Suitor is, that she
doesn't deserve to wear the locket, and the Suitor agrees.*

JENNIFER: I might let you down, sometimes.

SUITOR: You will let me down, many times.

JENNIFER: Well... I guess I could go visit my brother now.

SUITOR: It's a start.

*Their conversation goes on, and the play ends with another brief,
humorous pick-up attempt by the Suitor. (5)*

RESOURCE #6: A Jesus Affirmation: A statement
of faith for times such as these by Hope Douglas J.
Harle-Mould

> *I trust in Jesus, the Emmanuel, God-with-us,*
> *whose cross and empty tomb triumphed over*
> *the powers of death, the state, and established religion,*

254

who loves us so unconditionally and persistently
that eventually we will no longer be able to resist.

I trust in Jesus, the Rabbi,
whose teachings made the Scriptures come to life,
who sought followers among the ordinary,
out of whom he called forth the extraordinary.

I trust in Jesus, the one who calls us not servants but
friends,
who knitted together
a family of those who lived out the will of the Abba,
who loved Judas, Zacchaeus, Mary of Magdala,
Thomas, Martha, the rich young man,
Simon, John, the Gentile woman,
the crucified Zealot, the centurion, and Saul.

I trust in Jesus, the Word Made Human,
who awakens in us the adventure
of being fully human, fully alive,
who unveils the meaning of life:
in losing one's self, one finds it.

I trust in Jesus, God's Servant and our Messiah,
who proclaimed and inaugurated God's kingdom
which had come in God's will being done,
where enemies learned to live together
and evil was overcome by good,
where the irreligious were accepted
and the privileged forgiven.

I commit myself to the koinonia,
the community of faith that is the Body of Christ,
in which we are confronted and nurtured
into a discipleship more costly and joyful
than we could know,
in which we grow more able to say to others

what Jesus said to us:

"I am willing
to let my life
be disrupted for you." (6)

ENDNOTES

Epilogue: Resources for Your Sketches of Jesus!

1. Joseph Girzone, a true story told in Girzone's own voice as the preface to the audio version of his book, *Joshua: A Parable for Today* (New York: Random House Audio, 1990).

2. Hope Harle-Mould, © 2009.

3. Malcolm Boyd, The Alleluia Affair (Waco, TX: Word Books, 1975), opening unnumbered pages.

4. Hope Harle-Mould © 2021.

5. Charlotte Heeg, "The Suitor," from a two-skit collection, "Otherwise Known as Jesus," (Colorado Springs, CO: Contemporary Drama Service, Meriwether Publishing).

6: Hope Harle-Mould, *A Jesus Affirmation*, is an excerpt from the author's longer confession of faith, "Affirmations," originally published by *Alive Now!* January/ February 1989.

Acknowledgements

My Beloved Mentor: Robert McAfee Brown

My lifelong pursuit of contemporary sketches of Christ was originally inspired by one article by one person, a man whom years later would become my favorite professor and mentor at Union Theological Seminary in New York City, **Reverend Dr. Robert McAfee Brown,** widely acclaimed as one of the greatest writers and teachers of theology from the 1950s into the 1990s.

Dr. Brown's article was titled, "From Fish to Clown: Contemporary Images of Jesus," in which he sketched eight images of Jesus of Nazareth to help us see and perceive Christ in our own time:

> *Christ the Clown*
> *Jesus the Revolutionary*
> *Jeshua bar Josef, the Teacher*
> *"The Man for Others"*
> *Christ the Offense*
> *Healer and Feeder*
> *The Clue to the Cosmos, or, the Picture in the Empty Picture Frame*
> *Christ the Fish*

One of his images, Christ the Clown, is featured in my chapter, "Sketch #20: Jesus, Our Crucified Clown: The Singing Clowns of Freedom."

I hope Dr. Brown's original words and all the Christ-sketches that he inspired me to discover and share with you, will provoke your imagination and catalyze your discipleship.

And a personal postscript: When Linda and I were married, we asked Bob to preach at our wedding service. But Bob chose a more creative, enlightened approach. He invited his wife Sydney (whom I had gotten to know and work with on her New-Ways-to-Work Project) to join him in preaching a dialogue sermon for us. Their message was both uplifting and practical, which might help explain why we're still together after 42 years!

About The Author

Mr. Hope Douglas J. Harle-Mould is a United Church of Christ (UCC) minister serving as a supply preacher ("the preacher with props") in churches throughout Western New York and is dedicated to a Ministry of the Pen — freelance writing. He is an active member of Pilgrim St. Luke's UCC in Buffalo, New York, which supports refugees and asylum seekers from around the world, and which is an Open and Affirming Church — welcoming all of God's LGBTQ children. He is involved with the Interfaith Climate Justice Coalition, the Network of Religious Communities, and the Western New York Peace Center.

Ordained in 1978, he has served as community organizer (farmworkers' movement), assistant prison chaplain, campus minister, youth and Christian Education pastor, visitation pastor, senior pastor, and founding director of an interfaith peacebuilding organization. He has done short-term volunteer service in Sierra Leone, Ghana, and Honduras.

Hope is co-author (with his wife, Linda) of *Talking with Your Child about God's Story* (United Church Press) and has written senior high materials for three different ecumenical curricula. His writings regularly appear in the devotional magazines *The Upper Room* as well as *These Days*, and in the Mennonite magazine *Purpose*.

His children's stories have been published in many religious periodicals and curricula: "The Shut-In Freedom Fighter," "The Parade of Misfits," "Ahmad's Hat," "The Girl Who Never Missed a Sunday," "The Boy Who Came in Last," "You Can't Promise Anything," "Just Pass It On," "The Land of Sharing," "Awakened by a Dream."

Hope received his B.A. in Religion and English from Carroll University in Waukesha, Wisconsin (and Schiller College in Germany) in 1975, and his M.Div. from Union Theological Seminary, New York City, in 1978.

He lives in Kenmore, New York (a Buffalo suburb), with his wife of 42 years, Linda, also a UCC minister. They have three adopted children and five grandchildren. Hope loves stargazing, hiking, playing Frisbee, the Green Bay Packers, reading, community theater, writing songs for guitar, performing poetry, and listening to the cooing of his white dove, "Gracie."

His unusual first name, "Hope," started out as a nickname at church camp where he was a counselor for two full summers. Afterward, when friends and his brother, Dave, continued to call him Hope, he realized that this was his spiritual name, his day-to-day calling. On the day after graduating from college at age 22, he legally changed his first name to Hope. *(See more of this story in the opening of Sketch #7: Jesus, Our Namegiver: What's Your Spiritual Name?)*

CPSIA information can be obtained
at www.ICGtesting.com
Printed in the USA
BVHW062130010322
630318BV00007B/533

9 780788 030161